Around the

• CORONATION STREET •

Houses

At the heart of the old industrial town of Weatherfield, life has never been easy on Coronation Street. Family names have come and gone but the Street has remained unchanged; those familiar cobbles have witnessed many a colourful scene over the years. From Pearl Crapper at No. 9 who buried husband and son after the Weatherfield Pit disaster of 1906, and Ena Sharples, battling caretaker of the Mission of Glad Tidings, to Samantha Failsworth, sultry barmaid of the Rovers Return, the Street has always bred strong characters who live long in the memory of its millions of fans.

Coronation Street: Around the Houses is the fascinating who-lived-where record of every house on the Street and their inhabitants from the day it was built up to the present day.

Daran Little joined Granada Television as Coronation Street's archivist in 1989, after graduating from Manchester Polytechnic in film and television production. In 1996 he was made Manager of Drama Serials, working with the producers and writers to build up profiles and histories for every Coronation Street character.

Daran is also the author of four other books on Coronation Street: *The Coronation Street Story - Celebrating 35 Years of the Street; The Ogdens of Number Thirteen; The Life and Loves of Elsie Tanner,* and *Life and Times at the Rovers Return,* and is co-author of *Weatherfield Life.* He is married and lives with his family in South Manchester.

Around the
• CORONATION STREET •
Houses

Daran Little

 B⬡XTREE

Coronation Street is based on an idea by Tony Warren

Published in association with

GRANADA TELEVISION

Dedicated to Sue, Toby and Isaac
for their patience and love

First published 1997 by Boxtree

This edition published 1998 by Boxtree
an imprint of Macmillan Publishers Ltd
25 Eccleston Place London SW1W 9NF
and Basingstoke

Associated companies throughout the world

ISBN 0 7522 1174 9

1 3 5 7 9 8 6 4 2

Designed by Maggie Aldred

A CIP catalogue record for this book is available from
the British Library

Printed and bound in Italy by Manfrini

Picture acknowledgements All photographs courtesy of Granada Television except the following:
Daran Little 9, 13, 14, 29, 31, 33 top left and right, 45, 47, 48, 51 right, 65, 67, 81, 83 top left, top
centre, 97, 98, 99, 102, 103 right, 105, 121, 123 top right, 137, 139, 153, 155, 156 right, 171
inset, 173 top right and centre; estate of Arthur Leslie 15 left; estate of Doris Speed 15 right;
estate of Jack Howarth 33 bottom left; Gabrielle Daye 33 bottom right; Daphne Oxenford 67
bottom left; Ivan Beavis 83 top right; estate of Avis Bunnage 83 below top right; Arthur Roberts
83 bottom left; estate of Joan Francis 103 left; estate of Pat Phoenix 123 bottom right; estate of
Maudie Edwards 156 left and centre; Ivy Cottage Church, Didsbury 173 left

• CONTENTS •

Introduction   6

Life Before Coronation Street   8

The Rovers Return   11

No. 1 Coronation Street   27

No. 3 Coronation Street   43

No. 5 Coronation Street   63

No. 7 Coronation Street   79

No. 9 Coronation Street   95

No. 11 Coronation Street   119

No. 13 Coronation Street   135

No. 15 Coronation Street   151

The Other Side of the Street   171

Residents of the Street   190

• INTRODUCTION •

Coronation Street is the world's longest-running television pro-gramme, delighting 18 million regular viewers by showing them glimpses into the everyday lives of the inhabitants of a small northern back street. The Street has become famous since the cameras first rolled on to the cobbles in December 1960 and boasts influential supporters. In May 1982 Queen Elizabeth II and the Duke of Edinburgh dropped in for a chat with the residents while passing through the area. Before 1960, the residents led a more private existence, coping with two world wars and starvation in the Depression years.

The Street has always bred fighters, from its early inhabitants such as Pearl Crapper, who buried two cardboard coffins after the Weatherfield Pit disaster, to Ena Sharples, the battling caretaker at the Mission of Glad Tidings. Family names have come and gone: some, such as Hewitt, lasted seventy years, others, like McDonald and Mallett, have yet to stand the test of time. No matter how long residents stay in the Street they share one common factor: they belong to the com-munity. It is this sense of community that bonds the neighbours, helping them to carry one another's burdens, to laugh and cry together.

This book chronicles the major events in the lives of the families, from the first inhabitants in 1902 through to those of today — Rita Sullivan, Fiona Middleton and Sally Webster to name only a few. The residents are grouped together in terms of the history of their houses. Some, such as Cissy O'Connor, lived only in one house, but others moved from home to home: Ken Barlow started life at No. 3, but has also lived at No. 9, No. 14, No. 3 (again), No. 1, No. 11, No. 1 (again), No. 15, No. 12 and is now back, yet again, at No. 1.

If you have enjoyed watching Coronation Street over part or all of the last thirty-seven years, then this book should be able to answer all the questions you've ever asked yourself about the inhabitants and their past lives.

It has been a great pleasure for me to research the parish records of St Mary's and I acknowledge the expertise of Mr J. Roach, the curator of Weatherfield Library. Also the following members of the Weatherfield Historical society — Mrs C. Reynolds, Miss S. Pritchard, Mr J. Stevenson, Mr P. Whalley, Ms S. Wadeson and local archivist

Miss A. Rose — have been most helpful. The records kept in the house of Woods Collins and the oral tapes of Miss Smallacombe have proved invaluable.

The biggest thank-you belongs to the residents of Coronation Street. They have invited me into their homes, shared the contents of their photo albums and opened their hearts to reveal secrets long hidden. I would especially like to single out Mrs Emily Bishop whose homemade shortbread helped me through the long evenings at the word processor.

Daran Little, January 1997

• Valerie Barlow and Hilda Ogden enjoy a gossip (above), and Albert Tatlock celebrates reaching 80.

Life Before
• CORONATION STREET •

Coronation Street is situated in the centre of Weatherfield, a town that thrived during the industrialization of the north in the eighteenth and nineteenth centuries. The Street itself was built in 1902, and the story of its inhabitants is chronicled in the following chapters. There was, however, life on Coronation Street hundreds of years before the Hewitts and Makepieces moved into the new houses.

The first community to live on what would become the site of the Rovers Return was Roman. In AD79 the Governor of Britain, Cnaeus Julius Agricola, led the conquest of the north of England and established fortresses at Chester and York. A road was built between the two and another one to the northern frontiers. At the junction of these roads, he constructed another fort to serve as a communications post. Part of this fort lies buried under the cobbles of Coronation Street.

Around the fort, roughly in the area towards Albert Road and Bettabuy supermarket, a civilian settlement grew up. The farmers who dwelt on what had been forest land supplied food and other necessities to the troops. By AD250 the settlement had a population of about two thousand people.

When the Romans abandoned the fort, in favour of the larger one in Chester, the civilian settlement declined. Most of the population congregated at the firmer land in the north. Those who remained took over the disused fort and established their farmland around it. Over the next five hundred years the fort's stone walls collapsed and were pillaged for building materials. Some of the stones can be located in the foundations of St Mary's Church on Victoria Street.

The name Weatherfield was bestowed upon the farm settlements and the neighbouring land in the mid-fifteenth century. The name is an abbreviation of 'Bellwether Field' – the Field of the Belled Ram. The area was granted its Royal Charter and became a borough during the reign of Edward IV.

Wether Hall, on the site that is now occupied by Maureen Holdsworth and Rita Sullivan's shops, was used as a Royalist encampment during the siege of Manchester in 1642 at the outbreak of the Civil War.

The Bridgewater Canal was built in 1764 by the 3rd Duke of Bridgewater, Francis Egerton. Its terminus was only three miles from the heart of Weatherfield and another canal was built to the north of Coronation Street which linked with the terminus. This canal has claimed many residents' lives over the years, some accidentally and some as an easy way out of the misery of Weatherfield life.

The Weatherfield Main and Barton colleries were opened in 1786. The Barton pit had its entrance where Skinner's bookie's now stands on Rosamund Street, under which the pits ran. Although work closed on the site in 1880, the land has suffered quakes due to subsidence since then. The last, in 1965, helped dislodge the gable beams which demolished No. 7 Coronation Street. The more successful mine, the Weatherfield Main, occupied the land that is now North Cross Park, the cemetery and the Town Hall. It closed down after the disaster of October 1906 when 393 miners lost their lives underground, including Albert and Jack Crapper from No. 9.

On the junction of the two old Roman roads a coach house and inn flourished. Run by Dirty Dick Dawson, it gave refuge to Annie Marshall, the north's most notorious highwaywoman. On the site of the current Rovers Return, the old coach house was named the White Mare and lost its popular landlord when Dirty Dick was transported to Australia in 1869 for receiving stolen goods.

The land around the heart of Weatherfield was bought up by the Swinton family at the turn of the eighteenth century. New roads linked the area with Manchester, and in the 1830s the Great Northern Railway company constructed a viaduct across the land to carry passenger trains to and from the first railway passenger station in the world at Manchester's Liverpool Road. Although the viaduct still stands (Jim McDonald recently ran a bike repair shop in one of its arches) it is now disused. The line was closed after the 1967 disaster when a goods train ploughed off the track and fell into Coronation Street, killing three people and narrowly missing the houses below.

Sir Humphrey Swinton closed down the Barton colliery and Charles Hardcastle rented part of the land to build his cotton mill on the site that now contains the even-numbered homes on Coronation Street. The mills demanded labour, and families flocked to the area for employment. In 1900, Sir Humphrey oversaw the demolition of the dwellings on the old Roman road to make way for new shops, including the Queen's Parade, and the infirmary, which has since become Weatherfield General. The road became the main route into Manchester and was named Rosamund Street in honour of Sir Humphrey's mistress, Mabel Grimshaw, a variety singer whose stage name had been Rosa Hanbury. Unfortunately Sir Humphrey did not live to see the work completed. In his will he left the land surrounding Rosamund Street to Mabel, making her one of the richest inhabitants of Weatherfield. Charles Hardcastle convinced her that the slums in the shadow of his mill should be replaced with good-quality housing, so the tenements were demolished and new terraces were built.

The two centre streets, placed back to back, were to be called Mawdsley Street and Albert Street. The long street on which the mill entrance stood had already been named Victoria Street, and Albert Street was thought a fitting name for the smaller street behind the mill. The death of Queen Victoria, however, made the planners decide to rename Albert Street Coronation Street; it was completed just in time for the 1902 coronation of Edward VII. The public house built on the site of the White Mare was finally opened as the Rovers Return.

The workmen finished building Coronation Street on 8 August 1902 and the next day saw families moving into the fresh-painted homes, the day on which King Edward was crowned. Since then, over 300 people have lived in the houses and the street has seen drama, birth, marriage and death, but remains, as it always was, an ordinary street inhabited by ordinary people.

● *Charles Hardcastle and Mabel Grimshaw together were responsible for changing the heart of Weatherfield from a neglected backwater into a bustling industrial town.*

• THE ROVERS RETURN •

1902 – 1918
Jim, Nellie and Charlie Corbishley, with Pearl Crapper

1918 – 1938
George and Mary Diggins, with Edna Ellis

1938 – 1970
Jack, Annie, Billy and Joan Walker, with Concepta Riley,
Lucille Hewitt and Emily Nugent

1970 – 1984
Annie and Billy Walker, with Lucille Hewitt,
Emily Nugent and Fred Gee

1985 – 1987
Bet Lynch

1987 – 1992
Alec and Bet Gilroy, with Victoria Arden

1992 – 1995
Bet Gilroy, with Victoria Arden and Raquel Wolstenhulme

1995 —
Jack and Vera Duckworth, with Tricia
and Jamie Armstrong

It should have been called the Queen Victoria or, as Percy Oakes referred to it during brewery board meetings, the Queen Vic, but after the old Queen died a vote was taken to give the pub a name honouring the new King. As completion for the building was planned for the summer of 1902 the brewery bosses settled upon the Coronation, but they had to quickly rethink after it was decided to call the street 'Coronation Street'; two Coronations would be confusing. On the morning of Saturday 16 August 1902 the pub was opened as the Rovers Return Inn. The ceremony was performed by the young man whose repatriation from the Boer War had led to the new name, Lieutenant Philip Ridley, straight from taking battle honours at Spion Kop.

On that sunny day the new residents of the Street were each given a free tankard of ale and they crowded through the doors of the pub. Local landowner Mabel Grimshaw – or, as she was better known, Rosa Hanbury – stood behind the bar and helped to pour the first pints. Charles Hardcastle, the mill owner whose premises towered over the Street, was at her side. Behind them, staring in awe at the top hats and frock coats, stood the landlord Jim Corbishley and his wife Nellie. They had never seen the brewery bosses before – Percy Oakes, whose white moustache covered his mouth, dashing Aubrey Newton and severe-looking Leopold Ridley. James Corbishley, as he was called on the plate above the front door, was proud to run the third pub to carry the name Newton, Ridley and Oakes.

Jim Corbishley was a forty-three-year-old ex-grocer from Salford, who had been given the tenancy of the pub after three months' training and hands-on experience at the brewery's oldest pub, the Flying Horse. His thirty-seven-year-old wife, Nellie, had gone along with Jim's plans – he was head of the household, after all – but it was with a weary heart that she looked over the Rovers Return. The public-house side of the building consisted of three separate bars – the main public, the tiny ladies-only snug, where drinks were a halfpenny cheaper than they were in the public, and the select bar, which was waiter service and drinks were charged at a halfpenny more than they were in the public. A

cellar ran underneath the building and Nellie was glad that that was Jim's domain. At the back of the building were the family's living quarters: a living room and kitchen joined to the pub by a large hallway. Stairs from the hall led to four bedrooms and a laundry room. The Corbishleys occupied the front bedroom, their seventeen-year-old son Charlie another. Of the two remaining bedrooms, one was little more than a box room but the other was the largest of all and looked out over the barrels in the yard below. It was meant for paying guests and was required by law in order that the pub could be graded as an inn. All in all, as far as Nellie was concerned, the place looked like a lot of hard graft. Soon after moving in, she recognized

• • • • • • • • • • • • • • • • • • •

The select bar was waiter service and drinks were charged at a halfpenny more than in the public

• • • • • • • • • • • • • • • • • • •

that Pearl Crapper at No. 9 had a talent for cleanliness and at once she employed her to clean the pub from top to bottom every morning.

Charlie Corbishley had been happy to see the back of the Salford shop as at least two angry fathers were seeking him for seducing their daughters. At the Rovers he took on the job of potman, looking after the cellar, collecting jars from the customers and playing the piano in the evenings. Charlie was a looker and enjoyed the attention he drew from the local ladies. Men admired his drinking skills – he'd discovered spirits at fourteen – and women encouraged his wandering hands – he'd discovered women at fifteen. Unlike the other men in the area, Charlie was always well presented, never smelt of the mill or the pit and his fingers were as white as the ivories he tinkled. Jim thought his son a rake and encouraged him, boasting of his exploits to the male customers. He refused to meddle in the boy's affairs but gave advice when he saw Charlie heading blindly into danger. One such occasion was when Charlie started having ten minutes of passion in the back yard with Maggie Leeming from No. 5 down the Street. He dumped her for weaver

● *Jim Corbishley's pride in the exploits of his son Charlie made him nostalgic for his youth.*

Annie Rogers – to find himself fighting her fellow Daniel Grimshaw from No. 1. Next in line was Janey Atkinson, who moved in as resident barmaid. She claimed that Charlie was the father of her unborn child but Nellie realized she had been pregnant when she took the job and sacked her. A Weatherfield lass, Sarah Bridges, filled the vacancy and told Charlie on her first night at the pub that she kept a knife under her pillow and would stab him through the heart if he ever laid a finger on her. Nellie was happy to have no-nonsense Sarah around the place.

Jim Corbishley led a busy life, opening the pub at all hours and attending licensees' functions. He was happy as long as the till was full, and enjoyed dashing around behind the bar, pouring pints and dodging Sarah, while Nellie sat on a stool by the snug and Charlie collected the empties. It was a good atmosphere, and the Rovers became known as a place where you could spit on the floor in comfort and get a good pint among decent company.

In the summer of 1910 the brewery converted the laundry room into a bathroom and installed a zinc bath. No one else in the Street had a plumbed-in bath and Nellie enjoyed lording it over the other residents

●*Jim took out his frustration on his wife Nellie (above), drinking with his pals and then using his fists on his wife.*

until she received instructions that she was to make it a public convenience and charge local ladies a penny a bath. In the same year Pearl Crapper moved into the pub after her family left the area. She took on the role of housekeeper, and a bed for her was squeezed into Sarah's tiny room.

Nellie's health started to fail and she suffered violent bouts of sickness. As soon as she recovered from one attack another would come over her within a few weeks. She refused to see a doctor, believing that nothing much could be wrong with her as she always got better.

She was deeply saddened when Charlie, bored with serving in the pub, volunteered to fight in the war even before the call-up came. As the war gathered momentum the menfolk disappeared one by one, until only the old and infirm were left in the public. Nellie thought it stupid to keep the women pushing for space in the snug so she allowed them into the men-only bar too. Jim, kept back from joining the war effort by Nellie's illnesses, feared that once they had been let in they would never leave. He was right.

● *Mary Diggins feared that her husband George would lose them their licence when he took part in a prize fight against Jack Crawshaw at the Flying Horse. The police broke up the fight and George was arrested, but the brewery turned a blind eye: chairman Aubrey Newton had been at the fight.*

After she had undergone another violent attack of sickness, Jim insisted that Nellie saw the doctor. She was stunned to discover that over a number of years she had been slowly poisoned and the doctor suggested that she searched for traces of arsenic. The culprit was unmasked as Sarah, who declared that she had been trying to kill Nellie to free Jim for herself. The Corbishleys threatened Sarah with the police, but she escaped, taking with her the contents of the till.

Charlie Corbishley never returned from the war: wounded at the Somme he was taken to a Southampton hospital where he died. The news shattered his parents, and while Jim took to private weeping fits Nellie's anger at the waste of her son's life became public: she shouted abuse across the bar at women whose sons had survived. The brewery, recently renamed Newton and Ridley after the death of Percy Oakes, stepped in and Jim gave up the tenancy. The Corbishleys moved to Little Hayfield, taking faithful Pearl Crapper with them.

Retired police sergeant George Diggins, forty-five, was employed by the brewery to take charge of the pub. He and his wife Mary had no children and took on the tenancy to occupy their lives and take their minds off their loneliness.

Mary had always been fond of the music hall and decided to make use of the often empty select bar by having a stage built in it for performers. Throughout the 1920s she organized monthly attractions, with the help of Edna Ellis who had moved into the pub as resident barmaid. The Rovers became known as a house of good entertainment; beer flowed and the till

filled. Mary was broad-minded and made no objection to the bawdy songs sung by artistes such as Rickety Robert and Katey Hayes, the 'Salford Starling'. The most prestigious concert took place in April 1926 to mark the birth of Princess Elizabeth of York, when Mabel Grimshaw was persuaded to come out of retirement and took the stage as Rosa Hanbury, the 'Singing Sensation'.

Edna left the pub to marry Alfred Tatlock and moved next door to No. 1. Her job was taken by Avis Buck from No. 9 whose father-in-law, Ned, was one of the pub's best customers. George entered Ned in a contest against the Flying Horse, wagering a barrel of best bitter that Ned was the greatest drinker in the two pubs. Landlord Jack Crawshaw rose to the challenge and pitted his own champion, Armistead Caldwell, against him. The contest took place in the Rovers, and

● *Annie Walker's performance as Daphne in* The Knot is Sealed *coincided with her first wedding anniversary. Jack upset her by preferring to drink with his brother than to sit through the three-act melodrama.*

● *Billy Walker fought off Kenneth Barlow to take Christine Hardman to the Coronation Dance in 1953, but she stormed off after he spilt beer on her.*

Ned triumphed. He succeeded in drinking Armistead under the table.

During the unrest of the Depression years, George enlisted as a special policeman and was called on to stand against his neighbours when they marched on the Town Hall. The regulars boycotted the pub and, even though custom had fallen anyway during the harsh times, the Digginses felt the pinch. The brewery contemplated replacing George to bring back custom but George resigned from the specials on a matter of principle: standing alongside his unemployed neighbours, he won their respect by marching with them.

Just as the country was getting back on its feet George and Mary decided that they had had enough of running a public house. They cashed in their investments and bought a boarding-house in Blackpool.

John Walker, or Jack to his friends, was thirty-eight when he took over the Rovers' tenancy. He was a native of Accrington and had travelled to Weatherfield during the Depression in search of work. He was bitten by the licence-trade bug while helping out at his brother Arthur's pub, the Nag's Head, on Canal Street, before he found a job at a dyeworks and met his future wife when he tried to stop her killing herself – he didn't have to try hard because Annie Beaumont had only been looking at the shadows the canal water made and had had no intention of throwing herself in.

Annie was a leading light of the St Agnes Operatic Society and agreed to marry Jack on the understanding that he wouldn't stand in the way of her theatrical career. They were joined in matrimony on 23 October 1937 at the Mount Zion Baptist Chapel. They took lodgings in Ashdale Road, where their son William was born. When Billy was just a few months old the family moved into the Rovers Return.

Annie convinced herself that moving into the Rovers was little more than a springboard that would lead to a hostelry in the leafy Cheshire countryside where the Major and the Colonel would hustle for space at the oaken bar to laugh at her witticisms. She told Jack she would give the venture a year and would then decide if the back street suited her. In the meantime, she continued treading the boards, shining in Restoration comedy and proving a sensation in *The Desert Song*. At least, so she wrote in her diary; other critics were not so kind, one comparing her voice to coal stuck under an opening gate. All Annie's plans came to an abrupt end in 1939 when war was declared with Germany. Jack joined up to serve in the Fusiliers, while Annie was left with the pub to run and an infant to look after. The Operatic Society disbanded for the duration: "Where," asked Annie, "was the spirit of the Windmill?"

Joan Walker was born in 1940, delivered in the Rovers Return by a midwife whom Annie had bribed to stay at her bedside as she had no wish for the common lay midwife, Ena Sharples, to be present. Jack saw his daughter for the first time in 1942, but his leave was spoilt by an argument with his wife over a misplaced ration book. Annie spent the night in an air-raid shelter to spite him.

Annie hated her life at the pub, finding the customers uncouth and the local ladies too prone to gossip. Without Jack for support, she was forced to employ Ned Narkin from Mawdsley Street as cellarman. Ned was too old to fight abroad and too shifty to be in the Home Guard. He took liberties and Annie suspected he stole bottles of ale, but able-bodied men were scarce. When Ned's house was blown up in a gas explosion, Annie agreed that he could live at the Rovers on the understanding that he kept himself to himself and didn't eat her rations.

One night in August 1944, Annie was woken by the sound of a chair falling over in the living room downstairs. Fearing that Ned was drunk and would wake the children, she marched down to confront him – only to find a strange man searching through her sideboard. As she turned on the lights he pounced on her and held a knife to her throat, demanding the takings from the till and any valuables. She let out a scream, which was stopped by a hand over her mouth but which had been loud enough to wake Ned, who crept down the stairs and jumped from behind on to the man's shoulders. Annie rushed into the Street to wake ARP warden Albert Tatlock next door at No. 1 but by the time they returned the man was gone and Ned was sitting on the floor nursing a stabbed arm. Annie was ashamed she had condemned his character, but shortly afterwards he left to live with his daughter.

● *Widows Martha Longhurst, Ena Sharples and Minnie Caldwell took over occupancy of the Rovers snug, and here Martha died in 1964.*

After the war Corporal Jack Walker resumed his place behind the bar and Annie found that she resented the way he took command without a thought to the way she had soldiered on with the pub in his absence. Jack returned a stranger to his children, and six-year-old Billy found it hard to cope with having him around. He had been allowed to run wild during the war, collecting shrapnel and getting into fights with the Victoria Street gang. Annie put down his rough behaviour to the poor education offered at Bessie Street School and nearly came to blows with teacher Ada Hayes from No. 5 to whom she said as much in the pub.

When the children reached secondary-school age, Annie decided that they must be educated in a manner fitting to Beaumonts of Clitheroe. Ignoring the temptation to point out that Annie herself had received only an elementary school education, Jack decided to humour his wife. Billy was enrolled at the Mrs Dudley Henderson Private Academy while Joan was placed at the Weatherfield Girls' Grammar School. She fitted in well there and, having inherited her mother's desire for social climbing, made the most of rubbing shoulders with the daughters of bankers and solicitors. When asked her father's profession, Joan would say he ran a small hotel and that her mother was a retired actress. Billy, on the other hand, hated the stifling atmosphere of Mrs Dudley's Academy and was picked on because of his rough accent and manners. When criticized, he resorted to his fists and was soon expelled for fighting in a classroom, much to Annie's disgust. He finished his education at Bessie Street, and on leaving school took a job as a trainee mechanic at the Blue Bell Garage on Commercial Road.

On her forty-fifth birthday, in August 1954, Annie told Jack that she wanted them to retire from running

● *Jack Walker proudly cleaning his windows, and Annie snapped while holidaying in Majorca.*

● *Bet Lynch was Alec Gilroy's second wife. His first, Joyce, ran off with a footballer, taking their daughter Sandra with them.*

the Rovers and to find a more select country pub. Jack was aghast at the idea: the children would soon leave home and he didn't relish the idea of starting afresh with Annie in a strange area where he instinctively knew he wouldn't fit in. However, he knew how much Annie wanted to escape the back streets and agreed to view some properties. They drove out to Wilmslow in Cheshire and toured some of the public houses to get a feel for the place, but it soon became apparent that it wasn't just Jack whom the natives found common, rough and rude but Annie too. She was humiliated by the way in which the locals laughed at her affected airs and realized that she would be far happier staying where she was, as Queen of Coronation Street, than risking ridicule in pleasant surroundings.

Joan Walker completed her teacher-training course and found work in a secondary modern in Derby. Annie was pleased to find that her daughter's rented flat was situated in a select area of town and approved of her choice when she announced her engagement to Gordon Davies. Gordon, the son of a teetotal draughtsman, taught geography at the school where Joan was teaching English. She had decided to marry him, take out a mortgage on a modern semi and give up her job in favour of motherhood. Annie's one disappointment

● *Betty Turpin, whose secret hotpot recipe has proved a hit with countless customers since its introduction in 1973.*

was that her daughter had not found a husband who lived closer. Jack hadn't the heart to tell her that he had overheard Joan telling her friend Linda Cheveski that she had turned down a job in Stockport as it was too close to home and her overbearing mother. Joan had turned into a snob, just like her mother, and found the Street distasteful and beneath her. While Annie would agree with her, as she and her daughter sat in the living room sipping tea, she had no idea that Joan classed her as part and parcel of the northern back street she so desperately wanted to free herself from. In paying the huge school fees, Annie had unwittingly been responsible for driving a wedge between her and her perfectly poised daughter. Dublin-born Concepta Riley moved into Joan's vacant room in September 1960 as resident barmaid. Annie found in her the confidante she had always hoped Joan would become.

Jack gave Joan away when she married Gordon. He had never felt close to his daughter: after his return from the war she had hardly been around during term-time and he had left her to Annie during the holidays. When Billy returned from his National Service, Jack hoped that he would take his side behind the bar but his son moved to Chiswick to work as a mechanic.

The children having grown up, Jack and Annie found themselves growing older together. When the brewery offered them a new pub in the Cheshire countryside, Annie was thrilled. Jack was surprised when Annie turned the pub down; she knew that Jack would never feel comfortable in a place like the Royal Oak.

To ease the strain at the pub, the Walkers employed Martha Longhurst from Mawdsley Street as cleaner and gave Ivan Cheveski from No. 9 the post of potman. Concepta vacated her room in October 1961 to marry bus inspector Harry Hewitt. After the honeymoon she moved into his house, No. 7, and bowed to his wishes for her not to work any more. Harry had a teenage daughter and in 1964 when the family emigrated to Ireland schoolgirl Lucille was left in the Walkers' care until she completed her studies.

May 1964 found Martha Longhurst dying of a heart attack in the snug. Hilda Ogden from No. 13 took over as cleaner, and her daughter Irma became barmaid.

In 1966, the discovery of a framed oil painting in the cellar nearly changed the face of the pub for good. It was found when an old girder was removed, and featured an aristocratic woman. Jack wanted to throw it away but Annie fell for the romance of the picture, especially after finding a mask hidden behind the frame. The painting was of Mary Longford of Wether Hall, at the time of her marriage to Sir William Black in 1695, and had hung over the fireplace at the White Mare. The Rovers had been built on the old inn's

• • • • • • • • • • • • • • • • • • •

Annie had no idea that Joan classed her as part and parcel of the northern back street she so desperately wanted to free herself from

• • • • • • • • • • • • • • • • • • •

cellars and the painting had lain undisturbed for nearly two hundred years. If she had known this, Annie would have had the work restored and returned to the chimney breast but she got carried away with fantasies involving highwaymen and masked balls. The customers became bored with her romantic tales and got angry when she attempted to change the name of the pub to the Masked Lady. Jack took matters into his own hands by throwing away the valuable painting while Annie was visiting Joan.

Annie's aspirations grew when she stood in the local elections against builder Len Fairclough. She appealed for the women's vote, making the planting of inner-city trees her soap box. The voting ended in a tie and Len became councillor at the toss of a coin.

Lucille left Weatherfield Grammar with five O levels and decided to stay at the Rovers rather than be reunited with her family in Ireland. Jack was pleased, and Annie had high plans for her education. However, Lucille drifted from job to job, taking shop work, bar work and even dancing on bar tops during the go-go phase in the early 1970s. Her love life was just as fast moving, and she struggled to hold on to her virginity while adopting a worldly air that she thought was expected of her. She had a bad run-in with Borstal boy Ray Langton, who stole from the Rovers while he was

● *Raquel Wolstenhulme was given shelter at the pub after her father threw her out; he'd found semi-naked modelling photographs of her.*

there as her guest and threatened to rape her if she told Jack. Luckily his boss, Len Fairclough, discovered the truth and dealt with the youth down the back alley. Lucille came to look upon Len as a second father; he had been her father Harry's best friend and had been strongly supportive of her when Harry was killed in a car accident while visiting her.

In 1968 the Walkers were joined by another guest when spinster Emily Nugent took up residence in Joan's old room. Unlike Street-wise wise-cracking Lucille, Emily still looked for the goodness in all people and was willing to help anyone in distress. She had lived above the Corner Shop but lost her flat when the Barlows sold to the Cleggs. Some of her Mission-going friends were shocked at the idea of Miss Nugent living over a public bar but, as Emily pointed out, her Bible told her to live in the world. Annie was thrilled by

Emily's presence, trusting it would raise the tone of the pub, and called upon her reluctant guest to help out occasionally in the Rovers. Emily once calmed a room of roughnecks by refusing to serve them until they behaved like gentlemen, and often tried to act as a buffer between Annie and Lucille.

Lucille crossed swords with Annie when, at the age of twenty, she announced her engagement to Gordon Clegg, son of shopkeeper Maggie from No. 15. Annie thought the match highly unsuitable as Gordon had no money and few prospects. She tried to stop the marriage but the date was set. Eventually Gordon backed out of the engagement and told Lucille they were too young to settle down. Annie tampered successfully with another engagement when Billy showed off his fiancée Jasmine Choong. Annie refused to see her son tied down to an Oriental and collapsed behind the bar, taking to her bed until Billy 'saw sense'. Billy remained infatuated with beautiful Jasmine, but his prospective bride refused to marry into a bigoted family and broke with him. Billy told his mother that he would never forgive her, but he was quick to rush to her side in June 1970 when Jack died suddenly of a heart attack.

Annie took control of the pub, shrugging off suggestions that she should retire, and told Billy that she intended to act more as hostess than landlady. Betty Turpin was employed as senior barmaid with blonde Bet Lynch serving under her. With the two Bets behind the bar, Annie allowed herself evenings in her living room, mourning her lost energy. She had always relied on Jack to smooth over upsets she had caused in the pub and found that Billy couldn't fill the gap left by his father. He refused to be tied to the pub and shunned home life in preference to playing poker and gambling with the takings.

Even with help, running the pub was an immense strain on Annie, who insisted that her standards wouldn't drop. After thirty-six years of standing behind the bar she decided that the time had come to retire to Derby. The brewery were surprised when, after receiving her resignation, a petition arrived from the residents saying that they'd rather have her than any other landlady. Annie was touched by the gesture and agreed to stay on, while going through the petition at her own pace to work out who hadn't signed it.

As well as bar work Annie threw herself into corporate affairs when she became Mayoress to escort Alf Roberts as Mayor. She took elocution lessons and toyed with the idea of refusing to serve male customers who were not wearing ties but, as Billy pointed out, if she did that they would lose all their custom to the Flying Horse.

Billy left Annie alone at the Rovers when he took a hotel job in Jersey. He had planned to marry Deirdre Hunt from Victoria Street but that engagement fell through, too, and he decided to move away. Annie felt sure that Deirdre had no real feelings for Billy when, a few days later, she married Ray Langton at No. 9. Lucille also left the Rovers after falling out with Annie over her married boyfriend, Danny Borrows. When the relationship broke up, she took up residence with Concepta Hewitt in Ireland. Emily Nugent vacated her room when she married Ernie Bishop and moved into No. 3. (On the wedding day Ernie was late for the ceremony but Emily remained calm, feeling certain that he would eventually find the courage he needed to take a wife.) Annie struggled on at the pub but two incidents brought home to her that she needed a man about it. In the first she woke one night to find two youths ransacking her room for valuables. She stood up to them and saw them off into the yard where Len Fairclough gave them a beating. Afterwards the strain caused her to collapse but she refused to contact the police in case she was forced into retirement against her wishes. The second incident saw two of her regulars – Stan Ogden from No. 13 and Albert Tatlock from No. 1 – locked by mistake in the cellar. They spent a happy night supping from the barrels and singing wartime ditties but the brewery insisted that Annie take on a resident potman and appointed widower Fred Gee.

He gave up his job as storeman at Foster's foundry to move into Billy's old room. Annie worried that ex-paratrooper Fred would make a play for Bet Lynch: she was relieved to discover that Bet found Fred repulsive while he found her too 'common'. Annie doubted his

judgement when he took up with loud-mouthed Vera Duckworth, who was then separated from her husband, Jack, and on the prowl. Refusing to have her home turned into a bordello, Annie chaperoned Fred and Vera's every move.

Disaster struck the Rovers in March 1979 when a lorry driver suffered a heart attack at the wheel in Rosamund Street. His vehicle spun out of control and crashed into the Street, throwing its pile of timber straight through the Rovers' windows. Inside, Alf Roberts and Len Fairclough were trapped under the timber and glass while Deirdre Langton, from No. 3, feared that her daughter Tracy, whom she had left outside the pub only moments before, had been buried alive. Annie fainted at the sight of the devastated bar and the emergency services arrived on the scene to search for baby Tracy. When the timber was cleared, Tracy wasn't beneath it: she had been snatched before the crash by a psychiatrically disturbed girl.

Annie's staff continued to cause problems when she treated herself to a cruise to Casablanca. Refusing to leave Betty Turpin in charge, she took on a relief manager from the brewery. Gordon Lewis took an instant dislike to the staff but found the Rovers very pleasing. So much so that he decided he'd like to take it over. He suspended Fred for helping himself from the optics and caused Betty to walk out when he accused her of short-changing a customer. Bet followed in support. Annie was horrified on her return to find strange barmaids pulling pints and Gordon writing a damning report to his boss to the effect that she was too old to run the pub. After seeing him off, Annie relied on her old contacts at the brewery to have Gordon's report lost among paperwork.

Fred had always wanted a pub of his own, and after making an application to the brewery, was told he stood a better chance if he was married. After a whirlwind courtship, he married Eunice Nuttall in May 1981, only to discover that she was blacklisted by the brewery because, as a barmaid, she had been suspected of stealing from a till. George Newton told Fred that, with Eunice's record, they would never get their own pub. While the Gees argued, Annie grew tired

• *A happy holiday in Blackpool for Vera and beloved grandson Tommy, while Jack realizes a life's ambition: a trip to a brewery.*

of them taking over her home and ordered them out. When Eunice was employed as caretaker, they took over the community centre flat, but within months Fred had returned to Annie, his marriage over.

Annie's reign at the Rovers ended in October 1983 when she finally called time and moved to Derby to live with Joan. Her parting shot was to pay off Billy's £6,000 debts in return for him taking over the licence as she wanted the pub to stay in the family. However, Billy was not his father and saw no point in acting the gentleman behind the bar. He sacked Fred Gee and started an after-hours poker school in the back room. The pub was raided by the police and the brewery discovered that he was buying spirits from the cash-and-carry and not from them. Billy threw the brewery's disapproval in their face and told Sarah Ridley that the Rovers wasn't for him. He headed back to Jersey, leaving Annie disappointed.

Gordon Lewis returned as relief manager and, to the horror of the staff, applied for the licence. Urged

on by Betty Turpin, Bet Lynch applied too and was given the job of manageress. Bet had served at the pub for fifteen years and was well liked by the customers. Instantly recognizable by her blonde beehive and trademark earrings – she owned over 250 pairs – Bet refused to make any changes to the way in which Annie had run the place, although she wasn't so bothered about how the customers dressed. Bet, born and bred in Weatherfield, had never dreamed that one day she would be living in and running her own pub.

The Rovers Return was nearly closed for good in the summer of 1986. Cellarman Jack Duckworth attempted to mend a fuse with too strong a wire and the fuse box burst into flames. Bet woke at 5 a.m. to find her bedroom filled with smoke, which overcame her. Outside, Kevin Webster from No. 13 used a brick to smash the bedroom window and dragged her to safety. The pub was gutted and all that was saved was a plastic bag of earrings and hairpieces. Bet feared that the brewery would demolish the building but instead the decision was taken to renovate it. It was closed for three months before being opened again by Hilda Ogden, its longest-serving employee. Although the pub remained the same outside, inside the three bars had been knocked into one, the snug and the select disappearing for good.

Bet was thrilled with the new pub and decided to cement her interest by buying the licence from the brewery for £15,000. When she found that she couldn't afford to pay the interest the banks were asking, she borrowed from theatrical agent Alec Gilroy, with whom she had occasionally gone out. Alec saw Bet and the Rovers as a good investment but misjudged on one count: faced with huge monthly repayments, Bet panicked and fled the country. Alec panicked too, fearing that he had seen the last of his money, so he pleaded with his old pal Cecil Newton to give him the licence of the Rovers until the matter could be sorted out. Alec's name went up over the door and he took control with the help of Betty Turpin and young Gloria Todd from Ashdale Road. He finally located Bet in Torremolinos where she was working as a waitress. She assured him she hadn't touched his

money and he realized, with a shock, that it wasn't the money he was concerned about. He proposed to Bet, telling her that she could still run the Rovers if she was his wife. She accepted, unsure whether she wanted a husband or the Rovers. After the ceremony in September 1987, Alec gave her the pub as a wedding present. Bet's bridesmaid, Gloria Todd, left shortly afterwards, as did Hilda Ogden, who moved to Derbyshire after twenty-three years of cleaning the Rovers.

• • • • • • • • • • • • • • • • • •

The pub was gutted by fire and all that was left was a plastic bag of Bet's earrings and hairpieces

• • • • • • • • • • • • • • • • • •

Critics gave the Gilroy marriage only six months and were surprised to find the couple still together in 1988. They were drawn closer by shared grief when Bet miscarried their baby, and joined forces against the brewery when new boy Nigel Ridley announced plans to turn the Rovers into an American-style theme bar called Yankees. His plans involved knocking through into No. 1 and turning the upstairs of the pub into a carvery, all amounting to a huge increase in workload for the Gilroys. Bet and Alec refused to be part of the plans and barricaded themselves into the pub before a notice to quit was served on them. Luckily, at the last minute Cecil Newton flew in from retirement in Spain to announce that the Rovers would always remain a working man's pub.

Following the death of Alec's daughter, Sandra Arden, his granddaughter Victoria moved in, turning up her nose straight away at the smoke-filled atmosphere and larger-than-life Bet. She was a boarder at an expensive girls' school in Shropshire and Alec told her that she need spend only her holidays in Weatherfield. However, for Vicky it was light years from the lifestyle she had enjoyed in Cheshire, with her horse Saracen, and she planned to live with friends until Alec forced her to see that no one else wanted her.

September 1992 found Alec taking a job as entertainments manager with Sunliners Cruises, based in Southampton. Bet refused to leave Weatherfield and the Rovers so he went alone, putting an end to the five-year marriage. Vicky decided to continue to use the pub as her holiday base because her boyfriend, Steve McDonald, lived down the street at No. 11. Bet took command as manageress, supported by the ever-present Betty Turpin and new barmaids Liz McDonald and Raquel Wolstenhulme. Raquel didn't plan to stay at the pub for long as she had modelling ambitions. She moved into the Rovers after her boyfriend, Des Barnes, dumped her in favour of his ex-wife, and quickly became a surrogate daughter to Bet.

In 1994, both Bet and Raquel became casualties of love. Raquel rekindled her love for Des Barnes and moved into his home at No. 6 for a while before rushing back to Bet after finding him declaring his love for her fellow barmaid Tanya Pooley. Tanya convinced Bet and Raquel that Des had hounded her and threatened her with violence unless she slept with him, and kept her job. Bet, meanwhile, fell for country-and-western-loving lorry driver Charlie Whelan. He moved into the pub and Bet wondered if her future lay with him, but that fantasy was shattered when Charlie fell into bed with Tanya and they later drove away together.

Vicky Arden had better luck in the love stakes. Following her eighteenth birthday, on which she inherited £250,000, she eloped to St Lucia and married Steve McDonald, despite Alec and Bet's attempts to stop her.

Bet was stunned to discover that the brewery was selling off six of its pubs and that the Rovers was on the list. The asking price was £68,000 but she was told she could have it for £66,000, which was a sum Bet could never hope to raise. Newsagent Rita Sullivan contemplated buying the pub and starting up a partnership with Bet, but pulled out when she realized that Bet obviously wasn't a good businesswoman as she had no savings of her own. Vicky McDonald also refused Bet, as Steve didn't want to part with the money, and Bet decided to give up. She disappeared into the night, leaving no forwarding address. Betty Turpin was most upset, as two days later, at the age of seventy-three, she had to marry Billy Williams without Bet as her matron of honour.

The Rovers went under the hammer to whoever could come up with £68,000 first. Liz McDonald at No. 11 had her heart set on it but she missed out to Jack and Vera Duckworth, who sold No. 9 to buy the pub. As Jack feared that an old police charge would affect his application, Vera was granted the licence and became the eighth name to go up over the door. Raquel's job was safe but Bet's cellarman, Bill Webster, was shown the door and lost his room above the pub. Shortly afterwards Raquel also moved out: she married Curly Watts at No. 7.

Both in their late fifties, the Duckworths found that they had come to the licence trade too late in life and had to struggle hard to make a success of the pub. Vera hoped to make it a family-run business when their estranged son Terry arrived at the pub with his son, Tommy. But Terry was only after the pub's profits and disappeared again as soon as he discovered that the business ate all the profits and that he was expected to work long hours.

When Vera found out that her son had sold her grandson Tommy for £10,000 to relatives in Blackpool, she wrote him out of her will, and agreed with Jack that when they died Tommy would get the lot. However, Terry left behind a complication in the shape of single-mother Tricia Armstrong from Crimea Street. They had spent a night together, which left her pregnant – much to Jack's horror. Vera, though, was thrilled at the idea of another grandchild and took Tricia and her thirteen-year-old son Jamie under her wing. The Armstrongs moved into the Rovers when Tricia lost her job at Baldwin's Sportswear, and baby Brad was born prematurely in the back room, delivered by Betty Williams.

Tricia harboured hopes that Terry would marry her but when he did return it was only to attempt to steal the pub's takings and to point out that there was no way he intended to be struck with Tricia and her brats. Jack threw Terry out, and Tricia moved in with her boyfriend, decorator Ray Thorpe. Jamie was sad to leave – he had grown attached to Jack's pigeons, but Tricia had made her choice largely with her children's welfare in mind.

•Nº1 CORONATION STREET•

1902 – 1907
Percy, Aggie and Daniel Grimshaw

1907 – 1915
Thomas and Mary Osbourne

1915 – 1917
Alfie and Mo Marsh

1917 – 1918
Dinky and Madge Low

1919 – 1959
Albert, Bessie and Beattie Tatlock

1959 – 1981
Albert Tatlock with Ken Barlow

1981 – 1990
Ken, Deirdre and Tracy Barlow with Albert Tatlock

1990 – 1994
Deirdre and Tracy Barlow with Samir Rachid

1995
Tricia and Jamie Armstrong

1995 – 96
Ken Barlow with Denise and Daniel Osbourne

1996 —
Ken Barlow

When the houses on Coronation Street were handed over to the lucky new residents, Percy Grimshaw was the first tenant to be presented with a rent book. His pals from the pit cheered him as, face well scrubbed, he made to carry his embarrassed wife Aggie over the threshold while their nineteen-year-old son Daniel held the door open. Aggie's mother, Letty-the-Man, hung back from all the jeering, her shawl drawn close over her face. She had worked the pumps at the Tripe Dressers Arms in her youth and now she was sixty-five with ten illegitimate children, a humped back and a thick growth of hair hanging from her chin. She spat at the door as he shut it in her face and she uttered a curse against the house and all its occupants before shuffling along to Jubilee Terrace where she moved in with her unsuspecting daughter Florence.

Aggie had never before been alone in such space. During the day, when Percy and Daniel worked in the mine, she would sit with the sewing she had taken in. The house was sparsely furnished, and the one thing they had of which Aggie was proud was the oilcloth given Percy by a good friend at the pit. It covered the kitchen floor and made a change from the sacks that hid the wooden boards in the other rooms. Newspaper covered the old table and Aggie enjoyed looking at the print, trying to guess what each block of letters said. Letty had kept all her children away from schooling, pushing them out onto the streets and alleys to scavenge for food. Aggie had been caught stealing apples from a shop and taken away by a lady who wore gloves and smelt of lavender. She had been placed in an institution run by nuns and under their care had learnt to sew. Seven years later when she rejoined the family, her accent had mellowed and her fingers had become swift in needlework. Since then she had taken in orders for new clothing as well as mending.

Daniel Grimshaw worked hard, deep under the ground, sometimes side by side with his father. There had never been any question of Daniel not following in his father's footsteps: he would be the fourth generation of Grimshaws to work the Weatherfield Pit. When he wasn't working Daniel liked to play just as hard. He downed pint after pint at the Rovers Return and played billiards at the Flying Horse. He had an eye for the ladies too, and had his first sexual experience on his twentieth birthday in the back yard of the Flying Horse with thirty-five-year-old barmaid Moll Hardwick. Afterwards he saw Percy paying Moll for her 'present' to the lad and decided that he would never buy sex again. Percy encouraged Daniel to sow his wild oats while he could, and was disappointed when he announced he had fallen in love. The object of his infatuation was weaver Annie Rogers, whose house in Mawdsley Street backed on to No. 1.

Daniel wasn't the only Coronation Street resident with his eye on Annie: Charlie Corbishley from the

• • • • • • • • • • • • • • • • • • •

Letty-the-man spat at the door as it shut in her face and uttered a curse against the house and all its occupants

• • • • • • • • • • • • • • • • • • •

Rovers fancied his chances and made a play for her in the back alley between the two terraces. Daniel saw Charlie pinning Annie against the wall and rushed out of No. 1 to see him off. Punches flew as the lads rolled over the empty bottles in the Rovers' yard. Finally Daniel overpowered Charlie and thumped his face, sending him crashing through the Rovers' living-room window. A week later Annie accepted Daniel's proposal and Aggie looked forward to their wedding.

Percy convinced himself that Daniel getting married would be a big mistake and set about to save the boy from himself. Again he turned to Moll, who had warmed his bones on more occasions then he could remember. He sent a message to Annie, as if from Daniel, asking her to meet him at the back of the Flying Horse. All that evening he plied Daniel with drink and, at the given hour, Moll took him outside to her nest in the back yard. Daniel wasn't too drunk to see what was on offer and gave himself over to it, unaware that his beloved Annie was watching the whole sordid scene. Annie was not happy, but loved Daniel enough to forgive him.

Shortly after, Percy's body was attacked by TB and he soon died. And Annie was denied her wedding, as

• *Following the deaths of Percy (above) and Daniel, Aggie Grimshaw became an emotional wreck. She was barred from the Rovers for not clearing her slate after turning to drink for support.*

the wedding, he moved into the Tatlocks' home on Victoria Street. At the time he was forty-five and she was thirty-two. He found employment at a nearby tailoring factory, putting to use the skills that had been handed down to him. Mary worked at Hardcastle's as a spinner. When No. 1 fell vacant in 1907, Mary's mother, Louisa, secured the tenancy for her.

The Tatlocks were a close-knit family, and Mary had been devastated by the death of her brother William from TB in 1906, just months after his wife Emmeline. They left two boys, Albert and Alfred, and Mary saw it as her duty to help look after the youngsters. The boys lodged with their grandparents in Victoria Street and took part-time jobs at the mill. When Louisa and her husband Alfred also fell prey to TB, Mary organized lodgings for the lads – aged fifteen and eleven – over a shop in Rosamund Street. She had wanted them with her at No. 1 but Thomas saw the sense in making them stand on their own feet. Nevertheless, Mary kept an eye on them and cooked them a meal every Sunday.

It was a time for change all over the world as the war took hold across Europe. Nineteen-year-old Albert Tatlock marched off with the Fusiliers after depositing Alfred at No. 1. Thomas agreed with his brothers that it was a time for togetherness and moved Mary and Alfred out of the Street and into his family's large house in south Manchester.

During the workers' strike of 1911, when industry in Weatherfield was closed down and the police clashed with demonstrators, a few men refused to strike and crossed the picket lines. Called 'blacklegs' and 'scabs' by the strikers, they were praised by the management and the Government. Forty-seven-year-old Alfie Marsh was such a man. After the strike he was made up to foreman and promised the tenancy of a local house when one fell vacant. No. 1 Coronation Street was his prize.

The workers at Hardcastle's mill looked upon Alfie as more than a strike breaker – he was a nasty piece of work who bullied those under him and victimized them to get more work out of them. Those above Alfie turned a blind eye to his sadistic treatment of the unfortunate women under him.

Daniel was buried alive in the pit disaster that October. The earth seemed to swallow the men and only thirty-four miners emerged alive; 393 were killed. Aggie, unable to pay the rent, was turfed out of No. 1 and went to the workhouse on Baker Street. She was dead within the week.

Thomas Osbourne had broken with his Jewish roots by marrying a Gentile, Mary Tatlock, in 1895. All his life Thomas had been a good Jew, a fine scholar and a son to be proud of. Then he had committed the unforgivable sin of falling in love. From the moment he announced his intention to make Mary his bride the family disowned him and withdrew their support. After

In the spring of 1911 Alfie had married Mo Dowty and moved into her parents' home, 24 Inkerman Street. She had given up hope of ever finding a husband and couldn't understand what man-about-town Alfie saw in her. Alfie was never affectionate and only made love to her when he was drunk. When he was alone with her, he was often less than civil but if her parents were present he played his role as the doting husband. Alfie had married Mo believing Len Dowty to be a rich man and recognizing that Mo, as his only child, would inherit the lot.

One dark night in November 1914 Len fell down the stairs and broke his neck. The police were called in to investigate the death but could find no evidence to point to anything other than misadventure. Alfie awaited the settling of Len's estate with glee and was furious to discover that his father-in-law's affluent lifestyle had left him with debts and Mo with no legacy. Furthermore, he was faced with the prospect of supporting both Mo and Louise. He signed the tenancy agreement to No. 1 as soon as it became vacant and moved in straight away. Mo followed two days later after tracking him down, bewildered as he hadn't told her that he was leaving Inkerman Street.

Mo found work cleaning the Mission Hall and was a pathetic figure as she scurried across the cobbles every morning, her shawl drawn over her face. Alfie had told her that he believed a woman's place was in the home and she, eager to please in any way she could, kept herself to herself, never spoke to the neighbours and ventured out as little as possible. Alfie was happy to keep her prisoner at No. 1 while he sought sexual comfort in the arms of Sarah Bridges, the barmaid at the Rovers Return. Sarah eventually pushed Alfie to leave Mo for her, and the pair disappeared together with the takings from the Rovers' till.

Mo couldn't understand why Alfie should leave her and convinced herself that he would soon return. One day, however, instead of Alfie Marsh, Sybil Marsh turned up on the doorstep. She produced her marriage lines to prove that she was Alfie's legal wife, having made the mistake of marrying him in 1900. She now wanted to remarry and needed a divorce. Mo was horrified to discover that she had married a bigamist and locked herself away inside No. 1 fearing arrest. Two weeks later Sybil returned to tell her that she had traced Alfie to Bolton where he had married once more, this time to Sarah Bridges.

The shame was too much for Mo: after tidying and polishing her house, she made her way up to the canal and jumped into the icy waters. Her body was discovered floating by Plank Street Market.

The next couple to live at No. 1 had only a brief spell of happiness. Dinky and Madge Low moved in on their wedding day, 3 November 1917. They had been childhood sweethearts as they had grown up together in Jubilee Terrace and had both worked at Hardcastle's mill. They had been going to marry in 1914 but the war interrupted their plans and Dinky marched off to fight in the Fusiliers with his school chum Albert Tatlock. With Albert, Dinky had seen action on the Somme, had been decorated for bravery and made up to sergeant. He returned home on special leave to marry Madge at the Mission of Glad Tidings; the wounded Albert was best man. After the reception at the Flying Horse on Jubilee Terrace the Lows moved into No. 1 and had one night together before Dinky left for France. That night their baby was conceived.

Madge carried on working at Hardcastle's for as long as she could, but in the seventh month she collapsed in the Street with stabbing pains. Sarah Buck from No. 9, the local midwife, did all she could but the boy was stillborn. Three days later Madge died from internal bleeding.

Dinky returned from war a hero but his new home was empty; no cheery fireside awaited him. With him came Albert, who was looking forward to a new life as his sweetheart Bessie Vickery had agreed to marry him. Dinky decided that Coronation Street was not the right place for him to live and he stayed long enough only to gather together his possessions before catching the train to London where he planned to seek his fortune. Before he went, he arranged with the landlord that Albert and Bessie be given the tenancy of No. 1 and informed the happy couple that as a wedding present he had had a sideboard built in the house for them.

● *Three unhappy households at No. 1. Alfie and Mo Marsh (above) were not legally married, Mary (above right) lived with the knowledge that her marriage to Thomas Osbourne had ostracized him from his family. Dinky and Madge Low (below right) spent only one night together in the house before Dinky went off to war and Madge died bearing their stillborn child.*

Orphan Bessie had given up her job as an under-housemaid in Bury to marry Albert. They had met at the beginning of the war during his training in Bury, and he had proposed to her in a letter sent from the front. They married on 18 October 1919 and moved straight into No. 1, starting work together at Hardcastle's mill the next day. Albert was glad to have a job when so many returning heroes had nothing to come back to. He grew bitter at hearing of their treatment and was sickened to find wounded comrades begging in the streets. Albert had escaped the war with only a minor injury after shrapnel blasted into his leg and he knew he had been fortunate, but in his dreams he relived the moment when his pal Clarrie Ross had died in his arms. He had spent two days listening to the screams of another Weatherfield friend, Archie Sykes, who had been impaled on barbed wire and died slowly of blood loss because his leg had been blown off. Albert had wanted to try to help him but every time he lifted his head over the parapet of his trench he was shot at by the Hun. Safe at No. 1, at night he was tormented by the shrieks and suffered vivid nightmares.

Albert kept his service revolver and in 1920 he used it for the last time: a rabid dog, brought back to England by a lonely soldier, was found in the back alley of the Street. It trapped Ned Crapper in the back entry and onlookers feared it would bite him as he tried to lock it in the coal hole. Albert ran for his gun and shot the dog at close range. Afterwards he handed the weapon over to the policeman who carried the dog's body away.

In 1921 Albert's younger brother, Alfred, moved in. He had entered the war towards the end but had seen hardly any action, for which Albert was glad. Before 1914 they had been close, looking out for one another after their parents died. Now, seven years later, they were poles apart, Alfred still vibrant and gregarious, Albert withdrawn, subdued by all he had seen in the trenches. Alfred also worked at Hardcastle's, in the stores, but was a heavy drinker and spent long hours in the Rovers. He fell for the barmaid Edna Ellis and married her, against his brother's advice: Albert found her too worldly and ambitious and feared she would push Alfred too hard.

Both Tatlock couples were put under strain as Alfred moved Edna into No. 1 and the two women battled for space in the scullery. Eventually they worked out a rota and Bessie took on the cooking, Edna the cleaning. Edna continued to work at the pub but Alfred grew jealous of the attention her ample body received. He was pleased when she gave up the job to have their daughter, Joyce.

Poor Joyce was not long for the world and died during a scarlet fever epidemic in 1923. After the baby was buried, Edna went down with a tell-tale fever. Bessie

cared for her but Edna died two months after her baby daughter and was buried alongside her at St Mary's. Alfred stayed on at No. 1 for another year until he gave up his job for the post of junior station master on the Liverpool Road line. The job came with a small cottage and Bessie made it smart with curtains and feminine touches. When Alfred married Edith Brown in 1936, Bessie was matron of honour and the groom laid sprays of fresh flowers on his two family graves in the churchyard.

A new woman entered Albert's life on 21 August 1933, in the form of a six-pound baby girl. Bessie had believed she would never conceive and was thrilled with the arrival of little Beattie. The good news did not sustain them long, though, as Albert lost his job during the Depression. Bessie had lost her job when Hardcastle's mill had closed in 1931 and now there was an extra mouth to feed. Albert was adamant that he wasn't going to claim dole and was determined to find work. He walked as far as Wigan in search of a job, any job. He left home for five months, travelling around the region, taking whatever casual labour he could find. He sent money home until the postman, who realized the letters contained cash, began to steal it. He returned home occasionally with whatever he had managed to save and Bessie spent the money in keeping up Beattie's health. Albert finally secured a good job as manager of a print works and then found himself having to turn away other men, like himself, who needed work. Sadly the print works closed in 1935 and Albert signed on the dole for the first time. He looked after Beattie as Bessie traipsed around town, having heard that there were more jobs for women, who were cheaper to employ.

The outbreak of the Second World War coincided with Albert being taken on at the Town Hall as a clerk in the Highways Department. Suddenly he was at the hub of activity helping to organize the distribution of gas masks, the delivery of Anderson air-raid shelters to those with gardens and the erection of brick ones in many terraced streets. Albert built a shelter under the kitchen table for his own family's use. Bessie, however, had her own plans for Beattie's safety and agreed for

• Bessie Tatlock (above) struggled to accommodate her brother-in-law Alfred and his wife Edna (right) when they moved in with her and Albert at No. 1.

• Albert (left) had taken work harvesting beetroot the summer his daughter (above) was born. 'As red as the beets' when born, she got the name Beattie.

● Alice Pickens had lusted after Albert Tatlock since 1953
when he had won the knobbly knees contest at
the Coronation Celebration party at Weatherfield Baths.

the six-year-old to be evacuated with the rest of Bessie Street School juniors. Ada Hayes from No. 5 accompanied the children to Blackpool, and Bessie was sad to discover that, far from being distraught, Beattie loved the adventure and fell in love with her new family's pet dog. Bessie needed someone to mother and, with Beattie gone, turned her attentions to her young next-door neighbour Ida Barlow, who had a baby of her own, Kenneth. Ida was grateful for Bessie's friendship and glad to share the shelter with her. She stored her ration books and identification papers with the Tatlocks in the tin box under the shelter. In 1940 when the raids grew worse the women sought refuge in the basement of the Mission of Glad Tidings. Albert, as ARP warden, had the job of ensuring that the

● *The decor of No. 1 did little to cheer depressed Deirdre Barlow up. It was Samir Rachid (right), whom she met on holiday in Morocco, who brought the much-needed joy into her life. They had only a little time together to enjoy their happiness.*

residents were safe during the attacks and his cry of 'Put that light out!' was greeted with cheers.

While others suffered a miserable war, Albert and Bessie enjoyed the companionship it brought and settled into a routine. For them it came as a jolt when peace came and Beattie returned home. She had grown into an eleven-year-old with an attitude: five years of good living in a spacious home had turned her into a snob and she hurt her parents by making it clear that she viewed them as beneath her.

Albert and Bessie's middle years passed uneventfully. Bessie kept house and neighboured with the likes of Ida Barlow, while Albert worked hard at the Town Hall and started to collect rare coins. They lived in the kitchen of No. 1, surrounded by large, dark wooden furniture, the still of each night punctured by ticking clocks and crackling fires. They always left the back door unlocked for neighbours to pop in, and the kettle was always hot for a soothing cup of tea. They weren't bothered by the rush of consumer goods in the 1950s, ignoring television in favour of their wireless, forgoing a washing machine and a plumbed-in bath as they saw nothing wrong with the mangle and tin tub.

If they didn't, Beattie certainly did. After leaving school, she took a job selling perfume at Miami Modes Department Store and saved her wages, planning to leave the Street as soon as she could. In May 1953 she chose draughtsman Norman Pearson as her husband-to-be. He was startled by her wedding plans but too weak-willed to put up a fight. After the wedding Beattie chose a house in Oakhill and set about pushing Norman up the career ladder, leaving her bemused parents far behind her.

In 1960 Albert retired from the Town Hall just a few months after Bessie had died in her sleep. They had had great plans for their retirement, spending their days together, and Albert thought Fate cruel for robbing him of his lifelong companion. Still, he remembered her in every detail of the house and vowed never to change any of the furniture. Beattie tried to move him in with her and Norman, but Albert refused as she was such a fuss-pot. He knew that within a week they wouldn't be talking to one another.

Instead, he stayed where he was and tried to occupy himself to prevent himself from brooding. He helped out at the Mission of Glad Tidings as back-up caretaker and became a lollipop man outside Bessie Street School. In 1961 he was delighted when his niece Valerie moved in as a lodger, and even more pleased when she married Ken Barlow from No. 3 and made the Street her home.

Albert occupied his day with trips to the library, polishing his coin collection and reminiscing about the war to his ever-decreasing number of wartime friends. He met up again with Sergeant Boxer whose life he had saved on the Somme. Boxer had been taken on as curator of the Fusiliers' museum in Bury and offered Albert the job of his assistant. Albert took it for six months and let No. 1 to displaced widow Effie Spicer. She found the décor in the house too depressing, and Albert returned on a visit to discover that she had redecorated and changed his furniture around. Shortly after he gave her notice to quit and moved back in.

Old age did not mean that Albert led a lonely existence. In 1965, local char Clara Midgeley announced her intention to become the second Mrs Tatlock and he was flattered by the attention. They holidayed together in Cleveleys but he realized that she had annoying habits and he felt they were incompatible. A few years later Alice Pickens from Victoria Street started to call on him and told him she had always carried a torch for him. The affection wasn't mutual, and Albert found her overbearing and too excitable. However, he broke his arm and the doctor advised him to let Alice nurse him, the alternative being living with Beattie. To keep her around, Albert proposed to her and Alice gleefully accepted.

Albert got drunk on his stag night and was escorted home by a policeman after being found singing in the Street. But the wedding was cancelled when the vicar had a flat tyre and didn't turn up at St Mary's church. Alice took it as an omen against the marriage and told Albert that they had better not risk it. Rather than waste the honeymoon in Bridlington, she went alone.

In 1971, Albert was shattered by the death of his beloved Valerie and the removal of her children to live in Scotland with his brother Alfred. He tried to help the mourning Ken and told him to look upon No. 1 as his own home. For the next few years, Ken drifted in and out of occupancy of the house and Albert began to look upon him as his son. He had trouble with his daughter Beattie, when she announced she had left husband Norman. She planned to live permanently at No. 1 with her father, but Albert had grown used to his bachelor life and ordered Norman to take her back, telling them that a marriage had to be worked at.

For company Albert took in a pigeon called Gilbert and kept it in the back yard. He tried to train it to find its way home but the bird was eaten by Bobby, Minnie Caldwell's cat. Albert had known Minnie for years and realized that the best way for them to survive on their pensions was to join forces. When he told her that they would be financially better off, Minnie accepted his proposal and they planned a spring wedding. Their friend Ena Sharples didn't like the idea and felt left out. She persuaded Albert to pull out of the engagement by working out that actually he would be worse off with a wife.

• • • • • • • • • • • • • • • • • • •

Ken took a job teaching English at Bessie Street School and drifted from one woman to another

• • • • • • • • • • • • • • • • • • •

It took a long time for Ken Barlow to come to terms with the death of his wife and the absence of his children. He took a job teaching English at Bessie Street School and drifted from one woman to another, finding a few hours of solace in their arms. Albert was shocked at the number of women Ken pushed through his life and didn't like his attitude towards them. He longed for Ken to find a mother replacement for the twins so that they could return from Scotland, but Ken always seemed to be attracted to tarty women like Rita Littlewood, the local newsagent. Ken dumped shop girl Norma Ford to spend the night with Rita, and Norma gave him a piece of her mind, reminding him that he had children and challenging him about his attitude to them.

Albert agreed with all Norma had said, and was glad when the words sank into Ken. Ken decided that he had to put his children first, and straight away sought out a mother for them. Refusing Albert's advice to settle down with a homely girl like Norma, he looked to more spirited women and decided that Town Hall clerk Janet Reid was the right one. He took her to visit the twins and on the way back they called at her parents' home in Keswick and got married. Albert welcomed Ken's wife to his home, but straight away she turned up her nose at the tiny terrace and tried to persuade Ken to buy a house of their own.

Janet Reid was a fighter and always had been. She was well known in the Street for her affairs with Len Fairclough and Alan Howard from No. 11. Alan had been Elsie's third husband and everyone knew that Elsie had fought off Janet and they admired Janet's pluck in returning. She had always longed for a husband and saw Ken as her meal ticket to escape the dreariness of office life. She calculated that on his salary they could afford a mortgage on a big, detached house, but he was wary of committing himself. In the end they compromised and rented No. 11; away from Albert but not a big outlay. Albert was hurt, but also hoped that it would be like the old days when Valerie had been alive to look after him. He had a nasty shock when he invited himself to dinner and was told by Janet that he wasn't welcome.

In August 1975, Albert celebrated his eightieth birthday at a surprise party thrown by the neighbours. They contacted his old regiment, who sent along a bugler, and he was touched when they had a collection to raise the fare for him to visit the twins in Scotland. The children had remained in Glasgow as Janet had made it clear she didn't want them, and Ken's second marriage crumbled. He had made a fresh start, leaving teaching for middle management, running the Mark Britain Mail Order warehouse on Coronation Street. He had an affair with trade unionist Peggy Barton and resigned from the warehouse when the bosses refused to recognize the union. Albert was disappointed in Ken when he turned mini-cab driver for his next job, feeling that he should be pushing himself as hard as he could for the sake of the twins. He felt better a few months later when Ken took the post of community development officer at the Community Centre.

In February 1977 Janet Barlow returned to Ken and pleaded with him to let them start again, but he refused to pick up the pieces. He did, however, let her stay the night. In the morning he found her dead in bed: she had swallowed the contents of a bottle of tablets. Ken was filled with guilt at having rejected Janet, and his feelings were heightened when the police questioned him, suspecting that he might have killed her.

Albert became less and less active, limiting his outings to days on his allotment and his nights to a seat in the Rovers snug. One by one his old pals died and he resisted all of Beattie's attempts to move him into an old folks' home. He tried to explain that while he lived in the house he could look out of the window and see the ghosts of former residents and friends passing by. He knew that if he moved from No. 1 he'd lose that. While other people mellowed with age, Albert grew grumpier, sick of the way he was forced to struggle on a pension after fighting for his country, when others no longer stood up for the National Anthem and hordes of foul-mouthed football hooligans roamed the streets.

In July 1981 he was delighted when Ken married for the third time. His new bride was Deirdre Langton, who was divorced with a four-year-old daughter, Tracy. Albert had known Deirdre for years: she had grown up in Victoria Street and had lived at No. 5 with her husband Ray. Overnight No. 1 had a family once again, and the house rang to the cries of little Tracy. Albert gladly gave up his room to the newly-weds and moved into the downstairs parlour.

Deirdre worked at the Corner Shop for Alf Roberts and enjoyed the security that marriage to Ken brought her. He was so different from her tempestuous first husband and although she mourned the passion she had shared with Ray she appreciated Ken's solid reliability. At least, she did for the first year of marriage. Slowly, in her eyes Reliable Ken became Boring Ken and she embarked on an affair with factory boss Mike Baldwin. Mike poured attention on Deirdre, treating her to lavish meals and passionate encounters in his penthouse flat. He declared his love and urged her to leave Ken for him. At that time Ken had applied for promotion at work and was devastated when he learnt that he was not thought energetic enough for the post, and that he lacked drive. Deirdre didn't improve the situation by choosing that moment to break the news that she had a lover. Ken ordered her out of the house, telling her she had wrecked their marriage and accusing her of planning the whole sordid episode. She retaliated, saying that he never treated her as a woman and had never cared for her, denying her wishes to have more children. When Mike called round, Ken fought him off and Deirdre packed her bags. At the last minute she broke down, telling Ken that she couldn't go through with it and begged him not to make her go. The couple were reconciled and Ken told Mike to stay away from the house in future.

On 14 May 1984 Albert died, aged eighty-eight. In the last months of his life he sold No. 1 to Ken to stop the Barlows moving away. Beattie accused Ken of using blackmail to get the house cheap, but Albert assured her that she would inherit what he wanted her to have and not a penny more. She was mortified at the suggestion that Ken had meant more to her father than she had. The Barlows modernized the house, installing central heating and enlarging the kitchen. After Albert's death, they sold the old sideboard for which Dinky Low had paid and erected modern shelving.

Both Ken and Deirdre had a career change in the mid-eighties. He was sacked from the Community Centre for giving leaked documents on playground closures to the local free newspaper the *Weatherfield Recorder*. The newspaper admired his stand and offered him the chance to buy into the paper. He leapt at the chance and was made its editor, using it to alert the community to council scams and crooked deals of businessmen like Mike Baldwin. Deirdre hung up her shop apron to stand in the local elections. In May 1987 she beat Alf Roberts and became a councillor. From then on, the Barlows' marriage started to crack. Ken resented the amount of time Deirdre spent at the Town

• *Tricia Marsden had married Carl Armstrong when she was pregnant with Jamie. Eleven years later they moved to No. 1 in a bid to escape the violent Carl.*

Hall and felt pushed out by her influence. He had always been the people's champion, the power force, and now had to take a back seat as Deirdre took on the system. In the midst of this rivalry, Tracy suffered.

Deirdre came under intense strain when Ken started to print details from leaked council papers in the *Recorder*. The chief executive of the council suspected Deirdre of being the mole, and she became an outcast at the Town Hall, despite her protestations that she was innocent. When she discovered that the mole was the chief executive's secretary, Wendy Crozier, she broke the news and Wendy was sacked. Ken was outraged and employed Wendy to help him on the newspaper. They became lovers on his fiftieth birthday.

For a few months Ken tried to juggle his complicated love life, but Deirdre guessed what was going on. On New Year's Eve 1989 she confronted Ken and threw him out of the house, saying she was not prepared to fight for him. Ken pleaded with her to forgive him as he had forgiven her, but she had realized that their marriage was over.

Deirdre started divorce proceedings and Ken was forced to sell the newspaper to give her the house. Tracy was devastated by these events happening at a

• *Ken and Denise were distraught when she miscarried. Upset turned to joy when they learned the baby's twin had survived.*

time in her adolescence when she needed stability most. One evening, with Deirdre at a council meeting, she left the chip pan on too long and it caught fire. A passing electrician, Dave Barton, saw the smoke and dragged Tracy to safety. He put out the fire but the kitchen was gutted. Ken accused Deirdre of neglecting their daughter. Deirdre was grateful when Dave offered to install a new kitchen and attraction grew between them. They became lovers, but Dave grew frustrated by Deirdre's refusal to let him move in and finished the relationship. She was not alone for long, and Ken watched as she flung herself at local businessman Phil Jennings. When Deirdre lost to Alf in the council elections, Phil took her on to run his leisure company in the unit on Coronation Street. She grew alarmed as the company folded and then discovered that Phil was fleeing the country – with his wife.

• • • • • • • • • • • • • • • • • • • •

After years in grotty flats Tricia was thrilled to have the run of the house and her son Jamie was glad to have his own room

• • • • • • • • • • • • • • • • • • • •

Deirdre finally found Mr Right in the shape of a twenty-one-year-old Moroccan waiter called Samir Rachid. Tracy had left home when she turned sixteen and got a job in a local florist's. She fell for the delivery boy Craig Lee and, much to Deirdre's annoyance, moved into his flat. Finding herself back working in the Corner Shop, Deirdre decided she needed a break and had a two-week holiday in Agadir, Morocco. When she returned she was full of stories of handsome Samir, who had stolen her heart. While friends assumed that it was just a holiday romance, Deirdre couldn't stop thinking of Samir and borrowed £300 from Emily Bishop to send for him. When Samir arrived he moved into No. 1 with her, and took a job in a local restaurant although his visa forbade him to work: his pride refused to let him live off Deirdre. When the immigration people looked into his case he feared deportation, but Deirdre told him they should get married.

Tracy was disgusted to hear that her mother was marrying someone so young but Deirdre refused to listen to any doubts and believed that this time she had found her ideal mate. After the wedding in November 1994, the Rachids had a few short weeks of happiness before immigration officers swooped. They believed that the couple had married to keep Samir in the country. Samir was enraged that no one trusted him and pleaded with Deirdre to sell up and move with him to Morocco where they would be treated with love and respect. Deirdre was scared but decided that her love for Samir was more important than anything else. She sold No. 1 to Mike Baldwin for £15,000; he promised that he would sell it on and give her whatever profit he made. The Rachids left on New Year's Eve 1994, watched by Ken.

Mike let No. 1 to single-parent Tricia Armstrong. He knew that the rent was safe as it was paid directly to him from Tricia's housing benefit. After years in grotty flats Tricia was thrilled to have the run of the house and her eleven-year-old son Jamie was glad to have a bedroom of his own. Tricia's husband, Carl, had been arrested for GBH and sent to prison, and Tricia hoped he wouldn't be able to track down her and Jamie. She hoped the move to the Street would be a fresh start, and took a job cleaning at the Rovers. No sooner had she settled in, though, than Mike ordered her out.

Deirdre and Samir had returned to the area when Tracy had collapsed, having taken Ecstasy. It was discovered that she would need a kidney transplant, and while Deirdre was undergoing tests for compatibility with her daughter she urged Mike to sell No. 1 to the first buyer. She needed the money that the house sale would provide and pointed him in the direction of Ken Barlow who was offering a good sum: he wanted Albert's house as a home for himself and his girlfriend Denise Osbourne. Samir agreed to give up one of his kidneys when it was found that Deirdre's did not match Tracy's, but while he was walking to hospital he had an accident on the canal towpath, suffering concussion, and he died. His organs were kept alive, though, and the transplant went ahead, although Deirdre, grief-stricken, found she couldn't look at her daughter without blaming her for her husband's death.

• *Tracy was married from No. 1 when she became Mrs Robert Preston in 1996. The couple settled in Hackney, London, where Robert was a carpet fitter.*

Meanwhile, Tricia barricaded herself into Deirdre's house. When Mike tried to force the door, Jamie poured a chamber pot of water over him. Eventually Mike rehoused them in his flats in Crimea Street.

Ken and Denise moved into No. 1 with their son Daniel, and Ken hoped that in the family environment Denise would agree to marry him. She wasn't keen on the idea as she had had two husbands and, as Ken had already had three wives, figured that neither of them was a good advertisement for matrimony. At fifty-five Ken found looking after baby Daniel a bit of a strain and wondered what Albert would have made of the situation. As head of English at Weatherfield Comprehensive he had suffered complaints from parents over his lack of morals in fathering a child with Denise. Denise owned the hair salon across the Street and, following Daniel's birth, had tried to manage on her own, shutting Ken out of their lives. She agreed to

move into No. 1 to see if she and Ken could, after all, make a success of their relationship. Her big secret was that she had a lover, who was also her sister Alison's husband, Brian. Brian and Ken took an instant dislike to one another when they met at Daniel's christening, Alison and Brian being the baby's godparents.

Denise decided that Brian was getting too intense and tried to cool the affair, but he declared his love for her and told her of his intention to leave Alison. To put him off, Denise proposed to Ken and told Brian that they were finished. Ken gleefully arranged the wedding but then Brian told him that he was Denise's lover. Ken reacted violently, punching Brian and throwing Denise out of the house. When he told her she was an unfit mother, she agreed but begged him to take her back. He refused and she left with Brian, leaving Daniel.

Ken feared that Denise would return for the child while he was at school and employed an ex-pupil, nineteen-year-old Kelly Thomson, as a live-in nanny. She occupied the back bedroom and enjoyed being away from her parents as she could entertain her boyfriend, butcher's boy Ashley Peacock, at No. 1.

Following the death of her husband, Samir, Deirdre and Ken grew closer. When Tracy married in November 1996 they were drawn together as her parents and they both realized that they still had deep feelings for each other. Their love rekindled but suffered a setback when Denise returned to snatch Daniel, telling Ken he had no legal right to his son. Ken embarked on a court battle to secure custody of his son, but Denise lied to the court saying that Ken had always agreed that one day she would have Daniel. Eventually Ken was forced to settle out of court, with Denise agreeing to give him regular access to Daniel. Deirdre tried to help him through it all but he channelled his emotions into the fight and she felt cut off. She resented the way in which he assumed that they would just slide back into a comfortable relationship, and annoyed him by refusing to move back into No. 1 with him. He retaliated by sleeping with his headmistress, Sue Jeffers, and Deirdre realized there was no sense in raking over old ground. Their love was dead, even though they would always be best friends.

•Nº3 CORONATION STREET•

1902 – 1920
Samuel, Dolly, George, Thomas, Flo, Betsy,
Gertie and Molly Hewitt

1920 – 1930
Gertie and Molly Hewitt, with Billy and Flo Chad

1931 – 1938
Billy, Flo and Granny Chad

1938 – 1964
Frank, Ida, Kenneth and David Barlow

1964 – 1968
Unoccupied

1968 – 1970
Dickie and Audrey Fleming, with Ray Langton

1971 – 1972
Ken, Susan and Peter Barlow

1972 – 1980
Ernest and Emily Bishop

1980
Arnold and Emily Swain

1980 —
Emily Bishop, with Curly Watts and Percy Sugden

The largest family group taking possession of a new house in 1902 was the Hewitt clan. Mill worker Samuel Hewitt had married Dolly Pegg when she was just fifteen and pregnant with their first child. Dolly had grown up next door to Samuel in the tenement block their families shared with seven others on Barkers Lane. Samuel's father, Jake, had died when the lad was twenty-two and Dolly had comforted him in the small space under the shared staircase. When she announced that she was pregnant he readily married her and moved her into the two rooms he shared with his mother and sister. In 1902, when the couple moved out to live in Coronation Street, they had four children – George, Thomas, Flo and Betsy. Dolly was the envy of the Barkers Lane women as she oversaw the moving of their few belongings to the new Street. They wished her luck and she believed the family's fortunes were to change for good.

Cough, cough, cough. The rasping noise echoed through the house in 1905. All round Weatherfield the TB epidemic attacked households, grabbing hold of the young and elderly, the weak and infirm before breaking down the resistance of the strong. At No. 3 it was Dolly who started the coughing. She was heavily pregnant at the time and suffered terrible stomach pains as she clutched the bed sheets, coughing up blood. She died on 17 October 1905 and nothing

• • • • • • • • • • • • • • • • • •

With Dolly now dead, Gertie saw it as the most natural thing to take her sister's place, and Samuel allowed her to talk him into marriage

• • • • • • • • • • • • • • • • • •

could save the baby. The children had listened to their mother dying through the bedroom wall, and on the day of the funeral both nine-year-old George and four-year-old Betsy started to cough. The noise was too much for Samuel as he watched his youngest daughter contort in pain while she slept. He planned to help her out of her misery and one night covered her head with a pillow. Seven-year-old Flo woke up and saw what was happening. Her screams caused Samuel to drop the

pillow and sink to the floor in tears. Betsy died two days later, and George followed in February 1906. That was also the month when Samuel took another wife.

Gertie Pegg had known and admired Samuel since she was thirteen years old. She had been bridesmaid when Samuel had married her elder sister Dolly, and had continued to worship him from afar. As soon as Dolly was dead Gertie came to No. 3 to offer her condolences to Samuel and take on the role of mothering the children. Dolly and Gertie had always been close sisters and Gertie had been genuinely pleased for her when she'd married Samuel. With Dolly now dead, Gertie saw it as the most natural thing to take her sister's place and Samuel allowed her to talk him into marriage. He was surprised that such a young, carefree woman would want to be tied with someone else's children but was eager to have someone take on the responsibility of running the home. It was a quiet wedding on 22 February and the family wore black armbands to the ceremony, George having died on the thirteenth.

For a couple of months the household was happy, and Samuel entertained the customers at the Rovers as he played the piano. But then he, too, started to cough. Samuel's illness was the worst of all the Hewitts'. He was a strong man with powerful arms, used to pulling shuttles on the looms, but slowly the disease crept through his body, sapping it of its strength. He gave up work, with Gertie taking his place at his loom to maintain the family income. The noise of the machines was a welcome break from the sound of Samuel coughing as he sat in bed next to her at night. For nearly three years he spluttered and moaned, becoming bedridden for the last six months. Neighbours urged Gertie to send him to a sanatorium but she refused and, Flo helping her, nursed him day and night. Samuel died on 6 January 1909 aged thirty-five. He was buried alongside his first wife and two children. Three months later, Gertie gave birth to twins. She christened them Dolly and Molly, and six months after Samuel was buried, baby Dolly joined him in the same plot. Gertie prayed at the graveside that TB had claimed its last Hewitt victim and her prayer was answered.

• *Samuel Hewitt had two wives: Dolly (above)
and Gertie (below, with baby Molly).*

Gertie had been left a widow at the age of twenty-six; she had a six-month-old daughter, an eleven-year-old step-son/nephew and a ten-year-old step-daughter/niece. Thomas and Flo looked upon her as their mother and were happy to do all they could to help. With her they burnt all the furniture in the house, all the bedding and curtains, smashed the dishes and scrubbed the empty rooms with carbolic. The bare boards shone and the smoke from the fire in the back yard rose high into the air. It was time for the Hewitts to start afresh. Gertie's father, Harold Pegg, paid for new beds, a table and chairs for the family. He had wanted them to return with him to the family home in Barkers Lane but Gertie said there was no going back. She whitewashed and distempered the back yard, forced up a couple of flagstones and planted flowers and ivy. The house became well known in the area as being the one with the windows always wide open. Gertie saved what money she could and took the children on tram rides to the hills, where they would picnic on jam sandwiches and hard-boiled eggs.

Thomas and Flo left school and followed Gertie into the mill but their youth was cut short by the First World War. They went together to the Bijou Playhouse on Rosamund Street and sat through stirring performances as ladies with fine singing voices, dressed as soldiers, invited the men in the audience to enlist and fight for King and Country, promising each one a kiss. Bunting fell from the rafters and everyone cheered as men clambered over seats and down aisles. The orchestra played a rousing tune and Flo stood up and cheered as her sixteen-year-old brother hugged her before setting off towards the stage. He received his kiss and a soldier's hat was stuck on his head. It was joyous and wonderful: he was a hero setting out on a great adventure, women loved him and his King would honour him.

The men were taken off that night and Flo felt deflated as she walked home alone to tell Gertie that the man of the house wouldn't be back for a while.

Coronation Street was a strange place between 1914 and 1918: inhabited only by women and children it was similar to thousands of streets all over England, but Gertie's world began at the Rovers and ended at the Corner Shop and in her mind Coronation Street was unique. The lack of men forced the women into each other's company and Gertie often found herself near Ivy Makepiece, either in the street or the shop. Gertie had been heavily influenced by Samuel's hatred of the Makepiece family. She wasn't sure what had started the feud but she knew the family were no good and had often suffered Ivy's vicious tongue – the other local women waited to see the two come to blows.

The occasion arose in the first week of May 1917. After Harold Pegg's death Gertie's mother Bets had fallen on hard times and had been taken to live in the workhouse. Gertie had decided she couldn't help her mother as it was hard enough to feed Mary and Molly on her meagre wages from the mill. When Bets dropped dead, Ivy heard the news despite Gertie's attempts to keep it quiet. She voiced her condemnation of Gertie in the Street, calling the neighbours out of their houses to gaze upon a woman who would let her own mother die alone and be buried in a pauper's grave. Gertie tried hard to ignore the women but that night a brick smashed through the parlour window. She rushed into the street to find the culprit and saw Ivy. Ivy had seen that old Ned Buck from No. 9 had done it but wasn't about to inform on him. Gertie accused Ivy of throwing the brick and tossed the contents of her piss-pot in her face. Ivy sprang at her and the two women tumbled onto the cobbles pulling out chunks of hair, ripping dresses and smashing teeth. Molly and Flo tried to help Gertie but the Makepiece girls set upon them and soon the street was a sea of screaming women. The fight ended with Jim Corbishley from the Rovers throwing a bucket of water over them. Gertie claimed victory as Ivy hurried into her house but her cheers faded when the other woman returned with her rent book. She opened it and showed all the on-lookers that she had paid up to date and challenged Gertie to show hers to the crowd. Gertie had fallen into arrears and owed three weeks' rent: the shame of showing the book was too much and she collapsed. Molly and Flo carried her home.

Thomas Hewitt returned from war physically and mentally unscathed. He had witnessed men blown to pieces in front of him but had somehow forced himself to remain objective about the fighting. Now he had no job, no prospects and no money yet was happy to be back. But he was no longer a boy. Now aged twenty he noticed the local girls for the first time and decided that he was going to marry Mary Makepiece. Ignoring the feud that had raged for nearly ten years Thomas stated his intentions and set about wooing her. She let him see that she was interested by venturing into the Rovers just to be near him.

When he told Gertie of his plans she was furious and ignored him for the next three months, but when Thomas and Mary married on 16 March 1919 both mothers attended the service. On the eve of the wedding Thomas had forced them to listen as he told them of some of the horrors he had witnessed and made them see that the world was full of enough pain without them inflicting more. The feud ended and Gertie was pleased when Thomas took over the tenancy of No. 7 as she could keep a motherly eye on him.

Flo followed in Thomas' footsteps in 1920 when she married Billy Chad at the Mission of Glad Tidings. Billy was a bookie's runner who operated in the shadows down dark alleyways. He had dodged enlisting in the war and was eyed with suspicion by Gertie, who thought that he was no good and would break Flo's heart. Flo, however, was madly in love with the cheeky chap and admired his fancy clothes. He treated her to chocolate and bought her new dresses and she swore she'd reform his ways. Although he always seemed to have plenty of ready cash, Billy told Flo he couldn't afford to rent a house for them and talked Gertie into letting them stay at No. 3, taking over the front bedroom and parlour as their sitting room. Gertie was happy to oblige as she wanted to ensure that Billy made Flo happy. Each day Flo joined Gertie and Molly in the mill while Billy slunk off to meet with his gambling friends. Only once did he overstep the mark, holding a boozy poker game in the house while Gertie was out. She returned home to find one of Billy's pals trying to carry sixteen-year-old Molly into bed. Molly was screaming and hitting the man and Gertie walked past them into the kitchen, where she grabbed the bread-knife and held it against Billy's throat until Molly was released and the men left the house. After that Billy did his entertaining elsewhere.

Flo longed to have a baby and grew upset each month when she discovered that she still wasn't pregnant. Billy also wanted children and grew impatient with waiting, telling Flo that something must be wrong with her for not conceiving. He had always been unfaithful, spending the odd afternoon in bed with a local lass while Flo worked in the mill, but in the autumn of 1924 he began to look for a woman who could be a mother to his children. His eye fell on young Susie Makepiece, Flo's friend from the mill. She was keen on the idea of an affair: men were in short supply and you never knew where a flirtation would lead. This one led to infatuated Billy running off with

• *Billy Chad (below) knew it was not his fault that Flo had not conceived; he'd already sired a son by Fran Roberts in Kitchener Street.*

Susie. While Gertie rejoiced in his departure, Flo took the news badly. She refused to believe he was gone for good and continued to lay a place for him at the dinner table.

Gertie tried to bring Flo out of herself, and encouraged Molly to fill the house with young people. One of them, Will Makepiece, fell for Flo and wrote her a poem declaring his love for her. Gertie thought it a wonderful gesture and tried to push Flo and Will together but Flo barely acknowledged his existence. Will hung around the house in the hope of seeing her but Gertie advised him to leave her alone and was relieved when his attention was drawn elsewhere.

In March 1926, Gertie died of pneumonia. Flo and Molly stayed on at No. 3, with three places laid for dinner instead of four. Molly was amazed at her half-sister's resolve that one day Billy would return. She was doubly amazed when one day he did. He walked in, took off his hat and sat down in his chair to eat dinner. Molly waited for Flo to question her husband over the missing three years but she never brought the

• *During the war, with not much money coming in, Gertie (above) developed a talent for petty pilfering. She stole food mostly to feed her only child Molly (right).*

subject up. Billy was back for good and he wasn't giving any explanations, except to tell Ivy that her daughter was living in London.

The jazz craze hit Weatherfield later than it did most English towns. Skirts were raised and plaits were chopped into bobs. The old Alhambra Music Hall was transformed into a dance hall and on the opening night Molly Hewitt danced until her toes bled. Suddenly life didn't seem so depressing and the days in the mill sped past. Molly blossomed and the local lads started calling to take her walking or dancing. She enjoyed the company of the Weatherfield boys but found them too tame and longed for adventure. Even her brother-in-law Billy had settled down into a dull routine, driving trams, but Molly felt sure that a man somewhere would take her away from Coronation Street. He came in the shape of Artie Lonswaite.

Artie had been brought up in Mawdsley Street but had emigrated to Canada in 1911 along with his two elder brothers. They had taken their textile skills and knowledge with them and had been successful in business and shrewd investments. In 1929 Artie returned to Weatherfield to visit family, and fell for Molly Hewitt. She was immediately smitten by his husky accent and fine suit. He took her dancing and proposed after only two and a half hours. It was a New Year's Eve dance and Molly accepted him just as the chimes struck twelve and the dancers welcomed in a new decade. Cinders had found her Prince Charming at the ball but had no plans to run away. The marriage took place a week later, and by the middle of January Molly was on a ship setting off on the voyage to her new home.

In 1931 Billy lost his job on the trams. Jobs were hard to come by and he sought out his old friends who hung around the back-street clubs. His pal Ronnie Thorpe was planning a smash and grab, and Billy volunteered to drive the getaway car in return for the princely sum of ten pounds. The raid went well and Billy treated Flo to a new winter coat out of his 'earnings'. He told Ronnie he was willing to be of further assistance and was given three boxes of tinned ham to hide. Flo found the stolen food and insisted that Billy

● *Granny Chad, here with Flo, was devoted to her dead cat Ginger. She carried his stuffed body everywhere with her and used to open bottles in his mouth.*

got rid of it. He promised he would but was caught red-handed by PC Ratcliffe, the local bobby. Billy refused to say where the ham had come from and was charged with stealing it as well as with handling stolen goods. Flo watched in court as he was sent to prison for nine months, then pawned the new coat as she needed money to buy food. The next day a crate of tinned food was thrown into the back yard with a note from Ronnie saying that it was a thank-you for Billy's silence. Flo swore that she wouldn't touch the goods but when the pawn money ran out hunger drove her to break her vow.

When Billy returned with a prison record he found it even harder to find work. He promised Flo that he wouldn't contact Ronnie and struggled to make ends meet on his own. Ready to protest for his cause, he joined the National Unemployed Workers' Movement, unaware that it was led by the Communists. He marched with the group to Manchester and watched in horror at the violent clashes with the police. He despaired at the thought of being unable to support Flo, and thanked God that they had never been blessed with children.

Flo got a job at the Rovers as barmaid. The shillings she brought in saved the couple from starvation but their resources were drained when Billy's mother, Iris, moved in with them. Since her husband's death in 1927, she had travelled around Manchester living with her seven children at their different homes. Granny Chad was a familiar sight as she trundled from house to house with her battered suitcase, carrying the cage that contained her stuffed cat Ginger.

She had stayed at No. 3 in 1931, and Flo had hoped that she had seen the back of the critical woman, but Granny announced that after testing all the beds the one in the back room of No. 3 Coronation Street was the most comfortable. Billy's brothers and sisters heaved sighs of relief.

The Depression hit the Chads hard: with Flo's wages they did not qualify for Government assistance. Billy tramped the streets with a placard hung round his neck, advertising his availability for any sort of work. None was forthcoming. Granny scavenged in the alleyways of Oakhill for scraps, but during the harsh winter of 1936, she suffered pains in her chest and felt the cold worse than before. During the night of 16 December, she visited the outside water-closet and was found dead, frozen with cold the next morning, sitting bolt upright on the cludgy.

In the spring of 1938 Molly Lonswaite returned to No. 3. She brought presents for the Chads and whisked them off to the Imperial Hotel for a lavish lunch, but the rich food was too much for the couple who had grown used to cooked food only once every two days. They collapsed and Molly called a doctor. She was appalled by the diagnosis of malnutrition and decided she wasn't leaving England without them. The Chads didn't understand what was happening until they found themselves on the dockside with Molly, being waved off by Thomas Hewitt who wished he was going too: but anything was better than rotting in Coronation Street.

● *This photograph of Ida Barlow is Ken's favourite. He took it in 1957 with his first Brownie camera.*

● *Frank Barlow as a teenager followed his father into the Navy but later gave up the sea to look after his depressed mother.*

It seemed that as soon as the Chads had left for Canada work returned to Weatherfield. Factories started up and fresh orders brought prosperity to the area. It seemed fitting that a new couple should move into the house on this new dawn. Frank Barlow was a twenty-five-year-old postal worker. He moved into No. 3 the day before his wedding day, Sunday 1 May, carrying bride, Ida, over the threshold. She was twenty-two and a weaver at Earnshaw's mill. She had been introduced to Frank by his sister Marjorie who worked alongside her. Their courtship had been brief and she had been eager to marry and settle down with her new husband. She was delighted when her son Kenneth arrived on 9 October 1939. Marjorie delivered the baby: due to Ida's fear of bombs, he was born under the kitchen table, while she distracted herself from the pain by counting the knobs on the new gas cooker.

Frank was quick to join up and served with the 7th Cheshires. Ida's experiences of war were limited: she had been born in 1916 but her earliest memories were of her mother, Nancy, weeping over photographs of her dead father George, whom she had never seen as he had been killed at Loos six months before her birth. Ida had been brought up to dread war and now her worst nightmare had come true. Frank wanted her to leave the town along with the other mothers with young children. She and Kenneth got as far as the railway station but the heaving bodies frightened her. She told herself that she would wait a week or so and then evacuate, but when Frank wrote saying that the war would be over for Christmas she believed him and decided to cope at No. 3.

Marjorie Barlow, Frank's sister and Ida's best friend, moved into the spare room to keep Ida company and for a few months the load lifted off Ida. She and Marjorie carried on their work at Earnshaw's, with Kenneth being looked after by Bessie Tatlock at No. 1. At the mill, Ida was promoted to overlooker and supervised the other women as they worked on khaki and Air-Force-blue yarn. With Marjorie in the house and Kenneth toddling about, Ida looked forward to Christmas 1940 and saved up her coupons for a turkey. The festivities, however, were shattered when a couple of days before Christmas Day the sirens went off and the blitz of Manchester started in earnest. Ida always panicked when she heard the sirens. She decided to take Kenneth down to the shelter under the Mission Hall. Marjorie left the turkey in the oven and joined her, running across the cobbles. Suddenly the earth shook and Ida was flung to the ground, still holding Kenneth. ARP warden Albert Tatlock helped her up and pushed her down the steps to the basement where she screamed hysterically until Ena Sharples slapped her face. Elliston's factory had been hit, and a wall of bricks had tumbled into the Street. Marjorie, running just behind Ida, had been buried under it. When she was dug out she was dead.

Frank returned home on leave only a couple of times, on the first occasion leaving Ida pregnant. David was born in 1942 and Ida gave up her war work to nurse him and look after Kenneth, an adventurous infant. One night he wandered out of the back door during a black-out and frantic Ida spent three hours searching for him before he was found fast asleep

• • • • • • • • • • • • • • • • • • •

Due to Ida's fear of bombs, Ken was born under the kitchen table, while Ida distracted herself by counting the knobs on the new gas cooker

• • • • • • • • • • • • • • • • • • •

under a pile of barrels in the Rovers yard. David, too, gave Ida an anxious moment when, at one and a half, he unthreaded his cot blanket and stuck the wool up his nose. Ida rushed him to hospital where a doctor spent two hours carefully pulling it all out.

After the war Ida was thrilled when Frank returned, but was alarmed to find him changed. Gone was the laughing, carefree lad she had married: now he was a serious man who lost no time in criticizing the way she allowed Kenneth to hang on to her apron strings. He decided the boy needed a firm hand and tried to implement one. Ida handed over control of the children to her husband, believing it was his job to discipline them. She was glad he was not a drinker, like so many of the neighbours, and that he spent his

• *The Barlow boys were different in temperament: David (right) was carefree, easy-going and chirpy. From the earliest age Kenneth (above) was introverted, preferring his own company to playing with the local children. He spent much of his childhood at No. 5 with teacher Ada Hayes.*

evenings at home with her, but she wished he would loosen his collar now and again.

Frank resumed his work as a postman and was promoted to sorting-office supervisor. His wage improved but as it was still not enough to feed two growing lads Ida took a job cleaning at the kitchens of the Imperial Hotel. The children went to Bessie Street School and Kenneth surprised his parents by showing an interest in books. Next door, at No. 5, his teacher Ada Hayes told Ida she should encourage him, and Kenneth started to spend his evenings in Ada's front room where she taught him history and English. When she emigrated in 1949, her younger sister Esther carried on the good work, seeing Kenneth through his eleven plus. Ida was delighted when he became the first child in the Street to pass the exam and gain entry to the prestigious grammar school on Albert Road. Frank was not so happy: he thought education was fine for those who needed it but Kenneth obviously didn't. He was a working-class lad with working-class parents and his place was at his father's side, learning a trade, preferably in the GPO. David was much more to Frank's

liking: bright enough but not too smart, and willing to leave school as early as possible to become an engineer. A good honest profession, thought Frank, and one he understood.

While Kenneth studied and David played in the Street, Ida worked the occasional evening shift at the hotel and Frank became restless. He started to have the occasional drink in the Rovers and started a friendship with barmaid Lizzie Hewitt. Lizzie lived at No. 7 with her husband and daughter and Frank found her enjoyable company. She approved of his moderate drinking, so different from her husband Harry who often went home drunk. Over the bar, Lizzie chatted to Frank and confided that she often felt lonely. She said Harry never showed any interest in her and never went out with her, unless it was to the Rovers. Frank found himself offering to take her out and they arranged to go to the Luxy. One night led to several, and soon Frank and Lizzie were regular picture-goers. They kept their meetings secret, telling themselves that other people wouldn't understand their passion for Bette Davies and Clark Gable.

Then one night Lizzie didn't turn up and in her place came Rovers landlord Jack Walker. He warned Frank that Lizzie was seeing a lot more in the trips than mere picture-going. She had told Annie Walker that she planned to leave Harry. The news startled Frank, who had naïvely believed that he and Lizzie were just friends. It was true that he found her attractive, he confessed, but he had never promised her anything. Following Jack's advice, Frank asked Ida to stop her evening shifts, and spent less time in the pub and more at home. Lizzie never questioned his actions and their friendship cooled.

Kenneth Barlow had his first sexual encounter in the spring of 1955. He was fifteen years old, coming to the end of his time at the grammar school, and the girl in question was Margery Whithers. Frank Barlow couldn't understand why Kenneth's class should need a day in the country to study botany while David at Bessie Street spent his school hours crammed into a tiny classroom, the only 'fresh air' he inhaled polluted by the nearby mills and factories. As B5 set off, Ida worried over Kenneth's packed lunch. Normally he ate with the other boys in the canteen but the piece of paper carrying instructions that had been brought home asked for boys to bring their lunch with them. Ida's experiences of a packed lunch were restricted to the bread and jam butties wrapped in paper and the flask of hot tea that Frank took to work when he was on nights. She could hardly send Kenneth off on a geography field trip with the posh lads from Oakhill and a lunch wrapped in last week's *Gazette*. Poor Ida needn't have worried as the lunch was hardly eaten: lovesick Kenneth spent his lunch break exploring Margery, a pupil at Weatherfield School for Girls, rather than the landscape.

Frank harboured high hopes that when Kenneth turned eighteen in 1957 the Army would make a man of him. His eldest son disappointed him again, however, when his teachers secured him a university scholarship, delaying his National Service. While Frank grumbled about lack of commitment to the Crown, Ida had a secret weep and Kenneth moved three miles away into accommodation in the campus. Over the next two years his visits home became fewer as he flung himself into academic heaven, jazz clubs and sex. In his third year he considered moving into a flat with his lover, a French student, who influenced him with talk of Communism and revolution. They were part of the crowd that hung out in a basement café in Deansgate, smoking Woodbines and drinking beer. The Bohemian life was snatched from Kenneth's grasp in the summer holidays, when Frank was rushed to hospital with breathing difficulties. The doctors said it was a minor heart attack but Frank's father, Sidney, had died of a heart attack when in his mid-forties and Ida feared that her husband, now forty-three, would follow him. Kenneth offered to move home for a couple of weeks. Once he was back in his tiny bedroom, Ida waited on him hand and foot, and Kenneth allowed himself the luxury of living at home for his final year, despite Frank's quick return to health.

Meanwhile, at Ajaz Engineering, David was proving a hit on the firm's football team. He had always been in the shadow of his elder brother and had opted for the role of family joker, mainly to defuse atmospheres created by the feuding Frank and Kenneth and provide light relief for peacemaker Ida. Unlike Kenneth he was never interested in books, but he enjoyed listening to music, and seemed to mix well with both lads and lasses. His first date was with Linda Tanner from No. 11. They had grown up together, and she shared his interest in bicycling.

On Linda's nineteenth birthday, David borrowed a tandem from a friend's father and took her up into the hills. As they looked down over Weatherfield, the houses obscured by thick grey smoke, Linda let him kiss her on the lips before launching into the news that quickly cooled his ardour – that she and Christine Hardman at No. 13 were spending the evening in town with a couple of American servicemen from a nearby base. Out of frustration David remembered gossip in the Street and remarked that Linda was growing up like her mother Elsie, who had entertained more Yanks in the war than the Hollywood Canteen. Linda slapped him across the face and stormed off to find a tram, leaving him with the tandem.

During his final year at university, Kenneth grew passionate about the danger of nuclear war. Along with girlfriend Susan Cunningham, he took part in student demos and Ban-the-Bomb marches. Frank was horrified to discover his house had become a headquarters for beatnik students and felt Kenneth was turning into an anarchist. He gave Kenneth an ultimatum: give up the cause or leave home. For Kenneth there was no dilemma and he held his banner with pride. Frank climbed down when Ida pleaded with him not to drive the lad out. Frank's annoyance with Kenneth's behaviour stemmed this time from the realization that National Service was ending and that both his lads had escaped the experience that he felt sure would turn

• • • • • • • • • • • • • • • • • • •

Kenneth Barlow had his first sexual experience at the age of 15 and the girl in question was called Margery Whithers

• • • • • • • • • • • • • • • • • • •

them into proper men. Never a man to drink very often, Frank started to call in at the Rovers after work for a quick pint just to relax him before entering No. 3 and encountering Kenneth.

Nancy Leathers, Ida's mother, suffered a heart attack at her home in Arkwright Street. Her elder daughters Ethel and Vera had both moved out of the area so Ida nursed her and persuaded Frank that her mother should live with them. David moved in with Kenneth, his rock 'n' roll singles mixing for the first time with Kenneth's classical music collection. With his mother-in-law installed in his house, Frank settled into the Rovers after his tea as well as before. A whole new social life opened up for him and he joined the pub's darts team.

For a short while David took to drinking the odd mild with his father but then the unheard-of happened: young David, who had spent his life in the shadows, was picked by a talent scout to play for a second-division London team. He had been playing for Weatherfield County and the deal was struck between the two teams. Overnight David became a sensation in Weatherfield: not since Kitty Hardwick had been

plucked from her loom at Earnshaw's and thrown into silent films across the Atlantic had Weatherfield seen such success. Frank glowed with pride – and the amount of ale bought for him – and Ida wept into her handkerchief. Kenneth stayed aloof: as he believed football to be the sport of barbarians he could not get excited about his brother's career change. David packed his bags and left home but Kenneth was more interested in having his room to himself again.

For a while Ida was happy: David had done well and she lovingly cut out all the press reports on him; Kenneth had graduated, with a 2:1 degree, and was considering a career in teaching; Nancy was well; and Frank announced that perhaps they could take a holiday, their first in twenty-five years. On the afternoon of 11 September 1961 kind-hearted Ida decided to visit Beattie Pearson, whose ankle had been giving her gyp. It was only a bus ride out of town and she had the afternoon off from cleaning at the Imperial. Crossing the junction at Collier Street, she remembered she'd left her purse at a nearby café. She turned in the street and didn't see the bus as it ploughed into her, killing her instantly.

The funeral was a terrible occasion: Nancy took to her bed, and Frank shrugged off Kenneth's comforting arms, hurting his eldest son by wanting to wait until the last minute for David. But apparently David never came; instead, he watched from nearby bushes as his family buried his mother. Afterwards he told Frank that his legs wouldn't carry him across the graveyard but Frank never forgave him for not being at his side as Ida was lowered into the ground. Shortly afterwards, Nancy moved into an OAP bungalow, and Frank used the insurance money on Ida's life to have a bathroom installed in David's old room.

Now that he was alone in the house with his father, Kenneth had to adjust his plans. A private school in Surrey had offered him a position teaching English but Kenneth allowed Frank to believe he had lost the post and instead took a job at Bessie Street School so he could be near his father. This act of kindness greatly impressed Valerie Tatlock, who was staying at No. 1 with her uncle Albert. Kenneth found the girl stunning and recognized in her a kindness that reminded him of his mother. He proposed and she accepted, but panicked when she thought he was just looking for a mother figure. He assured her that he wasn't and the couple were married on 4 August 1962 at St Mary's. Albert gave away the bride and Lucille Hewitt was bridesmaid.

Suddenly Frank was alone at No. 3, the newly-weds having moved into No. 9. Over a drink in the Rovers Frank was startled when his companion Albert Tatlock commented that Frank was in the same boat as himself and offered to introduce him to the delights of dominoes. Horrified by the thought of spending his life stuck in a rut with nothing but the prospect of turning into another Albert, Frank willed himself to think young. He befriended the widowed Christine Appleby and suddenly found himself falling in love. Kenneth was appalled as Christine had sat next to him at junior school and was over twenty years younger than his father. But Christine obviously found Frank good company, and when he proposed she agreed to marry him. Frank looked forward to a happy future, believing that Kenneth would eventually come round to the idea. The date was set, but then Christine announced she'd made a mistake and called the whole thing off. Frank was devastated, but Christine's interest had proved to him that there was still life left in him: he left the Post Office and opened a DIY shop in Victoria Street. Frank's shop-keeping venture did not last long. In May 1964, he won £5,000 on the Premium Bonds. Realizing that this was his chance finally to enjoy life to the full, he sold the DIY business to a supermarket chain, put No. 3 on the market and moved to a detached house in Bramhall with a stream at the bottom of the garden.

No. 3 remained empty for four years. During that time it fell into disrepair and Ken decided it would never be sold. In Cheshire Frank didn't seem to mind – as Val pointed out to Ken, he hardly needed the money. Then, in 1968, an enthusiastic youngster viewed the house. His name was Richard Fleming but he liked to be called Dickie. At eighteen he was working through an apprenticeship and had plans to marry his childhood sweetheart Audrey Bright. At first the couple set their hearts on No. 9, which Ken was trying to sell for £1,000. That sum was too much so Ken showed them around No. 3. Part of the parlour ceiling had collapsed and the house was for sale at £400. Dickie borrowed the money from his father and the next week eloped to Gretna Green with sixteen-year-old Audrey.

Audrey was a petrol pump attendant on five pounds a week, the major breadwinner in the family as Dickie was on £4 2s. 6d. Money problems didn't bother the couple: they were young and in love and had their lives in front of them. However, after a while the romance went out of beans on toast so they took in a lodger.

Raymond Anthony Langton was a rogue. At twenty-two he seemed years older than Dickie; Borstal and the building trade had helped him develop hard muscles which attracted women like a magnet. He always had, ever since he had been lured into bed at fifteen by his mother's best friend. Compared to Ray, Dickie seemed immature and silly, or so young Audrey decided. Her marriage was less than a year old but the magic had already been replaced by a monotonous lifestyle in which she felt trapped. She couldn't even escape to the pub in the evenings – at seventeen she was too young to drink. Ray set about seducing her. The neighbours saw quickly what was going on at No. 3, and Ken felt sorry for Dickie, who reminded him of his brother David. He took the lad aside and advised him to get rid of his lodger before the lodger took over his place as head of the household. Inspired, Dickie tackled Ray and ordered him out. Ray decided the lad wasn't worth thumping and agreed to go. Dickie's stand impressed Audrey but not enough to sway her attentions and she decided that she would become Ray's lover when the opportunity arose.

It came during a Street outing to Windermere. Dickie sat in silence, aware of his own shortcomings, as Audrey sat with Ray, laughing at his jokes and not removing his hand as it slid under her skirt. The Street's gossips made no attempt to lower their voices as they commented on Audrey's antics, they'd seen it all before: weak husbands standing by while their passion-starved wives flung themselves on the powerful lads. The gossip was too much for Dickie and he sought out his wife at the secret place where Ray had taken her for sex. Dickie laid into Ray but straight away Ray overpowered him and they rolled around in the autumn leaves until Ken Barlow appeared to wrench Dickie away.

On the journey back to Weatherfield Audrey sat in silence beside her husband while cocky Ray stood in the aisle, a bottle in his hand, leading the singsong. Suddenly the coach swerved off the road, the brakes screeched, the bumper smashed into a tree and Ray was sent hurling through the air, through the windscreen and out onto the road.

• *The world of 1968 had much to promise young lovers Dickie and Audrey Fleming but the drag of their mundane lives soon broke their marriage up.*

The Flemings escaped serious injury, but Ray was paralysed from the waist down and the doctors said he would never walk again. Dickie took pity on him and moved him back into the spare bedroom. He believed Ray was no longer a threat, but Audrey found him even more attractive as he now seemed so vulnerable. She was horrified when he announced he was going to marry Sandra Butler from No. 11, and told him she wouldn't let him. She told him she loved him and pushed Ray to agree that he loved her too. Shopkeeper Maggie Clegg saw them kissing and decided that Dickie should be told, but this time Dickie was fed up with fighting for his wife. He packed a suitcase and told Audrey that their marriage was over. As he walked down Coronation Street for the last time, he bumped into Ray's fiancée, Sandra, and told her about Ray and Audrey's affair. Audrey had hoped that, with Dickie out of the way, Ray would finally be hers, but he decided that now she was a free agent he didn't want her and that he really did love Sandra. He moved out and she decided that she couldn't bear to be near him: it hurt too much. Giving the keys of No. 3 to Ken, she returned home to her mother in Preston.

Once again No. 3 was on the market, but buyers were scarce and it stood empty until January 1971. At the beginning of the month, Valerie Barlow was killed in a fire that gutted the Barlow home. While Ken struggled to come to terms with his grief, his neighbours arranged with Audrey for him to rent No. 3. Ken wasn't happy with this because he saw it as a step backwards, but he had his six-year-old twins to think of and knew that the neighbours would be willing to help out. He struggled to rebuild his life and allowed Val's mother, Edith, to take charge of his children Peter and Susan. Edith moved in as housekeeper and showed her disapproval when Ken came home late from a night-club drunk. When he refused to promise it would never happen again, she made plans to apply to the courts for custody of her grandchildren, believing Ken to be an unfit father. Ken didn't want to lose his children, but acknowledged that he had always left Val to look after them. His instinct told him that the twins needed a woman to care for them and that their grandmother would be a more suitable person than a nanny. With Ken's blessing, Edith took the children to live with her in Scotland and Ken sighed with relief as he ceased to be responsible for anyone but himself.

Just over a year after he had started to rent the house, Ken agreed to move out and joined Albert Tatlock at No. 1. No. 3 was sold by Audrey Fleming to newly-weds Ernest and Emily Bishop.

Ernest and Emily had married relatively late in life. For a number of years Emily had lived as a paying guest at the Rovers Return and had met Ernest at his mother Caroline's funeral in 1969. They immediately discovered they had similar interests, in literature, music and religion. Ernest was an experienced lay preacher on the Mission circuit, and Emily had devoted much of her time to secretarial work in the church. They were, as neighbours put it, a couple of do-gooders who wouldn't say boo to a goose. The pair had been engaged for a year, during which they had worked together as partners in a camera shop on Rosamund Street. They found it ironic that when they married they had to hire a rival firm to take the photographs.

Emily and Ernest, although very much in love, were rather stuck in their ways and struggled to adjust to married life. Emily enjoyed eating her meals in peace, but Ernest liked to listen to the Third Programme on the wireless; Emily slept with the window open, Ernest preferred it shut. Emily soon found Ernest naïve when it came to women, but she also discovered that women were strangely attracted to him, seeing in him a man who wasn't threatening and who did not impose himself. As Ernest came to the attention of local ladies, Emily slowly slipped into the role of his protector.

Ernest befriended night-club singer Rita Littlewood after she discovered he was a talented pianist. The pair would practise together in Emily's front room and she began to feel excluded. She was tight-lipped when Ernest ventured out into the sleazy world of clubs as Rita's professional accompanist, but refused to stand by when he innocently invited a stripper to practise in their home as her lodgings were too crowded. She pointed out firmly to Ernest that his relationships with other women were making her jealous and that she

wasn't prepared to share him. He couldn't see what all the fuss was about but found the sight of Emily, eyes blazing with passion, very attractive.

Emily's greatest regret in life was that she had never had children. She was the eldest of six and had spent her youth bringing up her siblings after her mother's death. Those years had revealed a maternal streak and sometimes she felt that that was what she found so appealing in Ernest: he was so absent-minded, so ineffectual, that he needed mothering.

The couple applied to be foster-parents and were quickly approved and registered. It was nearly Christmas and the Bishops were happy to help out when an emergency case arose. A baker from Jubilee Terrace was rushed to hospital and his young children, Vernon and Lucy, needed a home. Years later the Bishops agreed that they had never been so happy as the during two weeks they shared with the Foyle children. Even in the middle of the night as they stripped beds and changed wet sheets they did so with joyful spirits. Here was something they were good at, together, as a team. Emily cooked nutritious meals while Ernest read bedtime stories and played ball in the back yard. The couple spent lavishly on Christmas presents and filled the living room with a huge tree and trimmings. But just as they were about to sit down to eat Mr Foyle arrived to take his children home. Ernest and Emily's time as parents had been short but magical, yet they agreed to stop fostering as they had become too emotionally involved.

When the camera business folded, Emily took a job as a hospital porter. Ernest wanted to work alongside her but discovered he became sick at the sight of blood. He turned into a house husband, the first the Street had seen. Some residents pitied him as he emptied the carpet sweeper wearing his apron, but others admired his spirit as he rose to the challenge. His days of unemployment were few though, because he found a post as wages clerk with Londoner Mike Baldwin. Mike opened a factory in the Street, manufacturing denim outfits, and needed Ernest to act as his number two, looking after the workforce in his absence. Ernest was thrilled with the responsibility and

• Valerie Barlow's tragic death at the age of 29 left Ken struggling with the twins, Peter and Susan. He tried to cope with them at No. 3 but failed.

heavy wage packet. His first luxury was to have a telephone installed at No. 3, his second to have his piano retuned. Emily was pleased to see the spring in his step, but kept a watchful eye on his new workmates, especially mischievous Vera Duckworth.

The factory dominated the Street: from the Bishops' bedroom window, Emily could see right into Ernest's office as he sat going through the accounts. She found it comforting to keep that contact and, now that she'd given up her hospital job, she spent hours tidying the bedroom so that she could peep at Ernest

while he was working. On the morning of 11 January 1978, Emily wasn't in the bedroom when, at 11 a.m., two youths burst into Ernest's office, one holding a shotgun. They demanded that he hand them the wages he had just brought from the bank. He struggled to keep a clear head and did as they wanted, but as he was handing over the bag Mike walked in, nudging the arm of the gunman. The shotgun went off and the youths ran. As the smoke cleared, Mike saw Ernest lying on the ground, blood pouring from his chest. The ambulance rushed Ernest to hospital where he underwent emergency surgery.

When Emily returned from a shopping trip to find the Street full of police cars, she knew instinctively that something had happened to Ernest. As she stepped forward she heard Hilda Ogden pointing her out: "That's her, that's the wife." Neighbours gathered around her as Elsie Howard from No. 11 told her gently that Ernest was in hospital. The sky spun, her legs failed her and Emily hit the hard cobbles in a faint. She recovered in the hospital were she had once worked, to be told that she was now a widow.

Emily refused to allow No. 3 to become a house of grief. She was used to living on her own, having done so most of her life, but found it heartbreaking to cook for one, to have one side of the bed unslept in, to see the piano keys gathering dust. She needed to fill her life with someone and, as if in answer to her prayers, found that person in the shape of Deirdre Langton. They had been neighbours since the Langtons had bought No. 5 in 1977 and Emily was godmother to little Tracy Lynette. With Deirdre's husband, Ray, living abroad, she had been forced to sell the house and was homeless. Emily urged her to make use of her spare bedroom, and Deirdre and Tracy moved in. The two

• *Ernest Bishop and Emily Nugent had met in 1969 at Ernest's mother's funeral. Emily felt sorry for Ernie who obviously couldn't take care of himself.*

women were good therapy for each other, occupying the lonely hours and stopping each other feeling sorry for themselves. They decided to make use of their skills and went into partnership, forming the Coronation Street Secretarial Bureau. While Deirdre typed for clients, Emily dealt with their accounts. All went well until pet-shop owner Arnold Swain brought round his accounts.

Arnold was a charming man, a church-goer who was generous, kind to little Tracy, and made it obvious that he intended to sweep Emily off her feet. At first, Emily resisted: her heart was still with Ernest and she maintained that no one could take his place. But Arnold was persistent and had Deirdre on his side. Deirdre was certain that Arnold could make Emily happy again, could give her a secure future and fill her days. The second time Arnold proposed, Emily accepted.

Then Deirdre realized that she would have to find somewhere else to live. When Arnold and Emily returned to No. 3, Deirdre and Tracy were happily living above the Corner Shop.

Then the nightmare started. As soon as the wedding ring was on her finger, Emily found that there were sides to Arnold's nature that he had kept hidden. He was rude to her friends, had a violent temper and made plans without consulting her. Suddenly the neighbours had been told the Swains were moving to the country, that her home was too small, that the Street wasn't good enough for them. But Emily liked the Street and she loved the house; this was where she belonged, with her friends. But, as Annie Walker pointed out to her, she now belonged with her husband and if he wanted to move then she had to go along with his plans. Yes, thought Emily, she had a husband again, and it was a comforting thought.

A few weeks after the wedding Emily discovered that she did not have a husband after all: an insurance man called to talk to her about a policy on Mrs *Margaret* Swain, who, he said, was Arnold's wife. Emily tried to point out that *she* was his wife but the man was adamant that Mrs Swain needed her husband's signature on her documents. Emily's world crashed

● *When Emily married Arnold Swain she had no idea that he was already married. An insurance man revealed the existence of a wife, living in Bournemouth.*

around her as she confronted Arnold, begging him to explain what was going on. He broke down and told her that he had married Margaret fifteen years previously and had abandoned her during their honeymoon on the Isle of Wight, realizing he'd made a mistake. He had convinced himself that Margaret had died and that he was a widower; he had fallen in love with Emily and married her – she was his wife. Emily threw him out of the house, sick with herself for having become a bigamist and furious with Arnold for making her one. The next day Deirdre found her, after she had spent the entire night scrubbing the house to get rid of any trace of Arnold's presence.

A couple of months later Arnold returned, not to apologize or to plead for a reconciliation. He was clear-headed, knowing exactly what he needed to do – after

all, God had told him. It would be easy, he assured Emily, she wouldn't have to do anything, he'd take care of it all. They belonged together in eternity and he would help them on their way with some pills. Emily pleaded with him to let her go but Arnold over-powered her and promised that death would be painless. She challenged him to show her in the Bible that it was all right to take life, and as he went to fetch it from the bedroom she fled into the Street. The police were called and took Arnold to a psychiatric institution where he died ten months later. In his will he left £2,000 to Emily, but she refused to keep the money and gave it to the hospital to buy a bed. Shortly afterwards she received a visit from penniless Margaret Swain, who challenged Emily over the inheritance she believed should have been hers. Emily agreed, and wrote her a cheque out of her own account.

After Ernest and Arnold, it was hard for Emily to rebuild her life again, but she was determined to battle on. She laid one ghost to rest by taking on the job of wages clerk at Mike Baldwin's factory, her only request being that she did not have to use Ernest's old office. Binman Curly Watts moved into her spare room as a paying guest, and suddenly her life was full of young people and pop music. She started to bloom again as she nursed Curly, or Norman as she insisted on calling him, through love affairs and career crises. They shared out the household tasks: he would polish the silver while she vacuumed, he would polish the shoes as she made the beds. She introduced him to Beethoven, and he let her into his world of astronomy, allowing her to use his precious telescope.

In 1988 the sad day came when Curly announced his intention to move out and rent the Corner Shop flat with his girlfriend Shirley. Emily did not approve but forced herself to give the lad her blessing. She assured him that she would be content to live alone, spending her evenings sewing and drinking cocoa. In fact, she was looking forward to it.

Alas, it was not to be. A month after Curly's departure, No. 3 was invaded by Sergeant Percy Sugden, late of the Catering Corps, along with his budgie Randy. Emily had agreed to take him in as he had lost his job as caretaker at the Community Centre and was waiting for his OAP flat to be prepared for him. He would, he assured her, only be with her for a couple of weeks. After two months had passed, Emily decided to investigate the state of his flat and discovered it had been ready for six weeks. Percy said he didn't want to leave the Street where all his friends were, but Emily was furious at the way in which he had deceived her. She was also fed up with his domineering attitude, and the way he tried to reorganize her life. He had completely taken over the cooking and she had even found him ironing her underwear. She insisted that he moved into his flat and he sadly complied.

Percy had only been gone a week when Emily's conscience pricked her into visiting him. She found a sad, lonely old man fighting to hang on to his dignity. Before she could stop herself, Emily had offered him his bedroom back again.

Emily found it hard work living with the interfering Mr Sugden and struggled hard to maintain her own

identity. In 1992, she decided she needed a change of scenery and announced her plans to retire to Rhos-on-Sea. Percy was stunned when she told him that she wouldn't be taking him and put No. 3 on the market. He did all he could to put prospective buyers off the house but in the end Emily found a buyer, Percy moved out and Emily decided that she didn't want to

• • • • • • • • • • • • • • • • • • • •

**A month after Curly's departure, No. 3
was invaded by Sergeant Percy Sugden,
late of the Catering Corps, along with
his budgie Randy**

• • • • • • • • • • • • • • • • • • • •

leave the house after all: it had been Percy she had wanted to be rid of. Percy was hurt when Emily took the house off the market and poured out his heart to his new landlady, Winnie Dyson. He was comfortable at Winnie's house, except that she had a cat and he was allergic to its fur. He collapsed and was taken to hospital. Mrs Dyson was distressed but refused to get rid of her Fluffy. Emily realized that she couldn't see Percy homeless, and wearily aired his bed again. He returned and Emily knew that he was back for good.

In the summer of 1992 Emily had cause to be thankful for Percy. During the hot months he noticed that she was becoming confused: she would make arrangements then forget about them, letting people down, which was something she never normally did. Rather than question Emily on her actions, Percy started to cover up for her. Her appearance suffered as she became less interested in herself and withdrew into her mind, getting upset as she struggled to remember details of her childhood in Harrogate. She stopped eating and found it hard to sleep, and spent most days wandering around the house ignoring Percy. He tried to rally her friends but they thought he was just interfering and advised him to keep out of Emily's affairs. They changed their attitude, though, when he broke down after finding that Emily had disappeared in her slippers. The police were called, Emily was located and taken to hospital for tests. For weeks she went through therapy and took pills to subdue the depression she

● *Since moving into No. 3, Percy Sugden has crusted 267 pies, gutted and beheaded 439 fish and peeled 18,200 potatoes.*

both felt the need for companionship and planned a quiet wedding. To commemorate the fiftieth anniversary of D-Day they travelled to Normandy together and wept at the graves of friends and comrades. On their return, Maud admitted that she had wept at the grave of the young American who had been the father of her daughter Maureen. Percy was shocked that she had been unfaithful to her husband while he had been fighting and told her that he could not marry her.

He was astonished to receive an invitation from Olive to attend her marriage to Edwin Turner. He took Emily as his guest and it was at the service that she met the Reverend Bernard Mottram. She was flattered when he asked her to help him feed the homeless at Christmas and they started a liaison. When Bernard proposed, Emily decided that he was her last chance of happiness and accepted. Their wedding plans were shattered when he discovered that she had suffered a breakdown. He explained that he had nursed his mother through mental illness and was not prepared to go through it all again. She was heartbroken when he turned his back on both her and God.

Percy's budgie, Randy, was his main listening-ear before he moved into No. 3. Percy had bought the budgie for companionship after his wife, Mary, died in 1978. When, sixteen years later, he read that the average lifespan of budgerigars was fourteen years, he decided to write to the local paper to say that his Randy was at least eighteen. Emily stopped him writing by admitting that shortly after he had moved into No. 3 she had found Randy dead in his cage and, rather than upset Percy, had replaced him with an identical bird. Percy was stunned, both by Emily's behaviour and because he had not spotted the intruder.

Emily and Percy muddle along together at No. 3. Now that they are both retired, Emily tries hard to occupy her days with charitable work so that Percy is not always under her feet. She knows that he is becoming less able as he gets older, but he stubbornly refuses to acknowledge it. There will come a time, she is certain, when she will have to steel herself and suggest that he enters an old folks' home.

had been suffering. On her return home she thanked Percy for all he had done and told him he was a good friend.

Both Percy and Emily found romance late in life. He fell for Olive Clark, the widow of an old Army pal. He took her out on a regular basis and plucked up courage to propose. When she laughed at him, assuming he was joking, he put on a brave face and agreed it was a good joke. A year later he proposed again, this time to disabled shop assistant Maud Grimes. They

·Nº5 CORONATION STREET·

1902 – 1904
Jack and Maggie Leeming

1904 – 1908
Tom, Cissy, Mollie and Reg O'Connor, with Jake Matthews

1908 – 1952
Sidney, Alice, Ada, Fred, Esther and Tom Hayes

1952 – 1962
Esther Hayes

1962 – 1976
Minnie Caldwell, with Jed Stone and Charlie Moffitt

1976 – 1977
Mike Baldwin and Bet Lynch

1977 – 1979
Ray, Deirdre and Tracy Langton

1979 – 1985
Bert, Ivy, Brian and Gail Tilsley

1985 – 1988
Ivy Tilsley

1988 – 1995
Don and Ivy Brennan

1995 —
Don Brennan, with Josie Clarke and Ashley Peacock

Jack Leeming had a secret, which excited him. As he glanced around at his new neighbours moving into Coronation Street he was pleased to discover that they all looked like ordinary folk, the sort who worked hard and conformed, just like his parents and so unlike himself. He had been twenty-one in the summer of 1902 and had celebrated by telling his parents he had married the girl next door at Victoria Street, Maggie Baker. Jack and Maggie had grown up together, and she was two years younger, the same age as his sister Vicky. Jack had shared a bed with his sister since she was three years old and, just like Maggie, Vicky had fallen in love with him. They had drifted into sex around her thirteenth birthday when he was fifteen.

Jack and Maggie both worked at Hardcastle's mill – or, rather, Maggie worked and Jack spent as much time as he could off duty, smoking and exercising to keep himself in good condition. One day in 1903, during a singsong in the Rovers, Charlie Corbishley had decided that Maggie was ripe for some fun and she encouraged his advances. She had no qualms about being unfaithful to Jack: she had gone along with the pretence that she was married to him so that they could get a house together, but she had hoped that by the new year they would have exchanged vows. Jack, though, refused to be tied by a piece of paper.

Maggie was angered when Jack wanted her to have a baby so that he could announce publicly that they weren't married and shock the neighbours even more. Aware of this, Maggie was thankful that she had never conceived and prayed to God she never would. It wouldn't have mattered if Jack had loved her, but Maggie knew that he was only using her to make himself feel superior to the others: he was different, he had secrets, he was rebelling against society. She had had enough and moved out, telling Jack she was returning to her parents.

Jack wasn't bothered by Maggie's departure. He packed up the house and returned to Victoria Street and the welcoming arms of his little sister, living alone after the deaths of their parents. Next door sat Maggie, unaware that Jack had arrived to haunt her again.

In April 1904, widowed knife grinder Cissy Matthews moved into No. 5 with her six-year-old daughter Mollie, her four-year-old son Jake and her lodger Tom O'Connor. Tom had lived with the Matthews family in Butcher's Alley for seven years. He was an Irish immigrant and, since the summer of 1902, had worked as an engineer at Hardcastle's. His supervisor at the works had been John Matthews, Cissy's husband, and Tom had been with John when he became trapped by machinery at the mill. He had tried to pull the other man free but John's neckerchief had got caught in a retrieving machine and he choked to death. That had been in January 1904 and Cissy was given the tenancy of the house as soon as Jack Leeming had vacated it.

• • • • • • • • • • • • • • • • • • •

If anyone had asked Cissy outright, she would probably have given a straight answer, that she and Tom had been lovers since the night of John's death

• • • • • • • • • • • • • • • • • • •

Cissy had been a knife grinder since inheriting her father's grindstone in 1896. She enjoyed the work, wandering the streets with her stone and sharpening knives, scissors and axes. The children often accompanied her as she saw no point in schooling and thought it best that they learnt the rules of the street. Soon after moving into the Street, Cissy worked Palmerston Street and, as usual, had a liquid lunch of gin in the Eagle and Child. She left her equipment outside in Jake's care and settled down for some peace and quiet. Jake soon bored of guarding the stone and stool, and wandered off to watch the barges carrying coal along the canal. He watched the bargemen steer their load through the lock by Plank Lane Market and, when they were out of sight, leaned over the lock to throw pebbles into the water. He slipped and banged his head on the lock gate as he fell into the dark, dank canal. His body was found later that afternoon.

There was much gossip over the nature of the relationship between Cissy and Tom. Some commented on Mollie's resemblance to the lodger and noted that Tom mourned Jake as if he had been his own flesh and blood. Nothing was ever uncovered about the past but when Cissy married Tom on 25 December 1904, no one was surprised, although many wondered if the sleeping arrangements at No. 5 would have to change. If anyone had asked Cissy outright, she would probably have given a straight answer, that she and Tom had been lovers since the night of John's death and that reaching for him in the midst of her grief had been the most natural thing for her to do. But no one asked.

In 1907 young Mollie O'Connor – she'd followed her mother's lead and taken Tom's surname as her own – died of TB, just three months before Cissy gave birth to a son, Reg. Tom was thrilled with the birth of his son and gave him his own father's name. The affection the couple felt towards Reg was of no consolation in January 1908, though, when, after an evening of heavy drinking, Cissy rolled over in bed and suffocated him. The couple panicked and feared arrest for manslaughter. They waited until nightfall and then secretly buried Reg in St Mary's cemetery. As soon as the deed was done, they loaded their belongings onto a hand cart, stolen from the mill's store yard, and left under cover of darkness.

An altogether different couple took on the tenancy of No. 5 in February 1908. Sidney Hayes was thirty-two, and worked at the GPO as a clerk. Sundays found him in the pulpit at the Mission of Glad Tidings, where he was employed as lay preacher. His new bride, Alice, aged twenty-five, agreed with him that a woman's place was keeping house for her husband. She did, however, have her own pastimes, which included playing the organ and training the choir at St Thomas's.

The couple's happiness was cemented in 1910 by the birth of a little girl, whom they named Ada after Sid's mother. They organized a party to celebrate Ada's safe delivery and to welcome the neighbours at the Mission. For many it was the first time they had entered the building, but Ivy Makepiece from No. 11 was jealous to see the happy young family as she had recently lost a child by miscarriage. She told friends that she was surprised they could afford the delicious spread on Sid's wages. The gossips set to work and it reached Mission supervisor Thomas Hawkins's ears

● *Twenty-one-year-old Jack Leeming kept Maggie Baker hanging on for a wedding ring (above). Mollie O'Connor (below, with Cissy) was not Cissy's first-born; her daughter Kate had been trampled to death when the milk-horse bolted.*

that Sid had helped himself to the collection money to pay for his daughter's party. Sid's explanation – that he had saved hard for the party – was accepted by Hawkins, but, unluckily for Sid, mud had been thrown and some of it stuck.

The distant thunder of war disturbed Sid: he believed it was wrong to take arms against another man or nation and worried that he would be forced to compromise his beliefs if Britain entered the conflict. While other young men around him eagerly awaited the chance to battle against the Hun, Sid preached sermons on turning the other cheek to half-empty halls. Neighbours rushed to enlist, eager for the taste of conflict and a hero's homecoming, but Sid stayed at the GPO and, in 1915, celebrated the birth of his son, Frederick. What would the future hold for a child born into a warring world?

1916 brought conscription and Sidney, with Alice's blessing, refused to sign up. He was sent in front of a tribunal made up of local tradesmen and officials. His own boss at the GPO, Captain Warboys, was on the panel and Sid tried to explain why he would not fight. The local paper reported that he was a conscientious objector, shirking his nation's call, and a brick was thrown through the Hayeses' parlour window, the glass just missing Fred as he lay asleep in his pram. Sid refused to do manual work, building roads, and was sent to prison for the duration of the war. After two months he received a letter from Alice, saying that Fred had died of diphtheria.

Alice faced a hostile war alone with infant Ada. While her neighbours wrote patriotic letters to husbands and sons, Alice was shunned. Only Gladys Arkwright at the Mission cared for her and Alice spent many hours sitting with the old woman in her vestry.

In 1918 the war had still not finished with the Hayes family: after being handed a white feather by Ivy Makepiece, Sid was beaten up during a victory parade and, returning to work at the GPO, Captain Warboys told him that he would ensure he was never promoted above the post of clerk. Sid thanked God he hadn't been sacked when he looked around at all the ex-servicemen begging in the streets. He and Alice

opened a soup kitchen at the Mission and weren't surprised when none of the other residents volunteered their help.

At the end of the war Ada was eight years old and the time had arrived for her to start as a half-timer at the mill; she had received free education until then at Hardcastle's factory school. Sid wasn't happy with the idea of his young daughter dodging in and out of the looms, under weavers' feet, retrieving bobbins and threads, and facing the danger of being caught up in the machines. He sought the advice of her teacher, Gladys Long, who also taught Sunday School at the Mission. Gladys knew that Ada was a bright girl and suggested she kept her on at the school as her helper and gave the child extra lessons – perhaps one day Ada, too, would train as a teacher.

Two more children were born at No. 5 – Esther in 1924 and Thomas two years later. Thanksgiving Services were held for them both at the Mission. By the time Tom was born, Ada had left full-time employment and, under Gladys Long's guidance, had become a teacher. When she was seventeen, in 1927, she was taken on full time at Hardcastle's as teacher in the elementary class. Esther was thrilled to be taught by her big sister, but Tom hated it as he felt she was always twice as hard on him as the others.

Miraculously, both Sid and Ada managed to keep their jobs during the Depression years. While their neighbours faced starvation, Sid reopened the soup kitchen at the Mission where, helped by Ada, he distributed food bought from money donated by the Mission committee. For the first time since 1916, the neighbours accepted Sid's help and no longer referred to him as 'the conchie'. He also continued to operate the Band of Hope, giving free magic-lantern shows to local children with Esther operating the lantern.

During Esther and Tom's education at Hardcastle's, the school underwent a change of management. With the closure of Hardcastle's mill in 1931, the school, too, had faced its demise until the council stepped in and bought it as part of their education system. It was merged with the established council school at Bessie Street and Ada was promoted to teaching the older

● *Principled Sid Hayes (above) wasted years of his life in prison and his death turned Alice (right) into a bitter, cantankerous invalid.*

● *Both Esther (left) and Ada (above) had to look after Alice in her old age. Ada had given up hope of escaping when Matt proposed. She confided to Esther that she didn't love him, but he was her only way out. Esther knew she would never be so lucky.*

children – but still in huge classes of fifty. Esther left school in 1939 and took a job as a waitress at the Galaxy restaurant, where the ceiling was painted with stars and planets.

The autumn of 1939 found Ada helping to organize the evacuation of Bessie Street School. As part of the evacuation of 13,000 Manchester children to the coast and countryside, the 300 Bessie Street children were marched, *en masse*, to the railway station, each carrying their cases and gas masks. Ada was with them, her own case sent ahead on a lorry. While she was telling the children they were going on an adventure, she made sure that they did not see her own tears as she kissed her family goodbye, unsure when she would see them again.

In fact the bombing didn't start for another year. During that time Esther took a job as a Town Hall clerk while Tom fell in with a bad crowd and took to hoarding goods for selling on the black market. When the air raids began in earnest, Esther hated the day-time ones worst of all: she would sit in her bunker under the Town Hall not knowing how her parents, now in their sixties, were coping. Evening and night raids were easier for her as she shepherded them from their bed across the Street to join the other residents in the Mission basement where caretaker Ena Sharples kept the most comfortable easy chair for Alice.

Alice was sitting in that chair on the night of 24 December when Sid was caught in a raid while returning home from delivering a sermon at Booth Street Chapel. He sheltered in Gas Street's brick shelter and was killed outright when it caught a direct hit.

Tom was no help to Alice or Esther during the war years. He managed to dodge the call-up but was caught looting a bombed jeweller's shop in Victoria Street. Sentenced to three years in prison, he passed the war years behind bars, just as his father had – under different circumstances – from 1916.

After spending four years teaching in Blackpool Ada Hayes returned home to her shared bedroom with Esther. She had made occasional visits to No. 5 but had always been eager to return to her billet at the Rose and Crown public house, where she had had a

wonderful romance with French airman Alexandre Dupont. He had been her first lover and she had fallen madly in love with him. She hoped they would marry but when France was liberated he announced he was returning to his wife and son. Ada returned to Weatherfield, with thirty-six Bessie Street School-children still in her care, the others having returned after the Blitz. She got home to find that Alice had taken up permanent residence in bed. The doctor couldn't find anything wrong with her but she swore that whenever she got up her legs gave in and she felt nauseous. The doctor suggested to Esther and Ada that their mother was probably seeking attention and that they should humour her.

Tom also returned home, and his sisters were hurt at the welcome he received from Alice: she clambered out of bed to hug him and to say that he was the tonic she had needed since Sid's death. Tom, however, had no plans to support the family, only himself. He had had a pleasant war, making friendships with like-minded men who saw the system as oppressive and believed that the only way out of the gutter was to fight and steal. Ada was astonished to find stockings stored under floorboards in the scullery and tins of ham piled high in Tom's wardrobe. The girls asked him to settle

• • • • • • • • • • • • • • • • • •

When Alice's coffin was moved downstairs, it was the first time she had been out of bed for seven years

• • • • • • • • • • • • • • • • • •

down and take a job, for Alice's sake, but he just laughed and saw himself as a romantic figure, always keeping one step ahead of the law. But it didn't take long for the law to catch up with him, and in 1947 he was sent back to prison. Alice retired to her bed again.

When Matt Harvey proposed to her, Ada jumped at the chance. At thirty-nine she had resigned herself to spending the rest of her life teaching children and nursing her mother. Matt was a country boy, who had plans to farm sheep in Australia. His muscular build reminded her of Alexandre, her war-time French lover, and she never gave a second thought to the idea of

● *Ena Sharples was an occasional lodger in Minnie Caldwell's back room, but they were both too set in their ways to share No. 5 for long.*

leaving England; the country offered her nothing. They married at the Mission of Glad Tidings, and the only member of Ada's family present was Esther, Tom being 'away' and Alice in bed. After waving the couple off on their new life, Esther returned home downhearted, knowing that she was going to be Alice's nurse for the rest of her mother's life.

Although Alice maintained that she needed constant nursing, Esther clung to her job at the Town Hall and was made head of the library division. She was offered an exciting job in the south but turned it down out of duty to Alice. The neighbours felt sorry for

Esther as her youth vanished and she wasted away in No. 5. They took their problems to her, thinking her educated, and she occupied herself in trying to help them, just as Sid had helped those in need. On the morning of 16 February 1952, Esther took Alice's breakfast in to her only to find her mother dead in bed. Relief flooded over her and she fell to the floor in tears. When Alice's coffin was moved downstairs, it was the first time she had been out of bed for seven years.

Tom was released from prison and returned to Esther occasionally, mainly to borrow money or lie low for a night, but otherwise she lived alone at No. 5. When the chance came for her to take a new job, as head clerk at Mason's Department Store, she took it because it came with a flat on Moor Lane, which had its own bathroom. It was too good an opportunity to miss and Esther packed her bags merrily and shut the front door to No. 5 for the last time.

Minnie Caldwell had been widowed in 1935 when Armistead, her husband of ten years, died. She had been childless and, aged thirty-five, believed her mother, Amy Carlton, when she said no other man would look at her. Amy had moved into Minnie's house and there they had grown old together. Amy became bedridden in the late fifties and in 1960 Minnie retired from working at Earnshaw's mill. In the summer of 1962 Amy died, aged ninety-four, and Minnie decided that she could no longer live at 15 Jubilee Terrace. She asked Mission supervisor Leonard Swindley to help her move. She didn't want to go far as all her life she had lived in only two streets, separated by the Sally Army hall. To her, No. 5 Coronation Street would be ideal: she spent her evenings in the Rovers snug and her best friend Ena Sharples ran the Mission at the end of the Street. Swindley talked to the landlord and settled a fair rent for her and Minnie moved in with her cat, Bobby. She was surprised when Ena seemed put out by her arrival, but their friend Martha Longhurst put down her reaction to the fact that Ena was no longer the sole Grandmother of the Street.

Unlike her friends, Minnie decided against charring or caretaking to supplement her pension; instead she took in lodgers. Throughout the 1960s, many came and went, some staying days, others years. Her two favourites were petty thief Jed Stone and comic Charlie Moffitt. Jed looked upon Minnie as his mother and delighted her by calling her 'Ma'; her nickname for him was 'Sunny Jim', after the popular character on the Force Flakes packet. Jed was a native of Liverpool, and had been in and out of approved school and Borstal. As a youth, he had led Dennis Tanner from No. 11 into a life of crime, which had ended in them sharing a cell for six weeks in Strangeways, but the older Jed stayed clear of villains and made a living selling goods 'off the back of a lorry' on market stalls. He turned Minnie's front room into a store room for bottles of sherry, misshapen socks and sloppy Joe sweaters. While acknowledging that Jed brightened up Minnie's life, Ena felt that he was a terrible influence on the old woman, especially when he arranged for her to have a vacuum cleaner and television set on HP.

In 1966 Jed's criminal activities caught up with him when he was arrested for handling stolen blankets. The detective who came for him was touched to find him mid-preparation for Minnie's birthday party, and allowed him to finish the celebrations and tell Minnie he was leaving to see a sick friend. As soon as he left, Minnie burst into tears: his act had not fooled her for a moment, she knew exactly where he was going and that the chances were he would never return.

Charlie Moffitt was a completely different kettle of fish and arrived in Minnie's life just when she needed cheering up, Martha Longhurst having died of a heart attack. Charlie didn't come alone to No. 5 – he moved in with his greyhound Little Titch, six rabbits and eight pigeons. Minnie loved them all. Charlie 'Chuckles' Moffitt was a comic at the Viaduct Sporting Club under Elliston's raincoat factory. He had been born into showbusiness, his father being a trapeze artist, his mother a bearded lady, and all his energies were

● *Bet Lynch and Jed Stone had much in common: both came to the Street escaping the past – hers emotional, his criminal; both searched for love, and both were forcibly removed from No. 5 – she by her lover, he by the police.*

pushed into making people laugh. The unfortunate thing was that he wasn't very funny. After being booed off stage, he was sacked from the club and took a job as the local insurance representative. Minnie enjoyed mothering the accident-prone Charlie but wasn't pleased when he attempted to brew his own beer in her front parlour, telling her that it was tonic wine. Minnie opened a bottle, got drunk on the contents – and was more than startled when the other bottles started to explode. When he decided that insurance was not for him, Charlie packed his bags and left to resume his showbusiness career.

Minnie was a vulnerable old lady and people took advantage of her when Ena wasn't around to look after her. On more than one occasion she blew her pension on a new coat or fancy titbits for her cat, only to discover that she had no coal money and had to spend days wrapped up in bed, only venturing out to empty her chamber-pot. Her silliness over money reached a head in 1969 when bookie Dave Smith pushed her for repayment of ten pounds she owed in gambling debts – she had a passion for the horses. Minnie had no money to give him and disappeared, leaving a note for Ena in which she pleaded with her to look after Bobby. While Ena traipsed the snow-covered streets, searching for her friend, the residents rounded on Smith for victimizing one of their own. Minnie slept rough for a couple of nights on a park bench before being taken to hospital with pneumonia. She pleaded with the nurses not to tell anyone where she was but the doctor contacted Ena. Smith brought her flowers, promised to wipe the slate clean and limit her to two shillings a week betting money.

Minnie had known hardship all her life: as a child she had held her mother's banner when Amy toyed with being a suffragette, and they had been moved on in Albert Square. The Depression had robbed her of her husband and left her in a back-street hovel with an old bedstead, a rickety table and nothing else. The rest of her life had been no better and coping on a pension was hard enough without the introduction of decimalization in the early seventies. Neighbour Albert Tatlock felt he had the solution to their money troubles

when he suggested they married as they would benefit from a bigger pension. Minnie was keen on the idea, as long as Albert moved in with her at No. 5 so that Bobby didn't feel pushed out. For six months they had an understanding, until Ena broke the news that they would not be better off if they married. Albert said he didn't really mind if they went ahead anyway, but Minnie told him he had too many annoying habits, such as drinking tea out of his saucer.

In the mid-1970s Minnie's health started to deteriorate, and she spent more time than ever huddled in bed with Bobby. Ena became an on–off lodger, but she, too, suffered from failing health and passed most of her time recuperating at Lytham St Anne's by the seaside. In the spring of 1976 Minnie holidayed at Whaley Bridge, where her old friend Handel Gartside lived. Handel was happy to have Minnie keeping him company in his cottage and she enjoyed helping to tend his half-acre garden. It took little to persuade her to stay with him, and Handel arranged for her furniture to be moved out of No. 5.

Newly-wed Ray Langton decided that No. 5 would be the perfect house for him and his bride Deirdre. A builder by trade, he drew up plans to modernize the property. The landlord, Edward Wormold, put the house on the market for £4,500 and Ray knew he could afford it. The only problem was Deirdre, who refused to live in a back-street terrace. While the Langtons argued, Londoner Mike Baldwin stepped in and bought the house.

Mike was a barrow-boy made good, who had turned businessman at the age of twelve and had worked hard to drag himself up. At seventeen he opened a TV repair shop in his bedroom, the day after his mother's funeral. In 1973, at the age of thirty-one, he bought a factory in the East End and started to manufacture denim garments. He moved into Anne Woodley's house in Islington, became her common-law husband and looked upon her sons, Matthew and Jonathan, as his own. The need for expansion sent him searching the north for cheap premises, and in November 1976 he bought the old warehouse on Coronation Street, which had been empty since fire had gutted it a year earlier. No. 5 was handy for the factory, as it was directly opposite. Barmaid Bet Lynch was also handy and became Mike's lover. He told her he was married, and looking only for a bit of company during the week, but Bet convinced herself that he would fall in love with her and leave his wife for her.

Mike employed Ray Langton and Len Fairclough to modernize the house, using the plans Ray had drawn up. As well as knocking through downstairs, they removed the old Victorian fireplace and made an exposed-brickwork chimney breast. A telephone was installed and the third bedroom was made into a bathroom. Bet moved in, telling the neighbours she was Mike's housekeeper but everyone knew that only one bedroom was occupied.

After a couple of months, Mike grew tired of clinging Bet and invited Anne up for a visit. As soon as she walked through the door, Anne found strands of long blonde hair and smelt cheap scent. It was this that drew her to Bet in the Rovers and the two women faced each other across the bar. Bet wasn't prepared to fight Mrs Baldwin but was stunned when Anne broke the news that she wasn't Mike's wife, only his lover. Bet confronted Mike about his lies, and Mike told Bet that she didn't have a future with him as he considered himself married to Anne. She slapped his face and he ordered her out of the house.

Bet, however, refused to budge. Up to this point in her life, she had drifted from bedsit to flat and back to bedsit. Now that she had a proper house she was not going to give it up without a fight. Mike took up residence at the Oakland Hotel, had the locks changed on No. 5, and sold the house behind Bet's back to Ray Langton. Downhearted, Bet found her belongings in the back yard, shoved into bin bags. She moved into the flat over the Corner Shop, unaware that Mike had arranged with her landlady, Renee Bradshaw, that he would subsidize her rent.

Twenty-two-year-old Deirdre Langton was now happy to live in a back street after she had struggled to look after baby Tracy in a bedsit at the top of the house in Victoria Street where she had been brought up. Deirdre's father, Donald, had died when she was young and she had been raised by her corset-making mother Blanche. After their wedding in 1975 Ray had moved in with her and Blanche had let him section off the top floor of the house into a self-contained flat. Shortly afterwards Blanche had moved to the Midlands and now needed to sell the house. When Mike offered Ray No. 5, Deirdre knew it was their only chance to buy a good house at a reasonable price. Besides, Coronation Street was on her patch and she knew the residents well.

Deirdre did not have a happy stay at No. 5. In October 1977 she was molested under the viaduct while returning home from a keep-fit class. When she got back, she broke down, and told Emily that the man had tried to rape her. The attack drove a wedge between the Langtons as Deirdre shied away from Ray's touch and had a nervous breakdown. She disappeared from the house, leaving Tracy alone, and contemplated suicide on a motorway bridge. She was preparing herself to jump when a passing lorry driver asked her for directions and broke her concentration. She went home and tried to put the incident behind her but still refused to let Ray touch her.

Ray's patience with Deirdre grew thin. He still loved his wife but couldn't understand why she was punishing him for something another man had done. His roving eye fell on Janice Stubbs, a waitress at Dawson's bakery, and they embarked on an affair. Emily found out what was going on and dropped heavy hints to Deirdre, who finally understood what she meant. She felt that her whole world was collapsing and was filled with anger against Ray, Janice and herself. She told Ray she was leaving him but he begged her to stay, saying that Janice meant nothing to him. He swore his love was still hers and slowly won Deirdre round.

Deirdre told Ray that their marriage would survive only if they left No. 5, the Street and England. She told him she wanted to emigrate and left it up to him to find the right destination. Ray secured a job on a building site in Holland and the Langtons packed. The residents threw a farewell party for them, but during the evening Deirdre realized that she was running away, which was wrong. Ray was amazed when Deirdre told him she had changed her mind and wanted to stay. He felt he had taken all that he could from his mixed-up wife. He took the job and left the country, saying that the house would have to be sold because he needed capital. Deirdre was grateful when Emily took in her and Tracy as paying guests.

No. 5 was sold for £7,000 and in February 1979 a new family moved in. Forty-four-year-old foundry worker Bert Tilsley put down the deposit with money from his old landlord in Inkerman Street who wanted to convert his house into flats. Bert moved in with his wife, Ivy, and twenty-one-year-old son, Brian. Ivy was a familiar face in Coronation Street, having worked first

• • • • • • • • • • • • • • • • • • •

Bet moved in, telling everyone that she was Mike's housekeeper, but everyone knew that only one bedroom was occupied

• • • • • • • • • • • • • • • • • • •

at the mail order warehouse and now at Baldwin's Casuals. She was a staunch trade unionist and a regular church-goer at St Luke's Catholic Church. Brian didn't share his mother's faith and never attended Mass. Instead he spent his spare time in the gym and riding his motorbike. During the day he worked as a car mechanic but in the evenings he was a regular at the discos in Manchester. Just before the family had moved into No. 5, Brian had gatecrashed a party at No. 11 and had fallen for twenty-year-old shop assistant Gail Potter.

Shortly after the Tilsleys arrived in the Street, Gail celebrated her twenty-first birthday and Brian took the opportunity to turn it into a double celebration by proposing to her. Gail eagerly accepted but furious Ivy vowed to break the engagement. Bert Tilsley thought Gail a 'smashing little lass', and was certain she'd make a great wife, but Ivy was against her ostensibly because she was not a Roman Catholic but actually because Brian was her pride and joy and she didn't want anyone taking him away. When she discovered that Gail had had an affair in the past with a married man, she told Brian, thinking the news that Gail was soiled

goods would cause him to break with her. Instead, Brian confronted Gail and she told him how the man had taken advantage of her. Rather than being angry with her, Brian turned on Ivy for telling him in the first place. He packed his bags and walked out, causing Ivy to break down. As always, Bert found himself caught in the middle, understanding his wife's motives while supporting Brian's attempt to break free of the apron strings. He saw an ally in Gail and together they reconciled mother and son, at the same time forcing Ivy to accept Gail.

The young Tilsleys were married on 28 November 1979. Fatherless Gail was given away by her one-time boss, Mike Baldwin, and after honeymooning in the Isle of Man, the young couple moved into Brian's room at No. 5, Gail on the understanding that it was to be a short-term arrangement. Almost immediately, she and Ivy clashed over cooking in the small kitchen. When Gail discovered she was pregnant, she told Brian that she was not living in the house with a baby: they had to have their own home. The young couple decided to buy rather than rent, and signed up for a tiny one-bedroomed house on a new estate in Buxton Close, two bus rides away from Ivy. In need of a deposit, Brian borrowed £300 from his mother, unaware that it was his parents' holiday money. Gail was thrilled with the house and didn't mind its size: it would be her little nest and no one else had ever lived in it. The couple moved in just in time as, while visiting the Rovers on New Year's Eve 1980, Gail went into labour and was driven to hospital in an ambulance. Her son, Nicholas Paul, was born five minutes before the new year chimed in.

With the youngsters gone, Ivy and Bert settled down to life as grandparents, enjoying Sunday lunches in the bijou house and chatting about work. Ivy was made supervisor at Baldwin's and found her friendships with the workers compromised now that she was one of the bosses. Bert's life was shattered when the foundry closed down: he received £2,000 in redundancy payment, and Ivy tried to cheer him up by telling him he would find new work in no time. She was wrong, and Bert faced eighteen months on the dole.

● *Deirdre Langton had wanted her daughter named Lynette but Ray registered her in his choice – Tracy Lynette.*

The once chirpy man turned into a depressed, slouched shadow of his former self, until he was taken on at Longshaw's factory. It did not prove lucky for him. He slipped on some oil and fell, breaking his arm. After a while, he realized that the arm wasn't healing and asked the doctor what was happening. The news that he had had a mini-stroke shocked Ivy, especially when he told her he wasn't allowed to work with machinery again. Forced to leave Longshaw's, his spirits sank when faced with the dole again.

Brian took pity on his father and employed him at the garage. Bert was frustrated at feeling helpless and attempted to use a pressure gauge to blow up a tyre. The gas canister exploded and blew up the entire garage. Bert was taken to hospital in a coma. Ivy kept a bedside vigil until he regained consciousness, but the explosion had left him mentally disturbed. Once he returned home to No. 5, he quickly disappeared again. The police found him wandering in Bristol after sleeping rough and he was admitted to hospital for psychiatric treatment.

Gail and Brian moved in with Ivy after deciding to sell their house to invest in Brian's new garage. Ivy was

thrilled to have the house full again and loved having Nicky under her feet. The family were a great comfort to her in 1984 when Bert became very ill. She got to the hospital in time to be with him as he died but Brian, out on an emergency job, was too late and Bert's death affected him terribly.

Once the garage was up and running, Gail believed they would find a house of their own and was infuriated when Brian announced his intention of buying new equipment instead. She took Nicky and walked out on him. Ivy was appalled when, rather than begging Gail to return, Brian accepted her departure and announced that he was single again. It was only when Ivy threw him out that Brian realized he wanted Gail back. They were reconciled when he told her that he didn't care where they lived, just as long as they were together. Gail refused to return to No. 5 and they moved into a council house on Hammond Road.

Ivy was alone now at No. 5 and spent more time than ever in church. She became engaged to fellow attender George Wardle but broke with him when he confessed that he was a divorcé and not a widower. A true Roman Catholic, Ivy believed that that meant he was still married and she told him that she couldn't marry him. A couple of months later, however, she knew she still loved George and wanted him as her husband. She told him she was prepared to turn her back on the Church but by that time he had a new girlfriend and told her that he wasn't interested.

Bert's sister Veronica had emigrated to Australia in the sixties and her son Ian had been brought up there. When he came to England for a visit in 1986 he stayed with his auntie Ivy at No. 5. During his stay, Brian encouraged Gail to show Ian around the north. They fell for each other and had a passionate secret fling.

● *Ivy's two families: below, with Bert, celebrating the marriage of their son Brian to Gail Potter, and right, with Don. Don took in a greyhound, Harry's Luck, in return for a fare in his taxi. Their plans to race the dog failed when she turned out to be pregnant.*

Gail knew that the affair was doomed but was devastated all the same when Ian returned home to Australia. Shortly afterwards, she discovered she was pregnant and told Brian that she couldn't be certain if the baby was his or Ian's. Ivy was horrified when she heard and helped Brian move his things into his old bedroom. Ivy felt that her whole life was crumbling around her as the couple were divorced and little Nicky became caught in the middle of their battles.

Following the birth of Gail's daughter, Sarah Louise, Ivy was relieved to be told that Ian definitely wasn't the father. But Brian still refused to accept the baby as his and instead he snatched Nicky and made plans to leave the country for Ireland. As they were getting on to the ferry Nicky pleaded with Brian to take him home and Brian's resolve melted. He returned the boy to distraught Gail and Ivy. The incident made him realize how much he wanted his family and he finally accepted Sarah as his daughter. Ivy was thrilled when Gail decided to give Brian one last try and the couple were remarried.

Ivy herself was the next to say 'I do' when she married taxi driver Don Brennan in June 1988. They had met when he picked her up as a fare and romance had blossomed. Don's first wife, Pat, had died and he had three children, Maggie, Eileen and Gordon, whom he rarely saw. A good Catholic, he was the ideal man for Ivy and she was pleased when Brian approved of the match. It was only after the wedding that Ivy discovered Don's secret: he was a compulsive gambler. Just months later, she was stunned when Don lost his taxi in a poker game to Mike Baldwin. Ivy was forced to use her life savings to buy it back and Don promised to stop gambling.

In 1989 Ivy suffered her worst blow when Brian was stabbed to death outside a night-club. She found no consolation in the thought of him in heaven, especially when Gail refused to bury him alongside Bert and insisted on a Church of England funeral. Ivy felt that Gail was condemning her son to eternal damnation and hated her for it. To make matters worse Gail embarked on an affair with a lad ten years her junior, Martin Platt.

When Gail announced her intention to marry Martin, Ivy made a formal complaint to the courts saying that Gail was an unfit mother. She refused to accept that Martin should be allowed to adopt the children and became obsessed with them bearing the Tilsley name. The court battle turned Gail against her and made Don realize that the dead had more hold over Ivy than the living. He was deeply upset when Ivy made a will leaving their house to Nicky on the condition that he changed his name back from Platt to Tilsley. From that point, Don knew that he did not matter to his wife: rather than being content to be a Brennan, her heart was still with the Tilsleys, and he couldn't fight ghosts. He embarked on an affair with barmaid Julie Dewhurst from the Kit Kat Club and told Ivy he was leaving her. Ivy had been so wrapped up in fighting the adoption that she had no idea that Don had been leading a double life.

Don moved into a bed and breakfast in Clarence Street, telling Ivy that his life wasn't a shrine to Bert and Brian. She begged him to let them start afresh and convinced him that she meant what she said when she told him that she would be willing to sell the Tilsley house. Don returned home, telling Julie their affair was over, but agreed with Ivy that they didn't have to move – her gesture had been enough.

The rot had set in, though, and, no matter how hard Ivy and Don tried, their four-year marriage was over. Don saw Julie again in secret, and Ivy began to drink too much. She asked Don to renew their wedding vows but he walked out on her. He went to Julie but she told him she didn't want him. Rather than be with Ivy, he decided to kill himself. He drove the car at top speed through country lanes and smashed into a field, the car rolling over and over. The suicide attempt failed, but as a result of the injuries, his lower right leg had to be amputated.

Ivy swore to stand by Don but he tried to live alone in a bedsit, returning to No. 5 only when he discovered that Ivy had become an alcoholic. She agreed to stay off the booze on the condition he returned home, albeit into the spare room. The marriage was dead and the Brennans became two people just sharing a house.

● *Ashley left No. 5 after Don tried to frame him by telling the police he'd set fire to Mike Baldwin's factory. He moved in with his uncle Fred Elliott.*

Ivy announced her intention to spend some time in a religious retreat and moved into the St Catherine's convent. In her absence, Don began a relationship with doctor's receptionist Josie Clarke. He decided to tie up loose ends by divorcing Ivy and got a solicitor to write to her. A week later, Ivy died from a stroke brought on by the idea of divorce. Gail accused Don of killing Ivy, and fought him over the house as Ivy's will specified that it belonged to Nicky. Don refused to give up his home for a fourteen-year-old boy but, in the end, agreed to settle out of court and bought No. 5 from Nicky.

Josie had moved in with Don and given up her job at the doctor's surgery to become Mike Baldwin's supervisor at his new sportswear factory. She encouraged Don to invest in the future by buying Mike's garage. Mike knew they were interested and left a false valuation on Josie's desk. Both Don and Josie remortgaged their homes to buy the garage for £43,000, and Don took top-up loans to buy equipment. The garage became a terrible drain as Mike had run it into the ground and it needed money investing in it. Then Josie discovered from Mike that they had paid over the odds for it. She quit both her job and, later, Don. The receivers were called in and Don was disgusted when mechanics Kevin Webster and Tony Horrocks bought it for only £25,000.

Without Ivy or Josie around to blame, Don blamed Mike for his downfall. His theory that Mike was out to get him was, he felt, justified when he was caught driving his taxi drunk while Mike was a passenger. Don was fined £400 and lost his licence, and therefore his livelihood. On Christmas Eve 1996, penniless, jobless and hopeless, he broke into the garage and tried to gas himself. But even at that he failed because although the fumes knocked him unconscious he fell against the steering wheel and set off the horn. Martin and Kevin heard the noise and dragged him to safety.

Back at No. 5, Don continued to blame Mike for everything that had gone wrong, but he found a job at his taxi firm on radio control. He was already supplementing his income by taking in a lodger, Ashley Peacock, a twenty-year-old butcher's lad. Don decided to teach Ashley all about women so that the boy wouldn't make similar mistakes to his own.

While Ashley embarked on a passionate relationship with hairdresser Maxine Heavey, Don grew increasingly bitter. He attempted to hit back at Mike by setting fire to his sportswear factory, and was delighted when Mike was suspected of arson. When the police failed to charge Mike, Don went a step further and kidnapped Mike's wife, Alma. Driving her to waste ground he attacked her before trying to kill her by driving his car, with her inside, into the River Irwell. Both Don and Alma survived the crash but he was remanded in custody and charged with the attempted murder of Alma.

•Nº7 CORONATION STREET•

1902 – 1918
Ernest, Harry, Clara, Emily and Herbert Popplewell

1918 – 1948
Thomas, Mary, Alice, Harry and Frances Hewitt

1948 – 1961
Harry, Lizzie and Lucille Hewitt

1961 – 1964
Harry, Concepta, Lucille and Christopher Hewitt

1965
Collapsed

1982
Rebuilt

1982 – 1983
Len and Rita Fairclough, with Sharon Gaskell

1983 – 1986
Rita Fairclough

1986 – 1990
Rita Fairclough, with Alan and Jenny Bradley

1990 – 1992
Jenny Bradley, with Flick Khan and Angie Freeman

1992 – 1995
Curly Watts, with Angie Freeman and Andy McDonald

1995 – 1996
Curly and Raquel Watts

1997 —
Curly Watts with Samantha Failsworth

The building of the Weatherfield canal had begun in 1863 and been completed eight years later. During that time Ernest Popplewell had served as a labourer, helping to channel a course through the heart of what would become a busy town. In 1902, when he moved into No. 7, he was sixty-four, and fifty years of labouring had left his back twisted and his language and temper foul. His wife, Mary, had died of scarlet fever, leaving him to bring up their four children. The eldest had been ten-year-old Harry, whom Ernest kept, but he abandoned Kitty, Ernie and Alfie to the parish.

Harry was now thirty-four and worked as a storeman at Hardcastle's warehouse where he was responsible for storing the blankets and material made at the Coronation Street mill. His wife, Clara, worked there as a spinner, having learnt her craft at her mother's knee: they spun as outworkers before the mills were established. Their children were Emily, nine, and Herbert, four. Their grandfather, Ernest, earned money by pulling carts of slag from the pit face to his neighbours. It wasn't long after moving into the house that Ernest had the shock of his life: he called at No. 11 with slag for the Makepieces and saw Alfred Makepiece for the first time. He was the image of Ernest's dead wife and the old man collapsed in the street. He was taken to the infirmary and, believing he was going to die, told Harry the cause of his illness. Harry called on Alfred and asked him about his parents. When he learnt that Alfred had been brought up in the workhouse orphanage, Harry embraced him as his long-lost brother.

Ernest recovered and was soon back in the Street, ashamed of his actions and emotions. When Alfred called on him, he was shattered when Ernest told him that if he was his son he wanted nothing to do with him: Alfred had been dead to him for twenty-six years. Despite Harry's pleas to be reconciled with Alfred, Ernest ignored him and his family, crossing the street if ever he saw them.

This awkward situation did not last long as, during a game of dominoes in the Rovers, Ernest dropped dead on the table top. His opponent, Tom Schofield, complained as he had only one wood left to lay and had been about to win. No one mourned the old man's passing. Harry inherited his teeth while Clara got drunk at his wake and danced a jig on the table where he had died. With their father dead, Harry and Alfred started to build a brotherly bond between them.

Not long after moving in Ernest Popplewell had the shock of his life: Alfred Makepiece at No. 11 was the image of his own dead wife

The closure of the Weatherfield pit in 1911 sent the community into turmoil. Out-of-work miners scrambled for jobs at the mills and factories but only the youngest were taken on as cheap labour. The lack of coal cut a docker's work in half as there was nothing to transport. Their management responded by slashing wages and laying off men. Then the mill owners decided to exploit the situation by reducing pay as they knew people were desperate for work. Men roamed the streets and unrest grew in the town. The trade unionists urged those still in work to stand by their neighbours and take industrial action so the Popplewells and their workmates joined the strike.

Throughout that summer, Manchester faced famine and the Popplewells scavenged for food while temperatures soared to 97 degrees – Clara felt that if she didn't die of hunger sunstroke would get her.

When Fred Piggott led the residents in a march on the Town Hall she gladly took part. But the march turned into a riot when the crowd was met by a troop of armed police and shots were fired. Clara ran for all she was worth, but her heavy clogs slowed her down. When she heard horse's hoofs behind her, she glanced over her shoulder. As she turned a mounted policeman swiped at her with his truncheon. She felt the blow on her head and collapsed. When she woke, she was in the infirmary and Emily broke the news that she had lost her sight in one eye.

Herbert left school officially at fourteen in 1912 – he had left unofficially at eight when he had decided that school couldn't teach him anything. From then on he attended only in the week before Christmas when every pupil was given a free dinner with pudding. He spent his days otherwise at Plank Lane Market, selling chickens for an old Jewish trader who gave him twopence commission on every bird he sold. As soon as war was declared, Herbert signed up, eager to see action and as much of the world as he could. Harry, too, was swept away by the patriotism of the moment and rushed to enlist. When the recruitment officer told him that at forty-six he was too old Harry joined the back of the queue and tried again, this time saying he was thirty-nine. The officer turned a blind eye and Harry, like his son, joined the Fusiliers.

Clara and Emily stayed on at No. 7, both working at Hardcastle's mill. The shortage of men made the supervisor overlook Clara's impaired sight and she found herself operating a loom next to her daughter. However, Emily wasn't content to stay in Weatherfield and, after hearing a report about the horrors of the Somme, she volunteered to be trained as a nurse so that she could serve in a field hospital. Clara found herself the only member of her family left in England and, in her loneliness, took to spending her evenings drinking in the Rovers snug bar with Pearl Crapper.

When the armistice was declared, Emily wrote to tell her mother she had married and was living in a village near the Italian border. Just a week after receiving the letter, Clara had a telegram informing her that Harry, returning home from the war, had fallen overboard in the Channel and drowned. Herbert was the only member of his family to return home to her and he was now permanently deaf from the blasts of gunfire and shells.

As her neighbours celebrated the end of the war and the return of loved ones, Clara decided that she and Herbert could not stay in the Street. She gave up the tenancy of No. 7 and moved in with her invalid parents in Back Marriot Street.

As one war veteran moved out of the Street, another moved in. Thomas Hewitt was twenty when he returned to his family home, No. 3 Coronation Street. He was eager to settle down, find work and resume his peaceful existence. Within weeks of returning he noticed how beautiful Mary Makepiece had become in the four years he had been away. He started to court her straight away, ignoring an old feud that had raged between their families for years. Both he and Mary were relieved when their mothers, Gertie Hewitt and

● *Ernest Popplewell took against Clara the day she married his son Harry. Ernest had a foul temper which, when fuelled by drink, erupted into violence. Clara was relieved that at least the old man never took his temper out on the children, Emily (below right) and Herbert.*

Ivy Makepiece, buried the hatchet and attended their wedding. The women joined forces to give the young couple a wedding present and persuaded the landlord to let No. 7 to them. Thomas and his bride moved into the house in March 1919: after signing the register in the Mission vestry, they crossed the Street and let themselves into their new home. Each of them managed to get a job at Hardcastle's Mill.

Both Thomas and Mary came from large families and were keen to have children of their own. Their first daughter, Alice, was born in 1920, followed by Harry in 1921 and Frances in 1922. Little Frances died in May 1923 after an attack of scarlet fever and Mary hoped for more children but never conceived again.

Matthew Hardcastle was forced to close his dead father's mill in September 1931 after struggling for five months to find orders for his stock. Everyone believed that the Depression couldn't possibly last but one by one businesses ground to a halt. Hardcastle was one of the last mill owners to close down and he had incurred massive debts through trying to keep open. The workers were owed a week's wages when he finally halted production and the foremen gathered everyone together to listen to the boss's news. Mary was one of the women who wept at the word 'closure', and although a handful of men demanded the money they were owed, the majority realized how much it had cost Hardcastle to let them down.

For the first few months of unemployment, the Hewitts struggled to exist on their twenty-nine shillings dole money. Thomas tried to be optimistic about finding work but was only too aware that most of the adult population of Weatherfield was also looking for it. It wasn't just the adults: Alice and Harry had both been at Hardcastle's factory school and spent part of their week working under the great looms in the factory. While their schooling wasn't affected, the afternoons in the mill stopped together with the few shillings they earned. Mary tried hard to provide a nourishing meal each day but found she had to queue for whatever food was available. The family's possessions – ornaments, a clock, bedding and clothes – were pawned with no hope of being retrieved.

After drawing dole for six months, Thomas was turned away from the dole office and told that he would have to apply for assistance under the Means Test. An official came to the house, glanced around at the furniture and told the family they would be entitled to nothing until they had sold all but their beds and the table. By this stage Mary was beyond caring: and she sank to her knees and grabbed the man's arm, begging him for money to feed her children. The man shook himself free and walked out of the house while Alice tried to comfort her sobbing mother. Thomas spent the afternoon carrying the furniture to Benson's junk yard and received sixpence for all that the family had owned.

Then came the news that Councillor 'Black Jack' Elliston was buying Hardcastle's mill. He advertised for machinists and storemen and as soon as Mary Hewitt heard of the chance of a job she stationed herself outside the mill entrance on Victoria Street. She thanked God for the warmth of the summer as she slept at her post for two nights and only moved when Alice took her place for an hour in the morning and an hour in the afternoon when Mary hobbled home to eat. When Elliston opened the gates, he had forty posts to fill but insisted on seeing everyone who had queued as he wanted to give them hope. Mary was the first woman he saw and he was sickened by the sight of her: malnourished, her joints sticking out from her skin, her clothes hanging off her and her eyes deadened in their sockets. He had no idea if she could manage one of the sewing machines he had installed but understood instantly that here was a woman in dire need. She asked for a job for her husband too but Elliston knew that if he was to be of any help to the people living around the mill he could only employ one person from a family. Mary was signed up and became the only successful applicant from Coronation Street.

With Mary working full time, sewing sleeves on to raincoats, the dinner table began to look decent again. Thomas still spent all day searching for work, hating the idea that he was living off his wife's earnings. One evening, while drinking his daily ration of a half of mild in the Rovers, he was approached by local villain

● *The Hewitt clan: Thomas (above left) fell for Mary Makepiece (above centre) from No. 11. Their surviving children, Harry and Alice (above right), did not want to repeat the drudgery of their parents' lives.*

● *Lucille (above) was Lizzie's only child. Lizzie (left) was relieved when she suffered a miscarriage in 1954 – she had reason to believe Len Fairclough, not her husband, was the father of the unborn baby. Lizzie's own father had died when she was 3, and as an adult she still felt the absence sharply.*

Freddie Malone. No one asked where Malone got his money from – in the autumn of 1932 money was money no matter what its origins. Malone bought Thomas a pint and asked him if he was interested in a job. Thomas's eyes lit up and he thanked Freddie for singling him out. Freddie told him to be at the back of Elliston's factory at midnight.

When the hour arrived, Thomas was joined by two other men with jemmies, and they quickly broke open a window in the store room. Freddie propelled Thomas through the window and ordered him to pass out finished raincoats. Thomas stuffed garments feverishly into sacks thrown in after him but the stillness of the night was shattered by the rattle of police sirens. He was trapped inside as he heard the others running away over the cobbles. He heaved himself up and a hand grabbed him by the lapel of his jacket. He was hauled on to the cobbles and a torch was shone into his face by Special Constable George Diggins. Thomas pleaded with his old friend, the landlord of the Rovers, to let him go but before George could decide what to do for the best, regular constables arrived and took Thomas away.

Thomas pleaded guilty to breaking and entering. He refused to name his accomplice and was sent to Strangeways for five months. The family suffered a further blow when Elliston decided to take a hard line and sacked Mary.

When Thomas returned home he found Mary greatly changed. She was no longer the cosy wife of their youth or the determined mother who had fought for her family during the Depression. She had become cold and hostile towards the children and angry with herself for marrying a man who had let her down. Alice had left school and had found work as barmaid at the Rovers in the afternoons and the Flying Horse in the evenings. With mills and factories opening up all over Weatherfield, unemployment had ceased to be a problem but Thomas's criminal record stood against him. Eventually Solomon Jackson took him on at his chip shop in Victoria Street and Thomas had to grit his teeth when customers made a point of counting any change he gave them.

Harry Hewitt left Bessie Street School at fifteen and landed a plum job as a trainee clippie on the new bus system, which had just replaced the trams. He was thrilled, and after receiving his first wage packet went on a pub crawl, returning home after midnight with a large hole in his wages. He stumbled through the door into the hall but soon sobered at the sight of his mother, at the top of the stairs in her nightgown, the carving knife in her hand. She lashed out at him, slicing his jacket and his arm. Thomas appeared from the house and grabbed hold of his wife but she seemed to have superhuman strength: it took four neighbours to hold her down as she ranted and kicked. The doctor was called and a plain yellow van carried the sedated Mary out of the Street. Everyone knew where it had taken her and no one spoke of it in front of the Hewitts. Mary had brought disgrace upon them and the Street; many before her had suffered breakdowns and some had killed themselves but no one had ever been committed to the asylum. When she died, in 1936, and was buried at St Mary's, Harry refused to attend the funeral.

Alice had had great plans as a new bride for the winter of 1939 but the happiness of her wedding day, 3 September, was shattered by Neville Chamberlain's declaration of war. She refused to let the news spoil her day and she and her new husband, Sam Burgess, led the dancing in the Rovers select. However, immediately after the wireless announcement air-raid sirens started to wail and the residents panicked, expecting an immediate gas attack. Jack Walker ordered everyone down into the Rovers cellar and the party mood continued, thanks to quick-thinking Sam who smashed open one of the brewery's barrels of beer. Alice sat among the cobwebs and barrels and cried into her wedding dress, comforted by Ena Sharples from the Mission. When the siren stopped, Ena led the company in a hymn of thanksgiving. Sam expected to be called up immediately so the planned week-long honeymoon in Blackpool was cut to just a night. The next morning Alice returned to No. 7 while Sam joined the queues at the Town Hall to sign up. He entered the Army a full eight months before Harry.

• *Christopher Hewitt was a delicate child whose mother Concepta feared for his health. She moved the family to the Irish countryside in 1964.*

Thomas had often talked with disillusionment about the First World War and Harry was reluctant to be used as a pawn by the Government. He didn't enlist until the summer of 1940, his reticence shattered by the news of Sam's death at Dunkirk. Alice threw herself into mourning her dead husband, whom she had held in her arms for only one night. She refused to stay in the Street: if the bombs didn't get her, she reckoned that the grasp of the cobbles would and she would never be able to leave. She decided to take her chance while she could and fled Weatherfield for the open country of Stockport, where Sam's sister lived.

With Alice gone and Harry abroad, Thomas joined the Home Guard with neighbour Albert Tatlock and spent his nights on fire-watch duty. One night he was woken by a commotion in the Street. He looked out of the bedroom window to see the roof of Elliston's factory ablaze and rushed out to help put out the flames. It was only after the fire had been quenched that he realized he was still in his night-shirt.

Harry returned home from the war world-weary and anxious to get back to normality. His job had been kept open for him and during his first day back on the buses he noticed that many of the clippies were now women. He was greatly attracted to one, Nellie Briggs. He asked her out to the Luxy but she insisted on a double date, with her pal Lizzie Harding. Harry persuaded his drinking partner Len Fairclough to join them but was annoyed when Len made a play for Nellie. By the end of the evening both Harry and Len had had too much to drink and when Len patted Nellie's knee Harry lunged at him. They were still in the Rovers and started fighting on the floor, scattering tables and chairs. Thomas helped Jack Walker separate them and threw them out into the gutter. As Harry lay on the cobbles, nursing a bloody nose, he was put out to see Nellie making a fuss of Len and walking him home. Lizzie bent over Harry and pressed her handkerchief to his face. He smiled his thanks and made a date with her for the following Saturday night.

In December 1947 Thomas Hewitt died in his bed of a heart attack. Harry was sorry to see the old man go. After the funeral at St Mary's, Alice pointed out that Harry was the last Hewitt living in Coronation Street and that the terrace had never been lucky for any of them: apart from Thomas's, there were eight family graves in St Mary's alone. Harry refused to heed the warning and married Lizzie at the Mission of Glad Tidings. Len was best man and Nellie the bridesmaid.

Lizzie Harding Hewitt had grown up in Victoria Street and both her parents had been killed in the Gas Street shelter bomb in 1940. During the war she had avoided munitions work in favour of the buses as she enjoyed being in the open air. She was a keen cyclist and loved taking her bike on the train to visit the countryside at weekends. At first, after the wedding, Harry accompanied her, but after a couple of months his enthusiasm waned and he refused to let her go unaccompanied, saying it wasn't 'seemly'. Four months into the marriage Lizzie felt stifled in the airless, damp back street and the rosy glow in her cheeks faded. She gave up the buses to keep house, and in May 1949 gave birth to a daughter, Lucille. Harry was so happy with the new arrival that he promised Lizzie anything she wanted. She decided against a new coat or a night out at the dance hall and instead stated her desire to return to work. Lizzie sorted everything out, taking a part-time job at the Rovers as barmaid and paying Bessie Tatlock a few shillings a week to look after Lucille. Despite the noisy, smoky atmosphere in the pub Lizzie appeared to thrive there and became

● *After Len's death, Rita started a relationship with policeman Tony Cunliffe. He finished with her when she failed to invite him into her bed.*

a popular face behind the bar. When she worked evenings, Harry stood at the bar each night making certain no one took advantage of his wife.

Sometimes it felt to Lizzie that Harry wasn't thirty at all. He sat in his armchair, reading the *Evening News* and tutting at the headlines, expecting cups of tea and his supper ready on the table when he returned from work. Len Fairclough, though, was a cheeky rascal, with an exciting gleam in his eye. She felt sorry for him, married now to Nellie Briggs, who had turned into a real nag.

After the event, Lizzie couldn't remember when she had decided to become Len's lover, it had just sort of happened. One moment he was telling her his woes, the next they were nestling together in the doorway of Swindley's Emporium. With Harry working on the night bus and Lucille tucked up in bed, Lizzie entertained Len downstairs in front of the fire on the rag rug Mary Hewitt had made.

In January 1959 Harry moved from conducting on the bus route down Rosamund Street to the more complex Albert Road run. He had worked the 64 for five years and knew all the steep climbs and blind corners well. He spent his morning tea-break instructing the new clippie who was replacing him but forgot to warn her of the blind corner from Victoria Street on to Rosamund Street, at the corner of Hardcastle's warehouse. Maggie Clarke set off nervously – it was her first

● *The rebuilt No. 7 boasted a living room larger than the others in the Street. Rita Fairclough was proud of it until Alan Bradley attacked her there.*

day on the buses and she was as eager to make a good impression as was the new driver, Fred Ellis.

All went well on the first run-out, but on the return journey as the bus swerved on to Rosamund Street it skidded on ice and mounted the pavement. Fred struggled to gain control but Maggie was thrown on to the platform in time to see a woman being mown down by the front wheel. Maggie and Fred returned to the depot, shaking, with the news that the woman had died. Harry bought Maggie a cup of tea and let her cry on his shoulder, assuring her that there had been nothing she could have done to avert the tragedy. That afternoon he went home to find tearful a Lucille being comforted by Ena Sharples. As the older woman looked deep into his eyes he knew at once that the bus victim had been Lizzie.

Harry had no idea how to cope with grieving Lucille and agreed with her headmistress that he wasn't in any position to look after her on his own. A representative

from the council's Children's Office suggested that Lucille might be better off as a boarder in the orphanage on Regents Road. Numbed by his own grief, Harry allowed himself to be talked into sending his daughter away. For Lucille, the whole world had caved in.

Back in the Street Harry occupied himself with work and made plans to find a housekeeper. His drinking partner Len Fairclough told him he was stupid to think of paying a woman when he could have one for free by marrying again. There was no shortage of ladies interested in eligible Harry: Esther Hayes from No. 5, Elsie Tanner at No. 11 and Rovers barmaid Concepta Riley. Harry found Concepta attractive but shied away from her as she had taken Lizzie's job at the pub. He feared the local gossips would lay into the girl for stepping into his dead wife's shoes.

His immediate problems were solved in the spring of 1961 when his sister Alice returned to Coronation Street. Since the end of the war she had worked as manageress of the canteen at Howarth's mill in Stockport. When John Howarth closed the mill she had moved into his Cheshire home as housekeeper. When he died in February 1961, and left her £250, she decided against spending her nest egg and moved into No. 7, telling Harry she would look after him. Harry wasn't keen on having bossy Alice around but it did mean getting Lucille back from the orphanage.

Alice tried hard to get on with the sulky eleven-year-old but she had never liked children and her critical tongue often drove Lucille to bed in tears. When Harry always took his daughter's side Alice decided to move on. Rather than have Lucille sent away again Harry proposed to Concepta.

Concepta Riley was a devout Irish Catholic. In marrying her Harry had to agree that any children they might have would be brought up Catholics. Theirs was the first mixed-religion marriage in the Street and brought much comment from the local anti-Papists. Lucille was pleased for her father as she liked Concepta and knew she would bring happiness back into Harry's life.

Christopher Hewitt was born in August 1962 and Harry doted on his son. Lucille found she was no longer the centre of attention and took against her new half-brother, playing pop records loudly and staying out late at night. When the baby was only two months old, she took him out in his pram on an errand. After parking the pram outside Gamma Garments on Rosamund Street she chatted to a school friend and the baby was stolen. The police were alerted and a house-to-house search started. The detective leading the investigation suspected Lucille of damaging the baby out of jealousy, but she broke down under interrogation and swore her innocence. Concepta had to be sedated after she, too, broke down and ran screaming through the streets. Three days into the search, Elsie Tanner saved the day by discovering Christopher in the care of Joan Akers, a woman whose own baby had died. The police reunited Concepta with her son and Lucille promised her father that she would try not to be jealous.

Lucille turned her energies from brother-baiting to being a terrible teenager. She immersed herself in the music of the Beatles and fell for local window-cleaner Walter Potts when he was launched as pop sensation Brett Falcon. She made herself president of his fan club and even had his name tattooed on her arm. In the midst of all the arguments Concepta received news from Ireland that her father Sean had had a stroke.

· · · · · · · · · · · · · · · · · · ·

Suddenly, one summer day in 1965, without any warning No. 7 collapsed. Many other residents fled their homes in panic

· · · · · · · · · · · · · · · · · · ·

This, and Christopher's chesty cough, prompted her to talk Harry into the family starting afresh in Ireland. Harry agreed but was worried about breaking Lucille's schooling, which was when the Walkers stepped into the breach by taking in Lucille as their ward.

Lucille missed her father terribly. Jack Walker was kind but she felt she couldn't flare up at him or cuddle him as she had Harry. She took to slipping out of the Rovers and into her old home, where she would sit on the stairs, close her eyes and listen to voices from the past. Suddenly, one summer day in 1965, speculation that he was building an extension for his own house at No. 9. In the spring of 1982 he removed the coverings to reveal a new house in the space between Nos 5 and 9. It stood out from its neighbours: it had two upper floor windows at the front and a Georgian front door. Len had worked hard to create a beautiful home: the parlour had been replaced by a large hall with double doors that led to the sitting room and could be either left closed to make two rooms or thrown open to create one large one. His motive in making the house extra special had not been purely financial: as he worked all that winter he remembered the happy times he had spent in the old house and the evenings he had spent chatting with his best mate Harry Hewitt. The house was a showcase and in the summer of 1982 Len moved from No. 9 next door into No. 7 with his second wife, Rita, and their foster-daughter Sharon Gaskell.

Sharon was as pleased as Rita with the new house. At sixteen, she was looking forward to a long future as the Faircloughs' daughter and was grateful to them for taking her into their home. She worked at Len's yard as his apprentice and it was there that she met the man of her dreams, Brian Tilsley. The only blot on the landscape was his wife. Gail Tilsley was grateful when Sharon volunteered to babysit, little knowing that Sharon rooted through her house in their absence, looking for anything personal belonging to Brian. She would sit in his chair, drink out of his mug and rub her cheek against his T-shirts. Then, too, there was the bliss of having him drop her at home in his van.

Her eyes were opened when Brian told her she was just a kid. When she was offered a live-in job as a kennel maid in Sheffield Sharon saw this as her escape from the humiliation and gladly took it, although she was sad to say goodbye to the Faircloughs.

She promised Rita she would visit often but had no idea that her first return to the Street would be for Len's funeral. He died on the way home from Ashton on the motorway when he fell asleep at the wheel and his van crashed into a bridge. Sharon supported Rita through the funeral and returned to Sheffield, without discovering what Rita had found out: that at the time

●*Jenny Bradley studied environmental issues at Manchester Polytechnic where housemate Angie Freeman trained as a fashion designer.*

without any warning the house collapsed. Many other residents fled their homes in panic, fearing that the whole row would go but when the dust settled only No. 7 was affected. Fortunately Lucille had not been there – she turned up after visiting a friend. Builder Len Fairclough gave Edward Wormold, the landlord, an estimate for rebuilding and was surprised when he received instructions to pull down the whole house. Wormold said it wasn't worth rebuilding. Len cleared the site and made it safe, and as a short-term measure the council supplied a bench to fill the gap. It remained for seventeen years.

Towards the end of 1981 Len purchased the land on which No. 7 had stood. He removed the bench and covered the space with tarpaulins, which led to

● *Raquel married Curly in haste, fearing that if she didn't she stood to be hurt again by Romeo Des Barnes. The marriage lasted less than a year.*

of his accident Len had been returning home from seeing his mistress. Rita tracked down the woman, Marjorie Proctor, at her home and was surprised to discover that she and Len had been lovers for months, that Len had brought her happiness and that he had told her about his love for Rita.

The joy of having a smart new house meant nothing to Rita now without someone with whom she could share it and she was glad to take in one of her paper girls, Jenny Bradley, when her mother was killed by a car. Pat Bradley had been separated from her husband, Alan, since her daughter was eight and Jenny had not seen her father for six years. When Alan had been traced, and turned up on the doorstep, Jenny was full only of bitterness towards him. Slowly, over a

few weeks, Alan won Jenny round with Rita's help. He took Rita out to dinner and she was pleased to find she still enjoyed a man's company.

She began to see more of Alan and they moved into courtship. But he was never certain of her feelings as she avoided intimate encounters and he started an affair with barmaid Gloria Todd. However, when Rita tackled him about Gloria he decided to concentrate on Rita: he recognized her as the mother figure Jenny needed – and she had more money in the bank than Gloria. When Alan took a job in the Middle East, Rita looked after Jenny and enjoyed mothering her. Absence made the heart fonder and Rita was pleased when Alan returned home. He was glad to see her, too. He told her that he wanted to put their relationship on a proper footing and proposed to her. Rita felt that she wasn't ready to marry again but invited Alan to move into No. 7 as her lover.

The news that Rita Fairclough was living 'in sin' spread around the Street like wildfire. Still, mused Hilda Ogden, what else could you expect from a one-time night-club singer? Rita, though, was thrilled with her new domestic arrangements and encouraged Alan to take an interest in the shop. He opened a video library in the Kabin and developed ideas for a business of his own. He made one more attempt to marry Rita – by taking her to the register office on the pretence of attending a friend's wedding. When Rita discovered that she was the bride, she refused to be pushed into marriage and left Alan standing on the steps.

Meanwhile, Jenny was having more luck in the marriage stakes. Although she was only seventeen she travelled to France and fell for a medical student, Patric Podevin. He came to Weatherfield and the pair got engaged, but Patric promised Alan he would wait the three years until he had qualified before he married Jenny. Jenny enjoyed showing off her ring and swotted up on her French but the engagement was cancelled when he discovered she had been seen kissing a local lad at a party.

As Jenny's relationship cracked, so did Alan and Rita's. He was tired of Rita controlling the purse strings and found her increasingly cold towards him physically. Rather than talking things over with her, he left her for housewife Carole Burns.

For six weeks Rita cried herself to sleep and waited for Alan to return. When he did, professing repentance and love, she welcomed him with open arms, little guessing his true reason for coming back. Alan had enjoyed his sexual romps with Carole but she had no money. He planned to open a security firm, selling burglar-alarm systems, but Carole had no cash and the bank refused him a loan without collateral. He returned to Rita to fleece her. He started by borrowing a few thousand from her, manipulating her so that she thought it had been at her suggestion rather than his request. His next move was to find the deeds of the house and use them as collateral against a £15,000 bank loan, which he did by calling himself Len Fairclough. Rita was proud of his new offices on Rosamund Street and had no idea that she was financing the venture. Business was good for Alan, and Rita was pleased that he seemed so happy.

The bubble burst when Alan tried to rape his receptionist, Dawn Prescott. She went straight to Rita, who didn't believe her tale until she learnt of the letters Alan received in Len's name. She broke into the shop, looked through his files and uncovered the truth.

Rita chose the evening of Jenny's eighteenth birthday party to confront Alan, knowing that Jenny would be safely out of earshot in a local hotel. Then she calmly told Alan that the game was up. She had no idea how he would react but was unprepared for the savage attack he launched at her, smashing her across the face, throwing her into furniture and attempting to suffocate her. It was only Jenny's arrival home that saved Rita's life and Alan sped out into the night.

Rita recovered in hospital, with stitches in her bloodied face. Jenny stayed with her at No. 7, torn between loyalty to her father and love for Rita. After Alan was arrested and remanded at Strangeways they counted the days leading to his trial, Rita because she

● *Samantha Failsworth moved to the Street after the break up of her two-day marriage. She walked out on her husband and told no one where she was going.*

wanted to see him locked up, Jenny in the hope that he would be released. As Rita travelled to the court, she wondered if she would have the strength to give the evidence that would put Jenny's father in prison and was relieved when Alan changed his plea to guilty. But when the judge sentenced him to two years for assault and told him that, in view of his time spent on remand, he was free to go, she was horrified. She thought he would kill her, but Jenny was thrilled that he could start afresh.

Alan took a job as labourer on the construction site opposite No. 7, building the new houses. Rita knew he was spying on her and felt like a prisoner in her own home. Finally, she disappeared from the Street. Her friends believed that Alan murdered her and the police were called in to dig up the building site in search of her body. However, after two weeks she was found in Blackpool where she was singing in a hotel under her maiden name. Alan went there, intending to drag her back to Weatherfield to clear his name, but as soon as she saw him Rita bolted away across the prom. He

followed her and was knocked down and killed instantly by a tram. Jenny blamed Rita for her father's death and moved out after burying him on her own.

Rita decided No. 7 held too many bad memories. She bought one of the new properties across the street, and moved in both herself and the newsagent's. After she was reconciled with Jenny she allowed her to rent the house with a fellow environmental studies student, Flick Khan. Flick was the first Asian to live on Coronation Street but was thoroughly westernized in her views. During the summer of 1990 her younger sister Joanne came to stay and fell for Steve McDonald from No. 11. Flick didn't trust Steve and forbade Joanne to see him, but the youngsters rebelled by driving off together to the Lake District. Flick felt responsible for Joanne and worried that her parents would blame her for being too lax. After Joanne returned, her virtue still intact, Flick and Jenny went on a much-needed holiday to France. Away from England, Flick fell in love and decided to stay. Jenny returned alone and Flick's room was taken by her schoolfriend, fashion student Angie Freeman.

Angie's arrival at No. 7 coincided with a change in Jenny's character. She dropped out of the polytechnic and embarked on an affair with her dentist, a married man called Robert Weston. Jenny gained confidence as an older man's mistress and she discarded her comfortable slacks for tight-fitting dresses with plunging necklines. Rita was concerned for her, but Jenny told her that what she did was nothing to do with Rita and when Robert left his wife, Jenny moved in with him.

Angie continued to rent No. 7 and moved Curly Watts into the front bedroom to help share the bills. Twenty-nine-year-old Curly was an assistant manager at local supermarket Bettabuy. He had been lodging with the Duckworths at No. 9 and Jack Duckworth thought that by moving in with Angie Curly had landed on his feet. But Curly saw Angie as a good mate, someone to watch TV or drink a pint in the Rovers with, and Angie agreed. That was until they both had a disastrous day and reached out to each other for comfort.

Angie had graduated with a degree in fashion and burst herself into the rag trade only to find that some-

one had seen her designs at her final show and had copied the best ones for a fashion house. Curly offered to share a bottle of wine with her – he, too, was depressed: he had just heard that his girlfriend, Raquel Wolstenhulme, was leaving Bettabuy to embark on a modelling career. Angie and Curly ended up in bed together. The next morning Curly was on cloud nine but Angie was quick to apologize and said that nothing like it could ever happen between them again.

Although Angie was adamant that she did not want a sexual relationship with him, Curly tried all he could to ensure that she stayed close by. He bought No. 7 from Rita for £30,000, believing that his hold over Angie would be stronger if he was her landlord, but she continued to dodge his advances and he was hurt when she started an affair with builder Neil Mitchell. In another attempt to find his Miss Right, Curly joined a computer dating agency, Cupid's Arrow. He called himself Gerald Murphy, for 'security reasons', and met a 'Miss Shaw', who turned out to be his ex-fiancée Kimberley Taylor. Curly and Kimberley had originally met at Bettabuy and had become engaged while he was living at No. 9. Their relationship had finished because she refused to have sex with him until they were married. He felt he couldn't wait, they argued and she returned his ring. They hadn't seen each other for over two years but both felt that fate had brought them together again. Kimberley was impressed that Curly now owned his own house but did not approve of his female lodger. When his bosses advised him that he stood a better chance of promotion if he was married, Curly proposed to her again and the ring was replaced on Kimberley's finger.

Unfortunately it didn't stay on for long. Although Kimberley was now happy to share Curly's bed, he found the experience disappointing and couldn't stop longing for Angie's body. Then Kimberley schemed for Angie's room to be turned into a nursery and was staggered when Curly spent £3,000 having the loft converted into an observatory for his new rotating telescope – ever since childhood he had been fascinated by the stars. And Kimberley was one of the few people in his life who insisted on calling him by his baptismal name, Norman, which he didn't like: at school they'd called him Forty Watts – his head was shaped like a lightbulb – before he became Curly because of his straight hair. Neither did he enjoy Kimberley's cosy rug-making evenings by the fire. He would never have been content with her as a wife but he couldn't bring himself to tell her. When she called off the wedding he was much relieved.

With Kimberley out of the picture Curly once again tried to woo Angie. She objected to his attentions and, ignoring his declaration of love, moved out to rent a flat with Neil. Curly was alone.

Raquel Katherine Wolstenhulme had been brought up as a Catholic by a domineering father. When Larry Wolstenhulme found modelling photographs of his daughter semi-nude he called her a whore and threw her out. She took a job as resident barmaid at the Rovers and clung to Curly as a friend. Since the days when they had worked together at Bettabuy, Curly had worshipped Raquel. He had watched as her heart was broken by Des Barnes at No. 6, and when he felt she had picked up the pieces he proposed to her. Curly had reached a crossroads in his life: sacked from Bettabuy on a charge of sexual harassment, he was looking for a new career as well as for love. When she accepted him he was over the moon and showed his love by having a star named after her. They threw an engagement party at No. 7 but the evening ended in disaster when Des Barnes told Raquel she shouldn't marry Curly and proposed to her himself. She knew, deep down, that Curly wasn't right for her, but he was a good man and she was confident that she would grow to love him. But Des's proposal knocked her sideways and she ended the party by telling Curly that she couldn't marry him.

For the next year Curly stood by as Raquel drifted from one damaging relationship to the next. Nearly a year after she had broken off their engagement, Raquel told Curly that she had changed her mind and wanted to marry him – as quickly as possible. Curly threw all his doubts out of the window and the couple wed at the register office on 8 December 1995. Although he knew she had spent the minutes before the ceremony

sobbing in the ladies' toilet, Curly had no idea that Raquel had proposed to him after Des had used her for a one-night stand. Frightened of herself and her relationships with men, she had seen marriage to Curly as her only escape.

After honeymooning on the *QE2* the Wattses settled down to married life. Curly became manager of frozen-food superstore Firman's Freezers while Raquel gave up modelling and barwork to train as an aromatherapist. They planned to have children – a boy called Blake and a girl called Tiffany – but these plans were put on hold when Raquel enrolled on a ten-week course in Maidenhead. When she returned, Curly was startled by her new confident image: she discarded her mini-skirts and tight tops for tailored suits, and her long permed hair had been straightened and cut. Even her native Eccles vowels had softened.

Nearly a year after their marriage Raquel still felt she didn't love Curly, and she began to follow her own agenda. She applied to a firm of beauty consultants, who immediately offered her a job. The only problem was that it was in Kuala Lumpur. Raquel was torn between wanting the job and upsetting Curly. When she confessed to him that she had removed her wedding ring for the interview and told the firm that she had no commitments, he knew where her heart was. Telling her he had always known that she would leave one day, he refused to stand in her way. Their marriage had lasted only eleven months.

With Raquel on the other side of the world, Curly decided that it was time for him to do some travelling: there was no point in rotting in Weatherfield while there were mountains to climb, rivers to swim and lions to tame. He gave up his job, sold his car and let his house to barmaid Samantha Failsworth. The Coronation Street residents threw a farewell party for him at the Rovers and gave him a camera as a leaving present. Three hours later he was back, explaining that their love had made him see sense: he belonged in the Street. Samantha was appalled to see him and refused to give up the house so he became a lodger in his own home, moving from the front bedroom to the back with only his telescope for company.

· Nº 9 CORONATION STREET ·

1902 – 1906
Albert, Pearl, Jack and Ronnie Crapper

1906 – 1910
Pearl, Ronnie, Bertie and Rose Crapper

1910 – 1919
Ned, Sarah, Larry, Joe, Alice, Kelly, Jim and Ben Buck

1919 – 1926
Ned, Larry, Avis, Lucy and Ian Buck

1926 – 1946
Jack, Vi, Jim, Sally, Dot, Daisy and Clark Todd

1946 – 1950
Jackie Rigby and Alf Nuttall

1950 – 1960
Ted and Amy Gibson

1961
Ivan, Linda and Paul Cheveski

1962 – 1968
Ken, Val, Peter and Susan Barlow

1968 – 1977
Len Fairclough, with Ray Langton and Jerry Booth

1977 – 1982
Len and Rita Fairclough, with Sharon Gaskell

1982 – 1983
Chalkie and Craig Whitely

1983 – 1995
Jack, Vera, Terry, Lisa and Tommy Duckworth, with Curly Watts

1995 —
Gary and Judy Mallett

Albert Crapper was not employed at Hardcastle's Mill. In fact, none of the Crappers had ever crossed its threshold so they were surprised when they were accepted for one of the new houses. Albert was a native of Weatherfield and had worked down the pit since he was eight. Forty years on he still earned his daily crust hundreds of feet below the ground. Until August 1902, he had lived in Tile Street Alley, in two rooms backing on to the Pit public house. His wife, Pearl, had given birth to their sons, Jack and Ronnie, in the rooms and had washed the coal dust off Albert's body every night as he stood in the tin bath. Pearl was excessively houseproud and earned her wages charring and hawking flowers in the streets from Plank Lane Market. When she took possession of No. 9 she was amazed at the size of the house. As the family moved in, seventeen-year-old Jack eyed up his new female neighbours while delicate Ronnie coughed continuously into his handkerchief. Although only thirteen months younger, Ronnie's slight build was firmly overshadowed by his sturdy brother.

Jack worked alongside his father in the pit but Ronnie was thought too delicate to follow them. A bout of TB as an infant had left him with a weak chest and a rasping cough, and Pearl was adamant that he must steer clear of coal dust. Instead, he served an apprenticeship at Bright's pawn shop on the corner of Rosamund and Canal Street. The shop counter had booths set out along it and Ronnie served in one while Mr Bright took charge of the other two. The worst part of the job for Ronnie was unlocking the door first thing in the morning: as it swung open the women barged in, some shoving prams before them containing bundles. Each morning Ronnie had to run in front of them and vault over the counter to safety.

When Nellie Corbishley at the Rovers Return employed Pearl to clean the pub, she dropped the hawking and instead took advantage of Ronnie's position to open a pawn club, taking other people's items to the pawn shop for 3d commission to spare them the shame of being seen hanging around Uncle's.

On the morning of Monday 15 October 1906, the Weatherfield calm was shattered by an explosion that was heard throughout the town and sent a shudder to the foundations of the houses. People were knocked to the ground and windows broke. An underground explosion had caused the pit face to cave in and 393 miners were buried alive. Pearl and Ronnie waited all day and night for news of Albert and Jack but none came. Only thirty-four men emerged from the pit face, all deafened, some blinded, others lame.

After three days, the rescue operations were called off and Weatherfield was plunged into mourning. It was the biggest disaster that would ever hit the town and every street grieved for its losses. In the tight tenements surrounding the pit entire mining families had been wiped out, leaving only old men, women and children. The thing that upset Pearl most of all was not being able to see the bodies of her much-loved menfolk. She paid for cardboard coffins to be made and had them buried in St Mary's Cemetery in memory of dear Albert and Jack.

At the time she was four months pregnant and, in March 1907, she gave birth to a boy, whom she called Bertie after his father. She threw herself into charring at the Rovers, working with Bertie tied in a sling around her. Ronnie took on the responsibility of head of the household and told Pearl that he intended to look after her for the rest of her life.

Less than a year later, he was engaged. Rose Weaver was a timid creature who worked as a housemaid to Charles Hardcastle, the mill owner. As soon as she met Rose, Pearl approved of her well-scrubbed face and clean nails. Rose had to give up her job, though, as Mrs Hardcastle refused to employ married maids. Rose and Ronnie's wedding took place in February 1909 and Rose was happy keeping No. 9 spick and span under Pearl's watchful eye.

In 1910 the TB epidemic claimed Bertie as a victim and Pearl felt his loss even more than she had the others: the child had never left her side, day or night, and without him she broke down. Nellie Corbishley decided that Pearl's mind needed occupying and persuaded her to move into the Rovers as housekeeper, with four bedrooms, a bathroom, living rooms and three bars to keep clean.

● *Pearl Crapper (above,with young Sarah Bridges) moved to Manchester when she entered service. Her sons Ron (seated) and Jack were her pride and joy, although she feared for Ronnie's poor health. Ironically, it was Jack who never grew old.*

Ronnie and Rose did not stay long at No. 9. Ronnie was given a job as under-groom in the Hardcastles' stables and the couple moved into the mews, with Rose taking in the household's sewing.

July 1910 saw wife murderer Dr Crippen captured at sea and the Buck family moving into No. 9. Like most families in the Street, they were employed at Hardcastle's mill but this wasn't their only source of income. The neighbours soon saw how fortunate they were to have the Bucks on hand; while Sarah Buck helped people into the world her husband Ned helped them out. Sarah was a skilled midwife with secret knowledge about inducing labours and Ned's skills lay in the areas of embalming and making soft-wood coffins, a cheap equivalent to traditional hardwood but sturdier than cardboard.

The neighbours soon heard whispers of other talents possessed by the new family: there were rumours that Sarah aborted more unwelcome babies than she delivered, while Ned had tablets that could lift the burden of life from weary shoulders.

Ned and Sarah had three children, all of whom worked in the mill. Larry was eighteen, a quiet lad frightened by the lewd, bawdy women who called him handsome and groped him as he passed by their machines. His sixteen-year-old brother, Joe, was oafish and took after Sarah in looks – big-boned with a large body and small head. He worked in the stores at the mill, where he also looked after the donkeys that pulled carts to and from the dyeworks on Crimea Street. Fifteen-year-old Alice was a spinner, a pretty girl, much admired by the local menfolk. Alice and Larry were close and he kept an eye on her during working hours: once their neighbour, Ralph Makepiece, had cornered her in a quiet corridor and tried to force himself on her, pushing her into a cupboard. She screamed and Larry suddenly appeared and smashed Ralph over the head with a wooden shuttle.

Larry hated working in the noisy mill, where he operated a loom at which his fingers bled as he picked out pieces of cotton. The strike of 1911 was a blessing for him but he did not march on the mill owners demanding higher wages. Instead, he spent his labour-free days on a walking holiday in the Pennines, sleeping in barns and snaring rabbits for food. He later swore that he knew when the strike had finished because the noise of the mills and factories starting up again after weeks of silence had shattered the peace of the hills. He longed to stay but knew that the family needed his wages so reluctantly returned home.

● *Before they moved in No. 9 in 1910, Ned and Sarah Buck had brought up their children in a one-room tenement in Inkerman Street.*

Because of the nature of his job, Joe spent three afternoons a week at the dyeworks where his beloved donkeys were stabled. Although it wasn't part of his job, he would go to the stables early in the morning to change the bedding straw and make sure that the stable lad was giving the donkeys fresh water. During his afternoons checking the dyeing stores, he met a girl from Newcastle called Kelly who had been born on the same day as him. Her family had moved to the area in 1912 and Kelly was familiar only with the streets between her workplace in Crimea Street and her home on Collier Street. Joe introduced her to the more scenic areas of Weatherfield – the canal, the Rec and Plank Lane Market. She fell for Joe and determinedly steered him into an engagement. They were married on 9 March 1913.

At the time of her marriage to Joe, Kelly Smith had the most unenviable job in Hardcastle's dyeing shop: she stood all day in water as she manhandled yards and yards of material from the dyeing vats into clean water. She spent her wedding morning in tears as, although she had scrubbed them all night, her hands were blue and there was nothing she could do to cover them. On top of the blue colouring the scrubbing caused them to balloon in size. The Smiths were church rather than chapel so the ceremony took place at St Mary's and, as she walked down the aisle to reach Joe, Kelly felt certain that everyone was staring at her hands. She burst into fresh tears and blubbed her way through the service and the ham tea at the Rovers afterwards. Kelly moved into No. 9 on her wedding day, Joe having been given a double mattress to put on the floor of the larger back bedroom, with Larry moving into the front parlour where he slept in any available coffin. Joe's kisses stopped Kelly's tears and, nine months to the day later, she gave birth to a son, Jim.

Alice had asked Kelly about the facts of life but all Kelly had said was that it was a 'mucky business best left alone'. Once Alice had found Larry asleep in bed after injuring his leg, which was bandaged. Apart from a towel covering his groin, he was naked. She had crept up to him and lifted the towel. He had woken up

•Joe and Kelly Buck emigrated to Canada and settled in Newfoundland where their son Jim grew up. They were proud of Jim when he entered politics.

•Unknown to her mother, Alice's short life ended soon after Ned banished her: she died of TB in a London workhouse, and her son was taken into parish care.

•After settling in Newcastle, Larry (left) and Avis (above) had two more children, Joseph and Alice. Larry was killed in an industrial accident in 1948 but Avis is still alive and has celebrated her 100th birthday.

and pulled away, going red at the suggestion that she might like to touch him.

The war saw Joe and Larry joining up. Kelly had pleaded with Joe to stay with her and the baby, but he had been lured away by tales of overseas adventures and heroic deeds. Ned assured her it would do the lad good to go beyond the Ship Canal: he wished he was young enough to march to France with his lucky lads. Kelly took Jim and moved back to Collier Street so that her mother could look after the baby while she took a job as a conductress on the trams.

When Alice learnt that the Piggott twins at No. 13 had finally decided to enlist, she feared she would never be able to tell Vic of her long-held feelings for him. On the night before he embarked, she watched Fred Piggott take his sons into the Rovers and then, drawing a shawl around her, she crept into the night to wait for Vic to emerge. Finally he did, staggering: he wasn't used to drink. He stumbled on the cobbles and she reached out to steady him. He looked into her eyes and smiled. She smiled back and pushed herself against him. A minute later, he was kissing her and pulling at her skirts. She feared her mother would look out and see them, so pushed him round the corner into the back alley where she surrendered herself to him. The next morning she hid her head in her pillow so as not to see Vic and Robert leaving the Street, their hung-over eyes blinking in the bright sunlight.

When Alice discovered she was pregnant, the first person she told was Vic's mother Emma. As she stood inside No. 13, trying to form the sentences in her head, Alice knew that she shouldn't expect any help from the older woman. She blurted out the news much faster than she had intended and then looked down at her feet. With her head down, she had no warning of the slap across her cheeks that sent her spinning into the hard front door. Emma Piggott forced open the door and Alice was propelled into the street, landing on all fours on the cobbles. Emma called her a slut and told her she was telling lies: her son would never even have looked at Alice. The commotion brought witnesses to the scene, including Sarah Buck. She sprang to her daughter's defence, believing that Emma had launched into an unprovoked attack. When Emma told her Alice's news, she bundled the girl into No. 9 and out of the public gaze.

Alice refused to be ashamed of being pregnant and was certain that when he returned from France Vic would marry her. Sarah wasn't so sure as she knew that Emma had a powerful hold over both her sons. She tried to convince Alice that it would be best if the baby was done away with, hopefully without Ned discovering the truth. Alice refused to abort the child: she had helped her mother on a couple of occasions when she had freed other local girls of their burdens and she was not going to put herself through that hell.

• •

**In June 1916 Alice gave birth to
her son, Ben. So accustomed was she
to living in silence that she did so without
a single scream**

• •

When Sarah broke the terrible news, Ned Buck was furious with his daughter. He was all for casting her out of the house but Sarah begged him to be lenient. Ned agreed to her staying on but on the understanding that he never had to look at her or speak to her. In June 1916 Alice gave birth to her son, Ben. So accustomed was she to living in silence that she did so without a single scream, her mother delivering the baby with skill and care.

Ben's cries alerted Ned to the fact that he had a grandchild but he still refused to see Alice or the baby. Sarah didn't know if she could keep the family separate for much longer but the matter was taken out of her hands a week after the birth: Alice walked into the front parlour with Ben, unaware that Ned was snoozing in an armchair. He woke up as she entered and the pair stared at each other for what seemed like hours. Eventually Ned stood up and coldly and calmly told Alice to take her bastard and leave his house. Sarah had gone to the shop and by the time she returned Alice and Ben had gone. She never saw her daughter again nor ever knew what had happened, and from then onwards Ned acted as if Alice was dead.

After the armistice the Buck brothers returned home to find their sister gone and were told never to mention her name. Kelly and Jim, who was now nearly four, returned from Kelly's mother's and almost overnight the house was overcrowded, but still Sarah mourned Alice. Her fate tormented Sarah and she had nightmares in which she saw hounds devouring her daughter. When she began to have the same thoughts during the day, she drank to rid herself of them. It wasn't long before she was drinking out of habit.

Joe found that his job had been taken by an older man and the prospects of finding work soon became impossible. The Government promised its soldiers new lives in the colonies and he decided to take his chances in Canada. Kelly supported his plan, agreeing that England had nothing to offer them, and the doctor told her that the fresh Canadian air would help clear up Jim's chesty cough. The boat set sail just after Christmas 1918, and Sarah watched another of her children disappear.

The war had left Larry Buck scarred for life. In peacetime he had been a home-loving lad with a gentle nature; his only acts of violence had been in protecting his sister's virtue. He had belonged to the infamous Red Hand Gang as a boy, but had always acted as peacemaker and mediator in gang disputes. In the trenches, where he had seen friends blown to pieces, he had grown frustrated as he stayed inactive for week after week before rushing forward into the fire in a feeble attempt to gain ground. He had become aggressive and, out of loyalty to dead and maimed comrades, longed to smash the German ranks and damage the enemy. After the war he was restless and spent long evenings in the Rovers, drinking hard and trying to pick fights. He made a small progression from pub brawler to amateur boxer and soon found himself taking part in local bouts in a wooden hut on wasteland. Here, he was able to let loose his anger on an opponent and would try to smash the man to a pulp. He soon got a reputation for his punch and started to earn money for his fights. Sarah was upset to see him carried home, punch-drunk, and pleaded with him to stop, fearing that a boxer's fist would achieve what Jerry's bullets had not.

Larry's boxing career was cut short one night in November 1919, when he was billed against a London boxer called Fairfax. During the second round he received a blow to the nose which closed one of the passages and his face began to swell. He fought on for another round before collapsing in the ring, his face like a balloon. He was rushed to the infirmary where doctors cleared the blockage, but his brain had suffered from the prolonged pressure and afterwards his speech was slurred, giving the impression that he was always drunk.

The family suffered a further blow that November as Sarah died of alcohol poisoning at the age of fifty-five. Ned accused Larry of bringing on his mother's death by her worrying over his fighting. He told the lad that it was his duty to find a replacement for Sarah to look after them both. Larry realized that the house needed a woman in it so he proposed to mill drawer Avis Grundy who had been soft on him since school days. Twenty-four-year-old Avis gladly moved in and the pair took over the master bedroom. Ned approved of Larry's choice, and leered at poor Avis, spying on her as she bathed.

Avis gave birth to twins, Lucy and Ian, in March 1923. As a result of a complicated labour, she had to take time off work and lost her job. A little while later, she took an evening job as barmaid at the Rovers and was joined there most evenings by her husband and father-in-law. The babies were left alone in the house until one night a cinder fell from the grate and started a fire in the living room. Larry, coming home drunk, opened the door to find the house full of smoke. He raised the alarm but was too far gone to climb the stairs. Tommy Foyle pushed past him to limp his way up to rescue Ian while his wife Lil beat at the smouldering fire with a cloth. In the upset, baby Lucy was forgotten until Avis found her little dead body upstairs. After this incident Larry signed the pledge at the Mission Hall and swore on the Bible never to touch the demon drink again. For a while he joined Gladys Arkwright outside the pub, urging regulars not to enter, and disgruntled landlord, now George Diggins, took out his anger on Avis and sacked her. Larry's newfound convictions did not last long and Ned soon lured him back to the pub for a pint of bitter.

It was Larry and Ned's drinking bouts that caused the old man's death in 1925. There was a heated debate over naming the 1921 Derby winner and Larry had thumped his father across a table. As Ned fell, he smashed his head on the floor and died instantly. The coroner's verdict was death by misadventure and Ned was buried at St Mary's in the same grave as Sarah.

Larry felt that the neighbours blamed him for his father's death, which resurrected in him the blame he had attached to himself after his mother's death. He decided that he had to leave Weatherfield far behind and secured a job in a tailoring factory in Newcastle. The family packed their belongings on a hand cart and left at night without saying goodbye to anyone.

Ivy Makepiece at No. 11 secured the tenancy of the empty house for her daughter Vi. Since 1914 Vi had lived at 7 Mawdsley Street, whose back yard faced Ivy's, and it seemed as if she had never left the Street. She lived with her husband Jack Todd and his widowed mother Daisy. When the Bucks vacated No. 9 the number of Todds crammed into Daisy's house had grown to six people, two whippets and twelve rabbits. Daisy felt suffocated and was relieved when the tribe moved out.

Living at No. 9 meant that the children didn't all have to share the one bedroom, and seven-year-old Jim was moved into the tiny back room leaving six-year-old Sally and baby Dot to share the other. The whippets lived in the yard, but kept escaping to Daisy's, and the rabbits were housed in hutches by the coal hole.

Thirty-six-year-old Jack worked at the shunting yard, shovelling coal, while Vi operated looms at Hardcastle's. The family were glad of Jack's job during the hard years as they always had coal for the fire.

Vi had inherited 'the gift' from her mother and charged local residents to use her as a medium when they wanted to contact loved ones on the other side. She also saw into the future and predicted the great storm of October 1927, which ravaged the area and killed fifty in Lancashire. The Manchester *Evening News* ran an article on Vi's prediction and she became a local

● *Life was not full of laughs for the Todds: Jack (above) spent three years searching for work while Vi (centre) sold her hair to a wigmaker in Chorlton for money to buy food. Jim (right) survived the Depression only to be blown up in Africa.*

celebrity. The article brought her in a lot of custom and she gave up her job at Hardcastle's to concentrate on her gift. A few months later the customers stopped coming when Vi confidently used the local paper to predict a snow-free Christmas. The freezing blizzards that followed cut off food supplies for much of the country.

Vi managed to get back her old job at Hardcastle's and found herself the family's sole breadwinner when Jack lost his job in the autumn of 1930. The Depression took hold quickly and Jack spent his days walking the cobbled streets searching desperately for work. With the introduction of the Means Test, the family were forced to sell whatever they had of value for Jack to be entitled to the dole. The whippets had long gone and the rabbits were eaten in stews. Vi cut her food intake to a minimum to keep up Jack's strength while the children were fed by Daisy, who benefited from her state pension. In 1931, Hardcastle's closed and Vi lost her job too. Jack was stunned to discover that his dole would not be increased to support his wife. He took part in the march on the Town Hall and was beaten up by the police in Rosamund Street.

Eventually Jack found work at the bus company, working as a clippie. When Jim left school, he managed to have him taken on as well, only to find himself replaced by his son as the boy was cheaper to employ. Jack was forced to take a low-paying manual job, digging up streets for the council.

Sally Todd became addicted to the movies and when the Bijou Playhouse was reopened as a cinema in 1934 she took a job as usherette so she could see all the films for free while being paid as well. She often sneaked in Vi and brought some much-needed glamour into her mother's empty life.

The Depression had left Vi a broken woman. She withdrew into herself, going about her household chores as if mechanical. Her once brisk walk slowed to a shuffle and she wandered from room to room, her back bent and her head down. When Dot left school at fourteen Vi was only forty-four but looked as if she should be drawing her pension.

● *Dot's schooldays boyfriend, Len Fairclough, was best man when she married Walter Greenhalgh. Gregarious Sally Todd (right) was a hit at the US friendship dances held at the Greenvale where she showed off her talent for jiving.*

Jack approached the committee at the Mission of Glad Tidings and begged them to do something for his wife, who had worshipped at the Mission all her life. They agreed to help and paid for Vi to be sent to a hospital in Fleetwood for three months. Hardly anyone in the Street had visited the seaside before and Vi's departure was viewed with envy by some. She returned home a new woman, the sea air, good food and medication she had received having strengthened her. Sally burst into tears when she heard her mother laugh again.

The Second World War turned the Todd household upside down. Jim joined up straight away and served with the Desert Rats. Sally and Dot took jobs on munitions, and Vi gladly grasped the challenge of rationing: after the Depression she felt she could survive anything.

During the Blitz of Christmas 1940 Mawdsley Street bore a direct hit and Daisy was bombed out. The Todds moved her into Jim's bedroom, and Vi won the old woman's gratitude by braving the dangers of her wrecked house to rescue her husband's photograph and the ten-shilling note she had hidden in the frame. Jack joined the Home Guard with neighbour Albert Tatlock, and together they dug over the Red Rec to plant vegetables. Jack took the 'Dig for Victory' slogan further by taking up the flagstones in the back yard of No. 9 and growing potatoes. Vi converted what was left of the rabbit hutches into runs and kept a couple of chickens. To prevent them or their eggs being stolen, the birds lived in the scullery at night. The Todds' war was quite a jolly one – until news reached them in 1942 that Jim had been killed in action.

Jim's best friend was Walter Greenhalgh. When Walter had given up his factory job on the outbreak of war he had proposed to Dot. Swept away by the romance of the moment, Dot accepted him and wore his ring. However, the band of brass did not stop her from enjoying the company of other men and she joined Sally and their friend Elsie Tanner from No. 11 in their new pastime – Yanking. All three girls worked together making uniforms at Lewinski's Waterproofs and at the end of the day they crowded into the train to Warrington. Here US Army lorries waited to convey the girls to the base camp at Burtonwood where thousands of American men waited for dancing partners. Dot fell for handsome Gregg Flint and Sally paired off with his buddy, Oliver Hart. Oliver and Gregg became regular visitors to No. 9, their jeep parked outside the house. At first Vi and Jack were wary of the young men but the Americans won them over with their generosity and respectful behaviour. But while they might have seemed like gentlemen to the elder Todds, the men showed their animal instincts when they were alone with their daughters. Dot luxuriated in the presents Gregg gave her and felt she had landed her very own movie star. Sally, on the other hand, fell deeply in love with her Kansas beau and was thrilled when she discovered she was carrying his baby.

Sally only just managed to break the news to Oliver as without warning his platoon packed up and left the 8th Air Force Base Air Depot. She and Dot had planned a visit and found themselves caught up in the stream of wailing women as they raced to the railway station, running after the lorries that carried their sweethearts away. Oliver saw Sally in the crowd and leapt from his lorry to grasp her hand. She shouted the news of her pregnancy over the screaming hordes and he shouted back a marriage proposal.

Gregg Flint wrote to Dot and suggested they joined Sally and Oliver by making it a double wedding, but Dot realized that the gloss of Hollywood would soon disappear and that she was better off with safe, reliable Walt. When he came home on leave, he was surprised to find Dot eager to marry straight away on special licence. She hoped he'd arrive at the church in uniform and was disappointed by his civvy suit.

Vi and Dot delivered Sally's baby between them. She named her son Clark after her favourite film star and dipped his hand in ink to make an impression on the letter she sent to Oliver. Jack was shamed by his daughters' behaviour but stood by them when gossips attacked the girls in public. As Clark came into No. 9, Daisy left, dying in her sleep in the summer of 1943. Death hit the house again in January 1944, when Vi died of pneumonia after falling into the freezing canal during the blackout.

● *Ted and Amy Gibson's joy at winning the football pools was tempered by their neighbours' coolness towards them. They felt cut off from old friends.*

After the war, Dot and Walter moved into lodgings at 18 Victoria Street. Oliver sent money for Sally's passage and she joined the other GI brides at Liverpool docks, clutching the hand of two-year-old Clark. Jack and Dot waved her off and Jack returned home to the stillness of his once bustling house. He stuck it out for eight months, then gave up the tenancy to take the post of resident caretaker at Bessie Street School.

Jackie Rigby had lost his wife Iris during the Manchester Blitz in 1940. Since then, he had lived at 5 Crimea Street with Iris's father Alf Nuttall. They had lost their home when the Army found an unexploded bomb in the back yard and blew it up. Jackie had

nothing left but a battered brown suitcase, which he clutched to his chest on the morning of 17 April 1946 when he took possession of No. 9. He was employed as warehouse storeman at Elliston's factory and was well known by the other residents. The women found it touching that he still clung to the suitcase, unaware that it was not from sentiment but because it contained black-market nylons and perfumes.

Alf was sixty when he moved to Coronation Street and became potman at the Rovers, having served four years in the same position at the Tripe Dressers Arms. He took charge of all the cooking at No. 9 while Jackie worked in the stores at Elliston's by day and out of his suitcase in back alleys at night. Jackie was a big drinker – officially he was the Rover's best customer two years running – and he lost his stores job after goods were stolen when he was drunk on duty. A week later, drunk again, he tumbled into the canal and had to be rescued by Frank Barlow. Frank tried to sober him up and managed to get him a job as an insurance man – but Jackie drank away all his earnings and relied on Alf's wages for food.

Alf despaired of his son-in-law and tried to offload him on to widowed Ena Sharples. He pleaded with her to take on Jackie as a challenge, urging her to help him mend his ways. God-fearing Ena recognized that Jackie was in need of salvation and attempted to sober him up, deciding that the time had come for her to break in another husband. Jackie was amenable enough when drunk but as Ena succeeded in sobering him up the implications of her actions hit him and he bolted, telling her he would never marry again.

One Sunday morning in May 1950, Jack Walker was surprised to find that Alf had not turned up for work at the Rovers. He called at No. 9 to see if he was sick and found the house empty of people and furniture. Like the Bucks before them, Jackie and Alf had left under cover of darkness owing three weeks' rent. They were never seen again.

At forty-five, Amy Foster had given up all thoughts of marriage. She spent her days working on the fabric counter at Miami Modes, and would gaze wistfully at young girls and their mothers who handed over coupons for material to be used in wedding outfits. Then, in February 1950, she was introduced to Ted Gibson, a fifty-two-year-old bookie's clerk. Afterwards she said it was love at first sight and he must have felt the same because by the end of April they were married and living at No. 9.

Amy continued to work at Miami Modes, travelling in on the bus with Elsie Tanner from No. 11. She and Ted both believed in the Government's promises to build them new lives, better than any in the past. During the war Ted had worked for the post office but lost his job in 1946 to a younger man. He had been grateful to young Dave Smith, who employed him at his Rosamund Street betting shop, and saved as much of his salary as he could. The first thing Ted did after moving into No. 9 was get the landlord to agree to some home improvements. The neighbours thought his plans comical, none believing that Edward Wormold, the landlord, would agree, but Dave Smith was a friend of Wormold's and asked him to do the newly-weds a favour. Wormold approved the plans and, to Amy's delight, the back kitchen was extended, the scullery wall demolished and her kitchen became twice the size of the others in the Street. But Wormold wasn't all heart: as the house was bigger he put up the rent.

When Ted got all eight score draws up on his coupon he fainted from shock. He couldn't believe luck was in his favour as he had been struggling with the idea that retirement was just around the corner. His winnings topped the £20,000 mark and he threw a party in the Rovers to celebrate. Amy spent the entire celebration in tears in the snug, completely overcome with their good fortune. Suddenly Ted was the most popular man in Weatherfield and the postman delivered begging letter after begging letter, many from people the Gibsons knew. Ted felt that he wanted to help as many people as he could, but Dave Smith warned him against being too generous and brought his financial adviser to the house who talked to Ted about investments and bonds. The upshot of their conversation was that the Gibsons packed their bags and left the Street to embark on a world cruise before settling in Dorset.

When the Gibsons set sail in November 1960, Elsie Tanner waved off her former workmate. Returning home she glanced at the empty house and wondered who her new neighbours would be. She had no idea that within six months her own daughter would be installed behind that front door.

Linda Cheveski was a native of Coronation Street, having been born at No. 11 to Arnold and Elsie Tanner. She had been a wild, wilful child, who had sought out male companionship from an early age. When she met her future husband Ivan at the Ritz Ballroom in 1957, she had already been engaged to an American and had spent a weekend in Southport with a packer from Elliston's factory where she worked as a machinist. She married Ivan in a register-office ceremony, believing herself to be pregnant. She had no regrets when she discovered she wasn't as she viewed muscular, dark, handsome Ivan as something of a catch. What she wasn't prepared for was his desire to set up home in Warrington and his possessive nature.

Ivan was a native of Poland. He had been only three years old when Hitler invaded and smashed his secure family life. Throughout the occupation the Cheveskis

> **Elsie Tanner had no idea that within six months her own daughter would be installed next door at No. 9**

toed the line and believed that if they complied with the authorities they would be treated well. Unfortunately, Ivan's grandfather was found harbouring a Jewish doctor in his baker's shop. The Nazis burned it to the ground, with Ivan's grandparents still inside. It was across the square from Ivan's own home and the cries of his family haunted him through the night and stayed with him for ever afterwards. Shortly after this, the Cheveskis fled their home, afraid of repercussions.

After the war they arrived in Britain as refugees to live with Uncle Rizhard, who had lived in Warrington since before the war. The men found employment at the local steelworks but were persecuted by the locals who saw them as taking jobs that should have belonged to returning servicemen. When Ivan's father Kazimierz was killed during an industrial accident, his mother Biasia couldn't bear to live in an alien country without him and gassed herself. Ivan, just fourteen at the time, continued to live in his uncle's house and took his father's job at the steelworks.

After marrying Linda he brought her home to his community and found them a bedsit near his uncle's house. He had strong views on how a wife should behave, and he grew jealous when Linda attracted the attention of other men. She grew restless in the bedsit and became resentful as Ivan refused to allow her to work. She took to spending more and more time in Weatherfield, visiting her mother, and then, in 1960 told Ivan she was leaving him for good. She moved back to No. 11 Coronation Street to await his reaction. She was secretly thrilled when he came after her to plead for her return, pouring out endless laments of his love for her. They were reconciled when she broke the news that she was pregnant, and this time it was for real. Ivan was so delighted with the news that he told Linda he'd give her anything. She told him she wanted No. 9.

The landlord, Wormold, decided he couldn't be bothered letting the house again and told the Cheveskis he was looking for a buyer instead. Linda had her heart set on the house so Ivan borrowed the deposit from Uncle Rizhard and took a job at the local ironworks, as well as an evening post as potman at the Rovers to help raise the £560 to buy the house.

Baby Cheveski was born in June 1961. Ivan wanted to name him Rizhard but Linda settled on Paul. Their happiness was complete when Ivan surprised Linda with a television set bought on HP.

Ivan worked long, hard hours to support his family but Linda wasn't at ease in the Street. When Paul developed a chesty cough that refused to go away, she realized how unhealthy the area was. When Ivan broke the news to her that a friend of his had settled in Canada with a good job, Linda allowed herself the luxury of dreaming of a better lifestyle for her family. She was tantalized when Ivan received a letter from his friend with photographs of the huge detached house and modern fitted kitchen that he had bought. He told

● *The Cheveskis swapped the mangle at No. 9 for a plush top-loader in their new Canadian home. Elsie Tanner was shattered by their decision to go.*

Ivan he could arrange for him to have an equally highly paid job. It was just before Christmas 1961 when the Cheveskis set sail for Canada. Elsie Tanner bade them a tearful farewell and they promised to visit soon, but she believed that as they were going half-way around the world she would never see them again.

No. 9 did not stand empty for long. School-teacher Kenneth Barlow from No. 3 had married hair stylist Valerie Tatlock from No. 1 and, after honeymooning in London, the newly-weds moved into No. 9, Kenneth having sold his scooter to pay the deposit. The couple had big plans for their home and the neighbours watched with interest as Len Fairclough worked to transform the front parlour into a hair salon for Valerie. So that she could take bookings, Valerie had a telephone installed: it was the first local domestic line and the GPO had to dig up the Street to lay cables.

Valerie had been amazed when intellectual, good-looking Kenneth had proposed. She suffered from a slight inferiority complex and couldn't understand what he saw in her. At first she had feared he was after a mother replacement but he had convinced her of his love. She was thrilled by their intimacy as they spent long evenings by the fireside together, listening to his classical-music collection and dreaming of the day they would have enough money saved to buy a semi with a garden for children to play in. In their dreams there were always two children, a boy and a girl. They shortened each other's names to Ken and Val, and she felt safe. The only times she felt uneasy about the marriage was when she struggled to keep up with his intellectual friends who patronized her and laughed at her discomfort when they talked about world and domestic issues. She had no opinions about John F. Kennedy and Nikita Krushchev and these moments reinforced her sense of inferiority.

In 1963 the couple took a lodger. Val had never wanted someone sharing their home and when Dave Robbins arrived she was hostile towards him. Dave was a colleague of Ken's, teaching PE at Bessie Street School. Ken took no notice of Val's discomfort and encouraged his friend to make himself at home. He rarely gave much thought to domestic arrangements and busied his mind with what he considered more important issues. Dave, however, felt uncomfortable with the atmosphere at No. 9 and moved out to a flat over Frank Barlow's DIY shop. As soon as Dave left, however, Val missed his company. Unlike Ken, he never brought current affairs and politics into the house. He preferred Radio Luxembourg to the Third Programme and appreciated Val's plain cooking rather than challenging her to cook lasagne as Ken so often did. Furthermore, she missed his quiet, unassuming company and came to the realization that she had married the wrong man.

Tragedy struck the area in the early months of 1964 when Susan Schofield, a pupil of Dave's, was hit by a lorry while crossing Rosamund Street. She died of her injuries in hospital and Dave was devastated, blaming

● *Valerie Barlow was never certain if Ken loved her. She felt he saw her as a mother figure, and sought intellectual and emotional relationships elsewhere.*

himself because Susan had been in his care at the time. Ken pounced upon the incident as proof that a crossing was needed on Rosamund Street and spear-headed a campaign to fight for one. Meanwhile, Val was left to comfort the distraught Dave. Telling Ken that she felt he didn't love her and just saw her as a housekeeper, she packed her bags and asked Dave to take her in. Dave acknowledged he had feelings for her, but he was too weak to fight Ken for her. Ken arrived to take her back, and Val urged Dave to say he wanted her. When he didn't, she returned home to No. 9 and Ken.

Val closed down the salon in the early spring of 1965. It had never been a roaring success and her decision to train neighbour Dennis Tanner as a stylist had backfired when he bleached Lucille Hewitt's hair

blonde. Len Fairclough arrived to pull out the basins he had installed less than three years earlier and set about turning the room into a playroom in time for the arrival of Val's twins. Susan and Peter were born in Weatherfield General on 15 April. Val felt completely fulfilled as she gazed at her babies. Now, she felt, she had something worthwhile into which she could channel her energies; now she could seek escape from the long, uncomfortable silences that occurred too frequently when she and Ken were alone together.

While Val occupied her days with the twins, Ken grew tired of nappies and screaming babies. He became attracted to independent, intellectual reporter Jackie Marsh, whom he had met when she interviewed his brother David for the local paper. She had made it obvious to him that she was attracted to him. Val seemed so involved with the babies, feeds and changing that Ken felt out of place in the house. He spent time at Jackie's flat and, only six months after the birth of his children, embarked on a passionate affair.

Ken spent his evenings in Jackie's arms while Val soothed one twin to sleep only to have the other wake up and cry. She hardly slept as she woke at night to give feeds, and tried not to disturb hard-working Ken's sleep. He spent more and more time in Jackie's bed, after school, in the evenings, in free periods. But they became careless over the affair, and Elsie Tanner confronted Ken after seeing the pair kissing in the high street. He told her to keep out of his business, but all the same he was shaken by her interference. He had planned a weekend away with Jackie, letting Val believe he would be at a two-day teaching conference. Elsie threatened to tell her the truth so Ken decided to cancel the 'conference'. He decided to leave Val for Jackie and steeled himself to break the news. However, Val surprised him by preparing a packed lunch for his conference. When he saw the trouble she had gone to, when she didn't even have time to wash her hair, he realized he could never leave her, and instead he broke off his relationship with Jackie.

Since his days at university, Ken had been a highly principled man. He had a strong sense of what was acceptable in society and what wasn't and, unlike many of his peers, was prepared to fight for his principles. When he was denied promotion at Bessie Street School he took a post teaching English at the local college, Granston Tech. Here, he taught seventeen- and eighteen-year-olds before they went on to university. He saw himself in some of the more passionate, angry young men and urged them to fight for their beliefs. When the council attempted to stop an anti-Vietnam meeting, Ken not only encouraged his students to demonstrate but also took part. The police were called and Ken was arrested. He appeared before the magistrates and was fined five pounds. When he refused to pay up he was sentenced to seven days' imprisonment.

Val couldn't believe that Ken would put his principles before the interests of his family and begged him to pay the fine, saying she couldn't cope with the twins alone for a week, but Ken refused to listen to her pleadings, maintaining that his essential human rights had been taken from him. Val watched in disbelief as he was taken to Strangeways. When he returned, the incident was not spoken of and Ken never referred to his days behind bars.

The late sixties brought many changes to the area. Old factories and houses were demolished to make way for modern housing blocks and 'streets in the sky'. Opposite the terrace on Coronation Street, the bulldozers moved in to flatten the old Mission and Elliston's factory. Val watched the demolition with mixed feelings, looking forward to the future and housing improvements while feeling sad as the old ways were pushed aside. Just after the Mission was demolished, she discovered that the twins were missing from the back yard. Instinct told her that they were in danger and she rushed into the Street where she heard the bulldozer starting up to start smashing into the factory. She threw herself in front of the machine, causing the demolition workers to pull up sharp. As the engine stopped she raced inside and found the children huddled together in a dark corner.

The site opposite the terrace was bought by the council and new two-storey maisonettes were erected. They were airy and had huge rooms. Val asked Ken to get them one but Ken refused: they owned No. 9 and he did not want to sell up and pay rent. It was then that Val revealed that she had known all along about his affair with Jackie and said that if he wasn't prepared to forget his principles just for once she would leave and take the children with her. She was sick of struggling with a scullery kitchen and dark, damp rooms that never warmed through. Ken made enquiries and was amazed when the council agreed to allow him to rent a two-storey maisonette. He put the house on the market for £1,000, believing it was overpriced, and was astonished when just weeks later Len Fairclough announced he would buy No. 9. The Barlows packed and moved across the Street in April 1968.

Leonard Franklin Fairclough had been a builder all his adult life. He was well known in Coronation Street, mainly through his hard drinking at the Rovers. He had lived in Mawdsley Street since the end of the war, with his wife Nellie and son Stanley. When Nellie took Stanley and ran off with the insurance man, Len had proposed to Elsie Tanner but she thought their friendship was too good to be spoilt. He had other connections with Coronation Street: he had been best man when Walter Greenhalgh had married Dot Todd in 1942 and his best pal had been Harry Hewitt from No. 7. He was also a local councillor and Coronation Street was in the middle of his ward.

Len hoped to turn No. 9 into a bachelor pad where he would be able to entertain a series of women but his plans were sidetracked by the arrival of Marjorie Griffin, a publican's wife, with whom he had had a brief fling. Marj decided that Len was a better prospect than her husband Basil and moved into No. 9 with her pet monkey, Marlon. At first Len enjoyed having her around the place, cooking his meals and washing his

● *Builders Len and Jerry moved into No. 9 in 1968. Both had broken marriages behind them and Len had an estranged son, living in Nottingham.*

shirts, but she began to criticize his lifestyle and talked of changing the wallpaper. Len contacted Basil and asked him to take Marj back but Basil said he was enjoying his freedom and didn't want her. In desperation, Len paid two young tearaways to pose as his sons. Marj was horrified at the thought of having to act as their mother and returned to Basil. Len vowed never to let a woman move in again.

At his building firm, Len took on a couple of partners, Ray Langton and Jerry Booth. It made sense for the three to share the house as well as the business and the other two moved into No. 9. Ray reminded Len of himself when he was younger while Jerry took on the household accounts and chores. Despite the presence of the lads, his vow and the fact that Jerry slept in the front parlour, Len still strove to find a willing mate. He proposed to Town Hall clerk Janet Reid but she didn't love him. He went out with shopkeeper Maggie Clegg but knew he couldn't commit himself to her: deep down he was frightened of marriage and feeling trapped.

Life was never dull for Jerry Booth as he liked to fill his spare time with hobbies. He enjoyed walking in the country, cycling with the Weatherfield Harriers and swimming. In 1972 he embarked on an ambitious plan and built an eleven-foot sailing dinghy in the builder's yard. He named it the *Shangri-La* and dreamt of sailing in it around the coast of Britain. However, it sank on its maiden voyage. Shortly after this, he went through a bleak few weeks after pensioner Albert Tatlock was rushed to hospital from No. 1: Jerry had replaced Albert's old gas cooker with a new electric one and hadn't sealed the pipes properly. Gas had escaped into the house and Albert had to spend three days in an oxygen tent. When he came round, Albert assured Jerry it wasn't his fault but Jerry blamed himself and paid Albert's daughter compensation until Albert stopped him.

Len fell for the charms of night-club singer Rita Littlewood and bought an old newsagent's on Rosamund Street, installing her as manageress. The shop was called the Kabin and Rita employed timid Mavis Riley as her assistant. Mavis fell for Jerry and the

● *Rita Littlewood was Queen of the Capricorn Club. After years of working in a novelty trombone act she had branched out as a successful singer.*

pair became a couple, although somehow neither was able to summon up the courage to declare their feelings for the other one.

In the early seventies, terraced streets all over Weatherfield fell to the steel ball of the developers as tower blocks replaced the back streets. Len served on the council's housing committee and attended meetings during which it was agreed to demolish Coronation Street. He confided in Rita that the house owners would be offered money by Edward Wormold's property company and that the houses would be demolished by the end of 1974. Rita felt the residents had the right to be alerted and told everyone in the Rovers. A protest meeting was held but Len refused to attend. Emily Bishop at No. 3 was enraged that he didn't seem to be acting in their interests and threw a brick through his downstairs window. Eventually Len voted against the council plan, causing its defeat, but Rita disliked the way he had been prepared to turn against the residents and broke off their engagement. So that he would not be seen to benefit by the redevelopment, Len had put the deeds of the Kabin in Rita's name, and after finishing with him she refused to sign the shop back to him.

Councillor Fairclough then became involved with Lynne Johnson, who lived in Victoria Street and sought his aid in escaping her violent husband. Len tried to help but she refused to report her husband to the police and kept hanging around Len. He allowed her to take refuge in No. 9 while he was at work and it was there, in the living room, that Ray and Jerry found her body. Lynne had been violently beaten up and had died when her head had smashed against the hearth. The police cordoned off the house and arrested Len on suspicion of murder. Len swore his innocence but was held for two days in a cell until Roy Johnson confessed to killing his wife. Rita had refused to visit Len in prison, and barmaid Bet Lynch had been his only visitor. After his release, Len embarked on an affair with Bet, which was short-lived as he refused to commit himself to her.

After marrying secretary Deirdre Hunt at the register office, Ray moved out in July 1975. The same year, Jerry died of a heart attack and Len was left alone. Slowly he rekindled his relationship with Rita and proposed marriage to her, but she turned him down when she was offered a singing contract in Tenerife. Len drove her to the airport but she let the plane leave without her and they married on 20 April 1977 at St Mary's church. The whole Street turned out for the wedding, apart from Len's old flame from No. 11, Elsie, who couldn't bring herself to witness it.

After the honeymoon, Elsie continued to make waves when Rita objected to Len doing odd jobs at her house while tasks around his own went undone. She knew that Elsie had deep feelings for Len and was uncomfortable living next door to her. She didn't waste any opportunity to remind Elsie that she was a grandmother, but the backlash of this was that Elsie would remind Rita that she had no children.

Rita had always wanted a child of her own but a back-street abortion when she was fifteen had severely damaged her womb and she had been unable to conceive again. During the late sixties and early seventies she had lived as Harry Bates's common-law wife, mothering his two children whom she considered her own, but Harry threw her out when he discovered she had been seeing Len. She hoped to be a mother to Len's son Stanley, but Stanley was now a grown man and made it clear that he had no feelings for Len.

With no child to look after, Rita carried on running the Kabin and annoyed Len by keeping her evening singing jobs. As she was earning money Len said they didn't need, Rita treated herself by employing Hilda Ogden from No. 13 as a cleaner. Len objected to Hilda's presence as he believed it was Rita's job to do the housework. Rita pointed out that she was no man's skivvy and the two rowed. Both Len and Rita had passionate tempers, which flared quickly, and could be violent. One area in which they disagreed more than any other was the state of the house. Since he had bought it in 1968, Len had not made any improvements, seeing No. 9 purely as a place in which to doss down. Rita, on the other hand, regarded it as her home and wanted it to be comfortable and stylish. She made out a list of improvements, starting with the installation of central heating, and grew furious when Len laughed at it and tore it up. That evening she packed a bag and left.

Len had no idea where Rita had gone and turned to Elsie for help, but she pointed out that he had made his bed and now had to lie in it. After six months he located Rita working in a launderette in Blackpool. He begged her to return and promised to change his ways. At first Rita told him their marriage was over and that she wasn't coming back but then she had a change of heart. Len was grateful that she'd given him a second chance and installed central heating immediately.

Even with the home improvements, though, Rita wasn't happy and admitted to Len that she wanted them to have a child. The idea became an obsession and when she discovered they were too old to adopt she offered to buy a baby from a neighbour. However, after what seemed an endless parade of interviews, the Faircloughs were registered as foster-parents. They fostered two children: John Spencer, whose mother was in hospital, and the tomboy Sharon Gaskell, who loved working for Len and begged her social worker to let her stay permanently at No. 9. Rita was thrilled to have a daughter of her own, and the pair of them worked on Len to sell the house.

In 1981 Len bought the land next to No. 9 where No. 7 had once stood. With Sharon as his apprentice he rebuilt the house and planned to sell it at a huge profit. However, Rita fell for the modernized house and decided she wanted it herself. Len was amazed

● *Sharon Gaskell brought a breath of fresh air into the Faircloughs' lives. She even helped Len in the rebuilding of No. 7.*

when, over his head, Rita sold No. 9 to binman Chalkie Whitely and the Faircloughs moved next door.

Tom Whitely had been called Chalkie since before the Second World War. His wife Mary had called him Chalkie, as had all his family, his pals at the engineering works, where he learnt his trade, and from 1976 onwards, his workmates at the Corporation Refuse Department. He was Chalkie to everyone, except Phyllis Pearce. Chalkie and Phyllis had known each other for years, ever since they had lived in Cromwell Street together in the fifties and sixties. They were both married and both pitied the other's spouse for having to put up with their ways. Chalkie saw Phyllis as a cantankerous old biddy; she viewed him as a chauvinist with a roving eye, who liked to keep Mary chained to the kitchen sink. Chalkie never forgave his son Bob when the lad joined the Whitelys and Pearces in wedlock by marrying Phyllis and Harold's only daughter Margaret. For the next few years he had to share

Sunday lunches with Phyllis as she clicked her false teeth at him.

Chalkie moved into No. 9 in August 1982, without telling Phyllis where he was moving to. Harold and Mary were long dead, as was Margaret, who had died of breast cancer in the late seventies. Bob worked on an oil rig and Chalkie brought up his grandson, Craig, single-handedly. He would have liked to shut Phyllis out of their lives, but he conceded she had a right to see the lad as she was his grandmother.

As soon as Chalkie and Craig had moved into No. 9, Phyllis lost no time in tracking them down, urging Craig to leave the old fella and to move into her terraced house where it was 'nice'. Fourteen-year-old Craig, though, loved living with his grandad, who allowed him to come and go as he pleased. Craig soon caused the neighbours to complain when he unleashed his talents on his drum-kit. To help the lad settle in, Chalkie installed six pigeons and an old loft in the back yard. Craig was given the responsibility of looking after the birds, and he read up on how to race them. He never got a chance to see if they knew how to home because a few months after he had settled into the back bedroom he found himself on a plane flying to Australia.

Bob Whitely returned home from the rigs and caused a flutter at the Rovers where barmaid Bet Lynch took a fancy to him. She was as stunned as Chalkie and Phyllis when he announced that he was taking a job in Australia and that Craig was coming with him. Phyllis pleaded with Bob not to take Craig as she feared she would never see him again, and Chalkie choked back the tears as he waved his family off. Bob's last remark to his father was to tell him to sell the house, which had been bought with his money.

As Chalkie looked for lodgings, Phyllis aired her back room and decided that, despite his faults, he was a man and she needed a man about the house. Chalkie swore blind he wasn't crossing her threshold and hoped Elsie Tanner would take him in at No. 11. As it turned out he didn't have to find accommodation: after winning over £3,000 on a five-horse accumulator

● *Neighbours in the Street often pondered who meant the most to Jack Duckworth – his wife Vera or his pigeons. No one ever came up with a convincing argument either way, despite debating the matter with beer in hand in the Rovers Return.*

he put the house in the hands of an estate agent and booked a single flight to Australia. He left the Street in a taxi, and Phyllis broke down in tears as she watched the last of her family ties disappearing to the other side of the world.

The neighbours were appalled on the September day in 1983 when the Duckworths descended upon the Street. For years the loud-mouthed family had been a source of amusement in the Rovers as Vera's handbag flew through the air to bash husband Jack over the head. The regulars had witnessed her dumping his clothes on the bar as a gift for Bet Lynch, who had given Jack bed room. They had laughed themselves into a state watching Jack dressed up in his flared trousers, wide-lapelled jacket and frilled shirt to meet a mystery redhead at the Rovers, brought about by the Bill and Co. Video Dating Agency. The mystery red-headed 'Carole Munro' turned out to be Vera wearing a wig.

● *Shortly after moving into No. 9, Gary Mallett bought Jim McDonald's classic motorbike for £1,000 – the price Len paid for the house 27 years before.*

In 1983 forty-nine-year-old Jack was working as a taxi driver and Vera was one of Mike Baldwin's minions at the denim factory. They were well known in the Street, where the residents found them amusing – while they lived in Inkerman Street. The day they announced they had put £1,000 down on No. 9 and had a mortgage for the rest, long-standing residents swore that the housing value in the Street sank to an all-time low.

The Duckworths were new to house-buying. They had lived most of their married life in rented accommodation, which they only left because the landlord moved in with a bulldozer. They were given £1,000 compensation and Vera refused to let Jack blow the money on a car. Instead she insisted they use it as a deposit on No. 9. The main reason Vera wanted the house was to provide a stable home for the return of their nineteen-year-old son, Terry, who had been away from home for eighteen months while he served with the Paras. He returned to Weatherfield with a muscular frame, of which he made the most by wearing tight-fitting T-shirts. To keep in shape, he took a job humping carcasses around at the abattoir. Coronation Street was handy for work and boasted a good pub so he was happy.

Terry was never without a girlfriend but most of them were just sexual relationships. In 1985, however, he fell in love. Andrea Clayton lived with her family next door at No. 11. She was still at school, studying for her A levels, and Terry felt she wouldn't be attracted to him as he had no qualifications. He was pleased when she made it obvious that she was. Andrea's parents, though, were far from pleased, especially when she broke the news that she was pregnant. Her father, Harry, went for Jack in the Rovers, thumping him in the face and causing him to lose his false teeth on the floor.

When Jack lost his licence for drinking and driving, he had to give up the taxis. Vera refused to have him lounging about in the house and bought Stan Ogden's old window-cleaning round for him. Jack hated the idea of cleaning windows until he realized how friendly lonely housewives were. His ladders were often to be seen propped against Dulcie Froggat's windows at 45 Cromwell Crescent and he carried on calling on the lovely Dulcie long after he gave up the round to take the post of potman at the Rovers.

Terry also had a change of career when he took up selling household-cleaning goods door to door. He would call upon his experiences in the Paras to play on housewives' sympathies, saying he had been unemployed since fighting for his country in the Falklands War. Soon his selling brought him to Cromwell Crescent and Dulcie fell for her second Duckworth. It wasn't until Ralph Froggat gave Jack a thump in the face that he discovered was due to Terry that both men realized, with horror, that they had been seeing the same woman.

Vera's mundane days of work and bingo changed when she won a Vauxhall Nova in a woman's magazine competition. Jack had entered in her name and tried, in vain, to claim the car as his. The competition had been about the Perfect Husband and he had won it with the slogan: "My husband is husband of the year because right from the day we were married he has made my life one long honeymoon." The car gave Vera the freedom to travel wherever she wanted and she took Jack out for a romantic picnic in the hills. On the way home she decided to give her handsome husband a kiss. He was startled as she lunged at him and she was startled when the car lunged with her and hit a lamp-post. In the crash Jack's nose was broken and he successfully sued Vera for £600 compensation. As he didn't have a bank account, he allowed her to bank the cheque, only to have her spend the money on a bed, a washing machine and a microwave.

Terry left the Street under a cloud of shame when he ran off to Scotland with Linda Jackson, the wife of his best friend, but Jack and Vera weren't alone for long at No. 9. Vera's mother, Amy Burton, descended on them. She took a job cleaning at the Rovers but her stay was short-lived when Jack caught her stealing bottles of pale ale. Vera returned her mother to her Rusholme flat but felt awful when she died later. At the funeral, Vera was introduced to retired barber Joss Shackleton, who told her that she was his daughter. Jack thought that the old man was just trying to secure a cosy billet but Vera believed Joss to be her father and took him in. He soon shared with Vera the family secret: that his grandmother had been seduced by Edward VII and that his mother had been their offspring. The news that she was the Queen's cousin came as a revelation to Vera, who felt that her life suddenly made sense. She had always thought herself different from those around her, and this news clarified her position. Jack refused to believe the story and was relieved when the old man moved out.

Another family member moved into No. 9 in 1992. Terry reappeared to introduce his parents to his pregnant girlfriend, Lisa Horten, whom he had met in her native Blackpool where he had been working as a bouncer. Shortly after their visit to Weatherfield, Terry was arrested for GBH after assaulting a policeman at the night-club where he worked. He was remanded at Strangeways and Lisa moved into No. 9 to be near him. She became Mrs Terry Duckworth standing at the altar with two prison guards behind her. Terry was still on remand and was handcuffed throughout the ceremony. Afterwards, Vera talked the guards into taking the handcuffs off him for the photographs and Terry saw his chance. He ran off from the church, leaving Vera to face questioning and Lisa to ask herself if he loved her or had used her. Meanwhile, Jack sold the wedding pictures to the press for £100.

• • • • • • • • • • • • • • • • • • • •

When Ralph Froggat gave Jack a thump that was due to Terry, father and son realized they'd been seeing the same woman

• • • • • • • • • • • • • • • • • • • •

Terry wasn't on the run for long as he was caught on security cameras at Bettabuy's supermarket, where Vera now worked as a sales assistant. The police marched him off and he was sentenced to three years' imprisonment.

On 9 September 1992 Lisa gave birth by caesarean section to a boy, whom she named Tommy. Vera doted on her grandson but Lisa soon grew fed up with waiting for Terry's release. She started a friendship with Des Barnes from No. 6. They planned to move away with Tommy, but their dreams were shattered when Lisa was knocked down by a car in the Street. She died in hospital, without regaining consciousness, and Terry went for Des at her graveside. Little Tommy was taken in by Vera, who gave up her job to look after him as she waited for Terry to come home.

Terry was released from prison just before Christmas 1993. He had no paternal feelings for his son and went behind his parents' backs to arrange for Tommy to be brought up by Lisa's parents in Blackpool, striking a deal in which they paid him handsomely for the privilege of doing so. When he found out what had happened, Jack hit Terry and told him he was no longer his son.

The final family member to descend on the Duckworths was Jack's older brother Cliff. He admired the cladding Vera had had erected on the outside of the house in 1989, and decided to brighten it up even more by highlighting the occasional stone in bright blue. Vera was thrilled with the outcome but Jack and the other residents thought it an eyesore. Before Cliff was dragged home by his wife Elsie, Jack talked his brother into making a will with Jack as his sole beneficiary. Not long afterwards he was amazed to read in the paper that Cliff and Elsie had been killed in a car crash in Spain. At the time of their death they had had no savings but had taken out holiday insurance. Jack was sent a cheque for £30,000. The Duckworths decided that this was their one chance to make a difference to their lives. They sold No. 9 for £29,000 and bought the Rovers Return. When they moved Jack insisted on taking with him the pigeons he'd inherited from Chalkie Whitely.

It was the blue-highlighted stone cladding that attracted Judy Mallett to the house. She told her husband Gary that she wanted it and he was so keen to escape from living with her mother, Joyce, that he'd have bought a tent on the Red Rec. Gary had a job laying cables and Judy worked part-time in an amusement arcade. She had been a barmaid in the past, and put those skills to the test at the Rovers. Gary set up his drum-kit in the front room while the couple often startled the residents with their enthusiastic and uninhibited shows of affection.

Gary had always wanted children but Judy refused to plan for any until she was older. She changed her mind when she discovered that Gary had shown an interest in barmaid Samantha Failsworth. She decided it would make sense to have Gary's baby, in case he started to look around for someone more willing. Having made the decision, the couple were bemused when Judy didn't conceive straight away. As the months passed, it became obvious that all was not right. The couple were put off their stride by the sudden death of Judy's mother Joyce Smedley. With no one else to look after, they took in her dog Scamper, and lavished their excesses of love on the animal.

·Nº 11 CORONATION STREET·

1902 – 1918
Alfred, Ivy, Vi, Frank, Ralph, Mary, Lil, Will
and Susie Makepiece, with Hetty Harris

1918 – 1927
Ivy, Lil, Will, Susie and Iris Makepiece

1927 – 1938
Ivy Makepiece, with Jack Jinks and Henry Robottom

1938 – 1958
Arnold, Elsie, Linda and Dennis Tanner

1958
Ethel Myers

1958 – 1970
Elsie and Dennis Tanner, with Christine Appleby,
Walter Potts, Linda and Paul Cheveski and Sheila Birtles

1970 – 1973
Alan and Elsie Howard, with Lucille Hewitt

1973 – 1974
Ken and Janet Barlow

1974 – 1976
Ken Barlow, with Wendy Nightingale

1976 – 1984
Elsie Howard, with Gail Potter, Suzie Birchall, Martin Cheveski,
Audrey Potter and Marion Willis

1984 – 1985
Bill, Kevin and Debbie Webster

1985
Harry, Connie, Andrea and Sue Clayton

1986 – 1989
Alf and Audrey Roberts

1989 —
Jim, Liz, Steve and Andy McDonald

It was said of turn-of-the-century Weatherfield that every street had its rotten apples. In Coronation Street all the rotten apples lived together in one house – No. 11. The original meaning of the family name Makepiece – 'peace maker' – had been lost somewhere since the name first appeared in fifteenth-century Weatherfield. Far from being peacemakers, the Makepieces of 1902 were a warring tribe from the dockland area. Rough, ill-educated and drunken, they were regularly brought before the magistrates and six had been hanged from the gallows on Market Street.

Alfred Makepiece had been abandoned as an infant in St Mary's cemetery and had been brought up in the parish workhouse. At the age of seven, he had been taken in by Vera and Cody Makepiece of Bealer Street when the parish set up a pay scheme to encourage adoption. Cody spent his days in the docks with his sons and hired young Alfie to his brother Bert to use as his chimney-sweep boy. Alfred was given the family name and told he should be grateful.

Ivy Harris lived next door to the Makepieces in Bealer Street. The daughter of a docker and a char, she married Alfred and moved him into her family home when her father Joe was drowned. In the first eight years of marriage they had nine children, but only five survived. When Alfred broke from the docks to become an engineer at Hardcastle's mill they were allocated one of the new houses on Coronation Street and moved in with the children – Vi, eight, Frank, six, Ralph, five, Mary, three and two-year-old Lil. Will followed in 1904 and Susie made the set in 1906.

Ivy was twenty-nine when she moved into the new house but already her hair was turning grey and her sallow complexion aged her prematurely. To help feed the hungry children, she took in washing and always posted one of the children on guard as she didn't trust the neighbours not to steal items off the line to pawn. Alfred, although a year older than his wife, looked younger as his torso grew wider as he worked with the mill machinery. He had a shock when, shortly after moving into the Street, he discovered that his real father, Ernest Popplewell, lived at No. 7.

Ivy had always leant on her husband, had looked to him for guidance and strength, and his sudden death from TB devastated her. Left with seven children to support, she knew that she could either go under or fight to survive. She chose to fight. Taking a stall on Plank Lane Market Ivy traded in pegs and tin baths, drumming up custom by bashing a tub with her walking stick. At home the stick had another use: she lashed out with it, striking any child who disturbed her rest. Fourteen-year-old Vi, working full time at the mill, became the main breadwinner and took over the mothering of the younger children while Frank and Ralph stole what they could to boost the family income.

Another strain on the family came in the shape of Ivy's mother, Hetty Harris, who dumped herself at No. 11 when she was evicted from Bealer Street for not being able to pay her rent. She was a big woman and demanded twice as much food as the other family members. Ivy despaired of the cantankerous old harridan as she ate anything she found in the house. Hungry thirteen-year-old Ralph was caught stealing chickens from the market and was sent away to a reform centre: he had been Ivy's favourite and she blamed her mother's presence for him needing to steal. After a year of having Hetty in the house, Ivy decided to take action: she soaked fly-paper to remove the arsenic which she mixed into her mother's tea. It took two months to kill Hetty but Ivy's relief turned sour as the town was hit by strikes. The grave diggers weren't working and Hetty's body was left in the house through the hot summer months of 1911. The stench caused people to gag as they passed it.

In 1913 Ralph returned home after spending three years being knocked around in a huge Victorian building with bars in the windows. During that time he had been forced to do hard manual work but had also been taught how to read and write. He returned a sturdy sixteen-year-old, and reminded Ivy of her dead father.

Vi was the first Makepiece child to leave home when she married Jack Todd in 1914 and moved across the back alley to live with his mother, Daisy, at No. 7 Mawdsley Street.

In 1914 Frank and Ralph Makepiece marched off to war along with Jack Todd and many other young men.

• The Makepieces were
a bad lot.
Alfred (far left)
burgled the Corner
Shop, and Ralph raped
pretty Betty Cog
from Mawdsley Street
when she spurned
his advances.

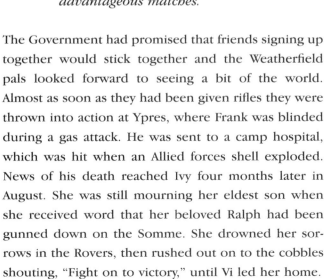

• Susie Makepiece (right) prostituted
herself in the back alley before moving on
to the streets of London, while Ivy (far
right) struggled to place her daughters in
advantageous matches.

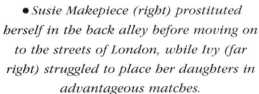

The Government had promised that friends signing up together would stick together and the Weatherfield pals looked forward to seeing a bit of the world. Almost as soon as they had been given rifles they were thrown into action at Ypres, where Frank was blinded during a gas attack. He was sent to a camp hospital, which was hit when an Allied forces shell exploded. News of his death reached Ivy four months later in August. She was still mourning her eldest son when she received word that her beloved Ralph had been gunned down on the Somme. She drowned her sorrows in the Rovers, then rushed out on to the cobbles shouting, "Fight on to victory," until Vi led her home.

During the war, Mary gave up mill work to serve as a conductress on the trams. She enjoyed standing on the open tops chatting to servicemen on leave and was amazed to find one who said he had been with Ralph before he died. The young man, Eric Walsh, invited her for tea, saying he would tell her more about Ralph's final days. Mary met Eric at his lodgings and before she had a chance to protest, he was upon her, tearing at her clothes and pushing her towards his bed. Her hand found a pair of scissors and she thrust them into Eric's arm and made her escape.

When the men returned home late in 1918 and early the next year, Mary found herself attracted to neighbour Thomas Hewitt at No. 3. They were married at the Mission of Glad Tidings in March 1919, and afterwards took on the tenancy of No. 7.

Ivy was happy to see Mary and Vi with husbands, and cast her eye around the other available men to see who Susie and Lil could catch. Both girls were considered beauties and she was certain she could find husbands for them with more than a few pennies in their pockets. Lil worked behind the bar at the Rovers Return, which suited Ivy as the girl was able to fill her gin glass when no one was looking, but Susie had always been a stubborn child and Ivy worried that when it came to matrimony she would go her own way. Ivy managed to pull off the coup of the century, as far as Makepieces were concerned, when she pushed Lil in the direction of bachelor shopkeeper Tommy Foyle. Lil agreed with her mother that a husband's looks weren't important as a pretty young wife could always find someone willing to entertain her behind her husband's back. Tommy was blessed with a healthy bank balance and was flattered when Lil came calling. He allowed himself to be manoeuvred into wedlock but immediately after the wedding service grasped what he'd let himself in for when Ivy demanded endless credit for her family as the girl's 'dowry'.

Now that her groceries were taken care of, Ivy turned her attention to the Rovers where landlady Mary Diggins was laid low with a fever that seemed certain to take her to her grave. Ivy tried to push Susie towards George Diggins and was angered when the girl refused to co-operate. Ivy demanded obedience and was furious when Susie ran off with Billy Chad, from No. 3, who had been her secret lover. Outraged that her master plan had failed, Ivy refused to let any of her children mention Susie's name.

Will was growing up fast. In 1924 when Susie left home he was twenty and worked in the docks with his cousins. On a hike over the moors he met nineteen-year-old Iris Morgan, who shared his interest in poetry. Ivy, however, thought Iris too weak-willed to be of any use to Will – she had always found that he needed someone behind him, pushing him. For once in his life, though, Will refused to listen to his mother and

married Iris in 1926 at the Mission. They moved to Bury where Iris's parents needed help in running a public house.

For the first time in her life Ivy was alone and she hated it. She was fifty-three when Will married and moved away, and although Vi, Mary and Lil lived nearby, they all had husbands and were beyond her control. Billy Chad returned to the Street with the news that Susie was living in London but Ivy wrote her off as dead until one day, in March 1929, she turned up on the doorstep of No. 11 dressed in a fur coat with a gentleman in a bowler hat waiting for her in a car. The neighbours stood in their doorways staring at Susie as she marched into the house and made a great show of kissing her mother. Ivy was sickened by the smell of Susie's perfume and demanded to know what she wanted. Susie said that she'd brought presents for the family and wanted them to share in her good fortune at finding a wealthy friend in London. Ivy called her a whore and threw her out.

When the Depression hit Weatherfield in the 1930s, Ivy was one of the few residents who managed to keep her head above water. She had her old-age pension, the one thing the Government couldn't touch, and took in a series of lodgers. She wasn't fussy, but made it a policy to insure the lodgers for fear they might die and she had to pay for burial. Her first lodger, Jack Jinks, *did* die after only three months in residence. Ivy was so surprised at the amount of money paid out by the insurance company that she joked in the Rovers she could kill off a few more tenants. Someone took her comments seriously and reported her to the police, suspecting her of doing in old Jinks. PC Henry Robottom was sent to have a word with her and ended up being talked into renting the spare room himself. He stayed for a couple of years.

In 1938 the old woman's reign as Queen of the Street came to an end when she died in bed of a stroke. She had no money to leave, after drinking away the insurance she'd put aside, so the Todds had her buried on the parish in a pauper's grave.

During the Depression brute force became a commodity in Weatherfield. Unscrupulous characters, mainly bookies and landlords, built up gangs of rough-necks for their own protection and to act as debt collectors. Landlord Wormold had such a gang and the residents of Coronation Street made certain they kept up to date with their rent payments to avoid a visit from one of the élite. They all felt uncomfortable when Wormold gave the tenancy of No. 11 to one of his men, a burly brute called Arnold Tanner.

Arnold was the first resident to wear a suit when it wasn't Sunday. He tried to make friends with the local men at the Rovers but they didn't trust him and resented his presence. Their reaction wasn't the same to Arnold's sixteen-year-old bride, Elsie. Here was a

● *When Elsie Tanner first came to the Street she was 16 and a new bride (bottom right). Baby Linda soon arrived, and Dennis followed two years later. Elsie was relieved when, after an initial period of mixing with villains, Dennis settled down.*

woman who spent every moment she could at the Bijou, who felt Laurence Olivier was the sexiest man alive and who modelled herself on Barbara Stanwyck in *Stella Dallas*. Already pregnant when she moved into No. 11, Elsie loved to sit in front of the mirror saying over and over again Stella's line: "Who says I'm not fit to be a mother?"

Arnold had married Elsie because, although in his moral code it was fine to threaten violence to elderly debtors, he believed that a man had to stick by his mistakes. Elsie had been a mistake, made when he had been drunk. Elsie, the eldest of ten, had grown up as a mother's help, looking after the younger children while her mother nursed the babies. Her pregnancy was indeed a blessing: it gave her a strong man to look after her and now, after months spent living in a caravan in Bamfirlong, she had a home of her own. She wasn't the sort of woman who lavished hours on keeping the place clean and tidy, and besides, she knew that

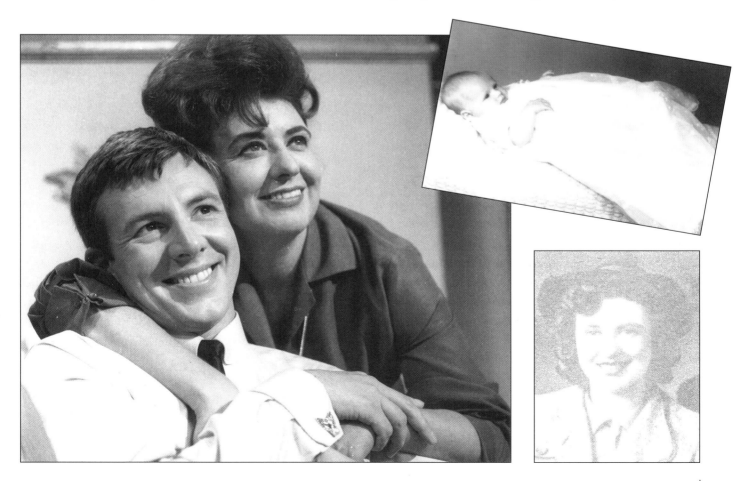

Arnold only wanted it as a base, somewhere to eat and sleep, but she decorated as best she could, covering the bedroom wall with pictures cut out of her movie magazines. It was November 1939 and Elsie was reading all about the most magnificent picture ever made. *Gone With The Wind* was to première the next month and the magazines were full of photographs of Vivien Leigh and the gorgeous Clark Gable. Elsie had already decided that if the baby was a boy she'd call him Clark and that a girl would be called Linda after glamorous Linda Darnell. While Elsie lost herself in creating her Hollywood bedroom, Arnold joined the Royal Navy and announced to Elsie he was off. They had lived together in the house for just seven days.

Although her family lived in Gas Street Elsie never saw them, and felt cut off in her new home. She told herself she'd be able to cope when the baby arrived but once in labour she found the pain too much and panicked. She managed to make her way to the Rovers and gave birth in Annie Walker's living room. The girl was christened Linda, as Elsie had wanted, and, two years later, after Arnold's only wartime visit, baby Dennis was born, this time as planned at No. 11. At nineteen Elsie had two children, an absent husband and worked long hours making service uniforms with her neighbour Dot Todd.

Leaving the children to fend for themselves, Elsie set about making the most of her war. The Americans were offering the most fun so Elsie joined the trail of girls making their way to Burtonwood and soon became the sweetheart of the 8th Air Force Base Air Depot. A string of American airmen danced with her and when they had the chance spent the night in her bed. Her love of the period was twenty-one-year-old Steve Tanner, who told her it was fate as they had the same surname. He was all for marrying her and looking after the children, but Elsie found her feelings for him too strong and stopped seeing him, fearing Arnold's actions if he ever found out.

Private Robert Riley caused a scene in the Street when he overstayed his leave to warm Elsie's bed for a week. When the Military Police caught up with him, he leapt naked from the house and tried to dash for

● *Alan Howard kept secret from Elsie the fact that he had a son, Mark. That was until Mark turned up and tried to break the couple apart.*

freedom across the cobbles only to find himself cornered by Mission caretaker Ena Sharples, who attacked him with a coal shovel while ordering her daughter Vera to keep her eyes closed. Elsie's reputation in the Street sank to an all-time low when, on VJ Day, two naked men appeared at her bedroom window to hang out a banner saying, 'God Bless Monty and the Lads'.

In 1946 Arnold returned from sea to see Dennis for the first time, and revealed that Ena had written him several long letters chronicling Elsie's 'war effort'. He told his wife that he was joining the Merchant Navy and she should consider herself a free agent, as he now saw himself.

Meanwhile, Linda found herself having to guard her honour from some of the more lustful of her mother's friends. When she was thirteen, one 'uncle', Chuck Nelson from Victoria Street, tried to trap her in her bedroom when Elsie was out. Dennis heard her screams and sprang on to the man's back, sinking his teeth into his ear. By the time Chuck had fought off the eleven-year-old blood was pouring down the side of his face and he doubled over when Linda kicked him in the groin.

Elsie took a job selling dresses at department store Miami Modes, and set up Linda with a job in the same department. However, Linda refused to work with her mother and started as a trainee machinist at Elliston's raincoat factory. She went out with neighbour David Barlow, but found him too tame. She'd inherited her mother's taste in men and became engaged to Roy Newman, an American sent to Burtonwood, in 1956 – Ena Sharples saw the jeep outside No. 11 and thought herself in a time warp. The relationship didn't last.

Dennis took part in a raid on an office in Rosamund Street. He tried to hide the money he stole from the safe in the coal hole at home but the police called on all known young offenders and the money was discovered. Elsie was distraught when he was sent to Borstal for a year and reproached herself for having been a bad mother.

When Linda married Ivan Cheveski, Elsie was left alone at No. 11. She became ill and the doctor, having diagnosed depression, advised her to take a long holiday. She closed the house and went to stay with a cousin in Hartlepool.

No. 11 was let for six months to spinster Ethel Myers: she managed Snapes café on Rosamund Street and needed somewhere local to stay. After she had been in residence for three months she woke in the night to hear someone creeping around. Her screams alerted the neighbours, who came to her aid to find a bewildered Dennis, who had been released early from Borstal and was trying to work out who the woman in

● *Ken Barlow's second wife Janet was not happy about renting No. 11 from Elsie; in 1971 Janet had failed in her attempt to break up Elsie's marriage to Alan.*

his mother's bed was. Dennis asked Ethel if he could stay in his old room but she refused and he was taken in by Ena Sharples.

Just before Christmas 1958, Sylvia Snape took over managing the café and Ethel left the area to live with her niece in Scarborough. Elsie returned to No. 11 and was reunited with Dennis, who in 1960 was caught in the middle of breaking into Biddolph's newsagent's with his friend Jed Stone. The pair were sent to prison for six months. On his release, Dennis took a job as front-of-house manager at the Orinoco Club, a seedy back-street working-men's club where his fresh-faced looks went down well with the strippers and exotic dancers.

After an absence of fifteen years Arnold returned seeking a divorce so that he could marry sweet-shop owner Norah Dawson. Elsie was forced to agree when he threatened to divorce her anyway for adultery, producing his letters from Ena.

There had never been a shortage of men in Elsie's life but, in October 1961, she met the one man she believed would be the love of her life. He was Chief Petty Officer Bill Gregory and they met during Harry

and Concepta Hewitt's wedding reception. Bill was from the south and while he stayed on duty in Manchester he took Elsie out. She kept expecting him to propose to her and had already decided to accept but he never asked the question. It was Ena who told her that Bill had a wife. When Elsie confronted him he said that the marriage was long dead and told her he would leave Phyllis for her if she wanted. Elsie had always had one rule – not to take another woman's husband. She let him walk out of her life.

With Linda settling in Canada and Dennis trying his luck as a theatrical agent in London, Elsie felt lonely at No. 11 so took in Christine Appleby as a lodger. Christine had grown up next door at No. 13 and had been a close friend of Linda. She had left the Street to marry Colin Appleby in June 1962, but now, only three months later, she was a widow: Colin had been killed in a car crash. Elsie also found her a job at Miami Modes, and Christine embarked on a relationship with

Frank Barlow, Kenneth's father, but eventually decided that it had been a big mistake to return to the Street.

Dennis returned from London and took over the running of the Lenny Phillips theatrical agency on Cross Street and was quick to discover the musical talents of window cleaner Walter Potts, whom he renamed Brett Falcon and lodged at No. 11 before launching him as a singing sensation. Elsie was surprised to find that Dennis had landed someone with real talent. Walter's first record 'Not Too Little Not Too Much' zoomed up the charts and Elsie was horrified to find hordes of teenage girls encamped on her doorstep screaming for their hero. Success frightened Walter, who amazed the regulars at the Rovers by earning fifty-four pounds in one week's record sales. In early 1964 he left Weatherfield to embark on a European tour while Dennis gave up the business to train as a hair stylist. Walter tried to pay back Elsie's kindness by sending her money to have a bathroom and toilet installed at the house. She had some cash left over and used it to install a red lacquer telephone.

In 1966, when Linda returned with her son Paul having separated from Ivan, Elsie had a full house. Their arrival coincided with Elsie letting the back bedroom to Sheila Birtles, who took a job at Elliston's, where she had worked until 1963 when she had left the Street after a failed suicide bid. Her old boyfriend, Jerry Booth, was pleased to see her back and she took him to see her little boy Danny, who was being fostered. Jerry offered to marry her and promised to take on Danny as his own son but Danny's real father, Neil Crossley, made a similar offer. Sheila chose him over Jerry and went to live in Sheffield.

When Paul fell in the canal and was rescued by bookie Dave Smith, Linda feared he would die. The cold water brought on pneumonia and he was placed in an oxygen tank, with Linda and Elsie keeping a bedside vigil. Ivan read about the accident in the local paper; and worry over Paul's health brought the

● *Elsie Howard in defiant pose:*
she was always ready to face whatever
the world threw at her.

• Kevin Webster moved into No. 11 with his builder father Bill three years after the death of his mother Alison.

Cheveskis back together. When Paul recovered, they all moved to Birmingham.

The Americans returned to Burtonwood in 1967 and Elsie was flabbergasted to find Steve Tanner among them. He was keen to pick up where they had left off in 1944 but Elsie felt she was too old. Steve convinced her that she was desirable as ever, and they had a fairy-tale wedding in a Warrington Methodist church. After honeymooning in Portugal, they rented a huge apartment in Altrincham, complete with a daily help, before leaving for Steve's home town of Boston in America. Dennis was left alone at No. 11 and decided to make extra money by letting it as theatrical lodgings. The plan backfired when a group of hippies moved in and set up a commune in the living room. After they

left, Londoner Jenny Sutton arrived looking for her sister Monica, who had been one of the group. Dennis fell for her and moved her into No. 11.

Elsie and Steve's marriage was doomed from the start: both had married a twenty-year dream and the reality was too harsh to take. Elsie, feeling out of place, sold her engagement ring to raise her flight money back to England and returned alone to No. 11. Dennis married Jenny at the register office on Clarence Street and moved to Bristol.

Steve followed Elsie to England, hoping for a reconciliation, but he got pushed down the stairs of his rented apartment and broke his neck. No one knew who had murdered him and the coroners brought in a verdict of death by misadventure. Elsie believed that one of her boyfriends, Len Fairclough, had killed Steve for her.

In 1969, shortly after Elsie bought the house from Wormold with money she had received from Steve's life assurance policy, sibling hairdressers Sandra and Bernard Butler moved into No. 11 to lodge with their auntie Elsie. Elsie too was employed by hair-salon owner Alan Howard. It wasn't long before she fell for his charms and they were married in 1970.

Sandra was less lucky in love. She agreed to marry Ray Langton, a local plumber, but on discovering that he was having an affair with Audrey Fleming at No. 3, threw his ring in his face and returned to live in Saddleworth with Bernard.

When they got back from their honeymoon in Paris, Alan broke the news to Elsie that his businesses were failing and he was insolvent. Before long, he also began to drink heavily. He turned his attentions to night-club singer Rita Littlewood but, as Rita told Elsie, she wasn't interested in alcoholics. In an attempt to lighten the atmosphere at No. 11, the Howards took in Lucille Hewitt as a lodger and she found herself caught in the middle of their arguments.

Hoping to start afresh, Elsie took a post at Mark Britain's Newcastle branch, believing that if Alan was in his home town he might stop drinking. The Howards moved to the north-east, Lucille returned to her old room at the Rovers Return and the house was let to school teacher Ken Barlow.

Janet Reid had married widower Ken Barlow in October 1973, after a short courtship. She was desperate for a husband while he needed a mother for his eight-year-old twins who, since their mother's death in 1971, had been living with their grandparents in Scotland. Ken's plan was to get settled in No. 11 then, after the honeymoon was over, send for the children. Unfortunately Janet had other plans. At thirty she was happy with the idea of having children but wanted her own, not Valerie's. Behind Ken's back, she looked into selecting a good boarding school to which Susan and Peter could be sent. When Ken found out he was furious. He had married Janet out of necessity rather than love, and once he knew that she wasn't prepared to take on his children the marriage was over. He moved into the spare room and Janet packed her bags.

With Janet gone, Albert Tatlock offered Ken lodgings at No. 1 but Ken decided to stay where he was and started to live the life of a bachelor. He seduced graduate Wendy Nightingale and she left her husband to live with Ken at No. 11, but her middle-class background set her apart from the neighbours and she felt uncomfortable with them. Her husband asked her to return, pointing out that in Weatherfield she was like a rose in a garden of thorns. Ken was stunned when Wendy left: he had thought they had been getting on fine.

After the collapse of her marriage Elsie Howard returned to Weatherfield. As a favour to her, Ken moved out of the house and she set about rebuilding her life again. With three broken marriages behind her, she decided that never again would her heart run away with her. She took a job as manageress of Sylvia Matthews's lingerie shop and took in her assistant Gail Potter as her lodger. When Sylvia's business associate took Gail out for lunch Gail fell in love for the first time. He was older and had money to buy her gifts and eighteen-year-old Gail took no notice of worldly Elsie who warned her that she would only get hurt. After giving Roy Thornley her virginity in the stock room, Gail was devastated when he admitted to being married. She finished with him, but his wife Doreen found out about the affair and named Gail as co-respondent in her divorce case. Elsie sorted the matter out by telling Mrs Thornley that Roy was having an affair with Sylvia Matthews. Sylvia retaliated by putting the shop on the market but Elsie talked Mike Baldwin into buying it as a retail outlet for his denim goods. He went ahead but she didn't get to keep her job. He told her that she was too old for the denim scene, and made her supervisor at his factory instead.

The back bedroom at No. 11 took in another guest when Suzie Birchall moved in with Gail after being taken on to help run Mike's boutique, which he called the Western Front. Suzie was from a broken home, and shortly after moving into No. 11, she learnt that her mother had left home after years of being abused by her husband Bob. Bob told Suzie she had to return home to look after him now that her mother had gone but Suzie fought back and refused. When he tried to bundle her into his car she was saved by delivery boy Steve Fisher, who fought him off.

Steve thought Suzie was wonderful and followed her around, but Suzie had no interest in boys, only men. Gail, however, fell for Steve, admiring his gentle ways and sensitive nature. She was heartbroken when, to demonstrate her control over men, Suzie seduced Steve in their bedroom then cast him aside.

Elsie worried about Suzie's sexual behaviour, seeing herself in the young girl. She tried to give her advice but Suzie just accused her of being jealous of her youth and beauty. When Gail married mechanic Brian Tilsley from No. 5, and Suzie left for the bright lights of London, Elsie found herself washed up and near retirement with no prospects, no money and no man to love her. The only jobs open to her were unskilled – café work and machinist – and she nearly

● *Trombone-playing Harry Clayton was well known as the Street's milkman, while Connie turned the front parlour into a dressmaking room.*

lost her life when she fell asleep on the sofa while smoking. She was saved when Hilda Ogden, from No. 13, called round to borrow sugar and found the house full of smoke.

A string of lodgers helped to occupy Elsie's life as she concerned herself with their affairs. First Linda's son, Martin Cheveski, stayed with his gran, making Elsie feel about a hundred. Then the back bedroom was occupied by Gail's mother, Audrey Potter, who stayed with Elsie while between men. She fled when grocer Alf Roberts decided to propose marriage. One lodger who did marry was florist Marion Willis, who wedded Eddie Yeats from No. 13 and then went to nurse her sick mother in Bury.

In December 1983 Elsie was surprised to receive a visit from her old beau Bill Gregory. He was amazed to find her still living at No. 11, and told her all about his new life in Portugal where he owned a wine bar. As Elsie had no ties he urged her to sell up and join him.

She realized it was her last chance of happiness and grabbed it, bidding farewell to the Street. She left the sale of No. 11 in the hands of her daughter. Linda had divorced Ivan after nearly twenty-five years of marriage and, as she had nowhere to live, moved into the house. She took a job behind the bar of the Flying Horse and tried to put people off buying No. 11. Elsie insisted on a sale being made so Linda agreed to sell to builder Bill Webster for £11,500 in the hope that he'd take her on as fixtures and fittings. When he made it obvious that he wasn't interested she left town.

Forty-two-year-old Bill had struggled to bring up his teenage children, Kevin and Debbie, since his wife Alison had died of cancer in 1980. He decided to buy No. 11 mainly to get the children out of their run-down tower block. At the same time, he broke free from his council job to start up his own building firm, renting Len Fairclough's old yard from his widow Rita.

Kevin was nineteen when the family moved into No. 11. He had just started as a mechanic in Brian

● *Alf Roberts married his third wife, Audrey, in 1985. She had borrowed his sports car and smashed it; when he rowed with her she cried, and he then proposed.*

Tilsley's garage and felt that the new house would give them the fresh start they needed. Sixteen-year-old Debbie had looked after her men since her mother's death and left school to work at Jim's Café on Rosamund Street. She annoyed Bill by going out with biker Dazz Isherwood. Bill maintained Dazz's bike was dangerous but Debbie liked to ride on the back.

The Websters' new start was turned on its head when Bill fell for Elaine Prior, the niece of community centre caretaker Percy Sugden. She was a hairdresser and had decided to open up a salon in Southampton. When Elaine agreed to marry him, Bill told the children that they would be moving south, but Kevin refused to leave his native Weatherfield. Bill and Elaine married in January 1985 and left for Southampton with Debbie, while Kevin looked for lodgings.

The house was sold to milkman Harry Clayton and his family. His wife Connie turned the front parlour into a work room for her dress-making business while their daughters, eighteen-year-old Andrea and fifteen-year-old Sue, studied at Weatherfield Comprehensive. The family found themselves caught up in a feud when Vera Duckworth at No. 9 refused to pay Connie for a silver lurex dress she had made for her. Connie agreed with Vera that she looked a right mess in the outfit but pointed out that it had fitted perfectly and was worth the forty-five-pound fee. Terry Duckworth tried to settle the matter by paying the bill but Connie refused to accept his money. Terry acted as peacemaker

● *The McDonald family had travelled around the world from one Army base to another before settling at No. 11, and in the early years of their marriage, Jim and Liz were mostly happy. The boys, Steve and Andy (below right), were very different in temperament considering they were twins.*

because the feud was interfering with his courtship of Andrea but the dress incident was forgotten when Andrea broke the news that she was pregnant with Terry's baby. Terry told Andrea he wanted to stand by her and support the child, but Andrea didn't want to be a member of the Duckworth family. The Claytons decided that after the baby's birth Connie would care for it while Andrea went to university. When Vera insisted on playing her part, the family packed up and moved, after only seven months in the house.

In 1986 sixty-year-old shopkeeper Alf Roberts paid £11,000 for the house, annoying his new wife Audrey, who had finally agreed to marry him and had had her eye on a detached house in Bolton Road, which was going for £44,000. Audrey had eventually married Alf when she realized that she was getting too old to keep flitting from man to man and that Alf was a gent of some means. However, he also kept a tight rein on the purse strings, and had the front parlour converted into a hair salon so that Audrey could earn her own

shopping money. Although a trained stylist, Audrey was not happy with making her living at hairdressing. After she had turned Hilda Ogden's hair bright orange, she was pleased when Alf closed down the salon.

Alf had been councillor for the St Mary ward since 1968 and it came as a terrible shock when he lost to Deirdre Barlow in the 1987 elections. While the neighbours celebrated Deirdre's victory, he suffered a heart attack. He recovered in hospital but was told to take things easy. Audrey tried to cope with running the Corner Shop but made a mess of it so Alf was forced back to work.

He had another shock when Audrey suddenly rushed off to Canada to nurse her son Stephen when he was involved in a car crash. He had had no idea that Audrey had a son – and neither did her daughter Gail. When she returned from Canada, Audrey assured Gail that her father had been a different man from Stephen's but that was all she was prepared to say on the subject.

Towards the end of 1989 Audrey talked Alf into giving up the house and buying something more in keeping with his status as an important member of the community. He saw her reasoning and the couple moved to Grasmere Drive, set on a hill overlooking the Oakhill golf club. No. 11 was sold for £25,000 to Jim and Liz McDonald.

For thirty-four-year-old Jim, No. 11 was the first house he had ever regarded as a home. All his married life Jim had served as an engineer in the Royal Signals. He had married sixteen-year-old Liz Greenwood in January 1974 and their twin sons had been born the following June. Liz had brought up Steve and Andy single-handed in Army quarters where Jim's senior officers had been allowed to inspect her housekeeping without notice. She had soon realized that she had married the Army rather than an individual, but stuck at it for the sake of the boys. When Jim's term of service came to an end in 1989, she made him promise to leave the Army and take his chance on Civvy Street. They moved to Coronation Street as Liz's mother, Nancy, lived locally and the boys could finish their schooling at Weatherfield Comprehensive. During their first week in residence the family made an impression when the boys started up a JCB and drove it into Alf's shop window, smashing the glass.

Jim took a job as a television-repair man and Liz found employment as a barmaid in the Rovers. In an attempt to make more of a success of his life Jim then went into business running a motorbike repair shop. He rented Unit 21, which had been built into the old viaduct arch at the end of the Street, and named it Jim's Bike Shop. When Steve left school with no qualifications, Jim took him on but Steve had no interest in working hard. Andy, though, was considered brainy and was pushed into staying on at school to get the A levels that would open up university for him.

In 1991 Liz was upset to discover that she was pregnant: with the boys leaving school, she had been looking forward to a peaceful life with Jim, and a baby did not fit into that equation. Jim, however, was delighted as he felt he had missed out on seeing the twins grow up – he had been serving abroad for most

• • • • • • • • • • • • • • • • •

Liz went into premature labour and gave birth to a tiny baby she called Katherine; the little girl died the next day

• • • • • • • • • • • • • • • • •

of their lives. With his support, Liz decided she could face going ahead with the pregnancy. Then Steve got caught up in gang warfare. Eager to earn easy money he had joined a gang stealing car radios and selling them on. Jim forced him to own up to the police and Steve was made to name the other gang members. In retaliation, the gang beat up Andy and broke a window with a brick. Steve lay low and Liz worried about his whereabouts. She went into premature labour and gave birth to a tiny baby girl she called Katherine, but the little thing died the next day and Jim blamed Steve.

The Bike Shop folded through lack of business, and Jim was forced to take a job as a security guard. He grew angry when Andy, doing computer studies at Sheffield University, announced after his first year that he wanted to give up his course. He reasoned that he wasn't a natural student and was only living out the family's expectations of him as 'the brainy one'. He took a holiday job at Bettabuy supermarket and was present when armed raiders stole the takings from Jim. When the gunman turned, Andy jumped him and was clubbed around the head with the shotgun. Although he wasn't hurt Jim was furious with himself for not having been able to protect his son.

After a spell managing the Rovers bar on holiday relief, Liz applied to Newton and Ridley for a pub of her own. Brewery boss Richard Willmore encouraged her and made her manageress of city-centre pub the Queens. Jim was thrilled to give up security work and moved in with Liz to help run the pub, leaving Steve and Andy at No. 11. Jim said he did not mind working for his wife but soon grew jealous of the easy way in which she chatted to the male customers. He believed Willmore had only given her the pub because he fancied her. He accused Liz of having an affair, and he punched Willmore. Willmore told Liz that the pub was hers for as long as she wanted it but that Jim would have to go. When Liz chose to stay at the Queens, Jim felt vindicated in his suspicions and returned to No. 11, telling the boys that their mother was a whore.

Liz started divorce proceedings against Jim, and the twins found themselves caught between their parents and expected to take sides. At first they were against bad-tempered Jim, but when Liz took her barman Colin Barnes as a lover they cast her as the villainess.

Andy started as a trainee manager at Bettabuy and moved out of Jim's way by lodging with his boss, Curly Watts, at No. 7, while Steve worked at Mike Baldwin's print shop. After being found guilty of perverting the course of justice when calling himself Kevin Webster to escape a motor offence, he was ordered to carry out 200 hours of community service.

Living without Liz made Jim realize how much he loved her and slowly he broke down her defences in an attempt to win her back. They were reconciled, she gave up the Queens and returned to No. 11. The twins had left home and the couple embarked on a honeymoon period. Jim worked as a mechanic at MVB Motors on Viaduct Street and Liz got a job behind the bar at the British Legion.

In 1995, the family celebrated when Steve married heiress Vicky Arden from the Rovers and set about spending her £250,000 fortune. When Liz worried about becoming pregnant again, Jim underwent a vasectomy but the marriage cracked when they failed to buy the Rovers when it came on the market. The Duckworths bought the pub and Mike Baldwin sacked Jim from the garage. He had a sad fortieth birthday throughout which Liz accused him of continuously dragging her down.

Liz took a job at Sean Skinner's betting shop but gave it up after falling for her boss, Des Barnes. She confessed to Jim about her attraction, hoping he would understand, but he accused her of being a whore and seeking out lovers. The final straw came when Liz admitted to having had an affair with Jim's best man, Johnny Johnson. Jim belted her across the face so she left him and took out a court injunction against him. When he tried to reason with her, she changed the locks at No. 11 so he tried to break in by smashing the living-room window with a spade. The police were called, and Jim was sent to prison for three weeks. Once again, Liz filed for divorce and felt that her world was coming apart when Steve was arrested for conspiracy and sentenced to two years in prison. His marriage collapsed.

In the divorce settlement, Jim bought Liz's share of the house with money left to him in his mother's will. He started up a business in partnership with Bill Webster, labouring and building. Andy returned to the family home after living with supermarket deputy manager Anne Malone.

Both Jim and Andy despaired of Liz when she took up with ganster Fraser Henderson. When Liz was suspected of informing on Fraser to the police, the three McDonalds found themselves trapped inside No. 11 by one of Fraser's henchmen, who threatened Liz with a sawn-off shotgun. Jim managed to jump the gunman and Liz beat him unconscious with her stilettos. After the siege Andy, furious with his mother, suffered a breakdown and turned to drink. Steve, at the end of his prison sentence, returned to the family home and the McDonalds tried to get back to normal.

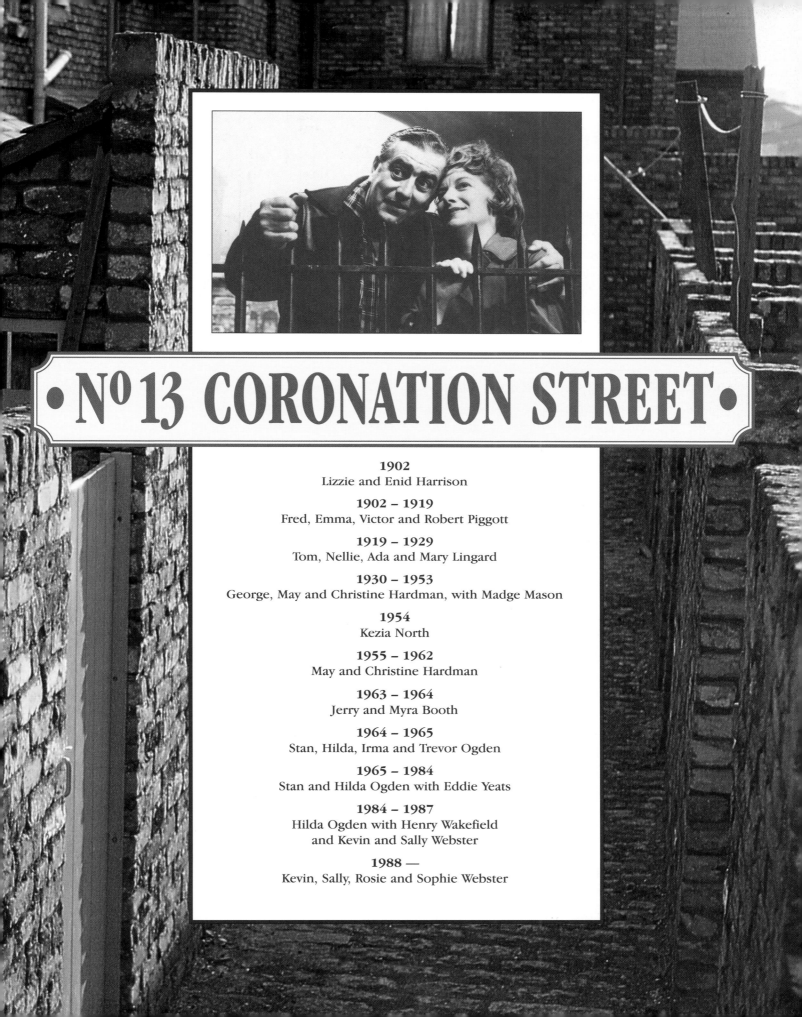

•Nº13 CORONATION STREET•

1902
Lizzie and Enid Harrison

1902 – 1919
Fred, Emma, Victor and Robert Piggott

1919 – 1929
Tom, Nellie, Ada and Mary Lingard

1930 – 1953
George, May and Christine Hardman, with Madge Mason

1954
Kezia North

1955 – 1962
May and Christine Hardman

1963 – 1964
Jerry and Myra Booth

1964 – 1965
Stan, Hilda, Irma and Trevor Ogden

1965 – 1984
Stan and Hilda Ogden with Eddie Yeats

1984 – 1987
Hilda Ogden with Henry Wakefield
and Kevin and Sally Webster

1988 —
Kevin, Sally, Rosie and Sophie Webster

On the August afternoon when the new occupants had taken possession of their homes, one remained empty. No. 13 stood vacant all that day and the next. The residents thought it awful that, when so many families lived in crowded conditions in the tenements, a house should be unused. They did not have long to wait though: on the morning of 17 August heavy curtains had been put up in the front windows and that evening gaslight shone through them. The new occupants had arrived.

Lizzie and Enid Harrison were sixty-seven-year-old twins. They never spoke to their neighbours and on the odd occasion that they were found in the Corner Shop ordered cautiously and whispered together in French. They were English but had travelled all over Europe as seamstresses and costume-makers to the most flamboyant music-hall stars. It was their talent with needles that had led them into friendship with Mabel Grimshaw, the one-time singer and now landowner of Weatherfield. They had retired and Mabel had presented them with No. 13 rent-free, as a gesture of thanks.

The sisters had always slept in the same bed and had never been interested in men. They did everything together and were watched by their wary neighbours as they shuffled down the Street, black shawls pulled tightly over their slight forms. They walked in step together, they ate together, slept together and, in a train crash, they died together. Only four months after moving the odd couple into No. 13, Mabel Grimshaw buried them at St Mary's.

Before Mabel's flowers had begun to wilt on the graves, No. 13 opened its doors to the Piggotts. Here was a family with whom the neighbours felt comfortable. Thirty-two-year-old Fred was a foreman in Hardcastle's weaving shed – in fact, the front bedroom of No. 13 looked directly into it on the second floor in the huge mill. Resident families, the Hewitts and the Makepieces, worked under Fred as did his wife Emma. The men liked him, admiring his commanding voice and his ability to down ten pints of ale a night with only the hint of a stagger home. Emma's front curtains were never closed and her front door was often left wide open all day, especially when the twins, Vic and Bob, ran in and out.

As Emma worked all day, the twins were cared for by Ivy Makepiece at No. 11. But the sad truth was that Ivy couldn't cope with looking after the boys and her own children. She had taken to drinking in the early morning and viewed the afternoon in a blurred state. Occasionally she threw bread and jam at the children but most of the time she let them run around unattended in the back yard. The twins often separated from the noisy Makepieces and climbed the dividing wall into their own back yard where they would spend hours sitting in the outside lavatory, huddled together for warmth. After a while, Ivy began hitting out with her stick, pinching arms and caning backsides – anything that interrupted her drinking was punished.

Emma eventually removed the boys from Ivy's care. The Piggotts decided to try to manage on one wage while Emma gave up the shed to look after her boys and keep the home fires burning for Fred. Slowly the twins came out of their shells and blossomed under Emma's loving eye.

One morning in 1911 the world changed for the women and children who spent their days in Coronation Street. Since it had been built, Hardcastle's mill had been a hive of activity from 6 a.m. to 8 p.m., six days a week and the occasional night shift. The noise of the machines blended with hooters and the buzz of other mills and factories all over Weatherfield. It was part of life, along with the soot that settled on clean clothes hung out to dry and the damp air that settled on the chest and slowly killed. On that particular morning, at 10.34 a.m., the machines suddenly stopped. Emma Piggott was so startled by the change in noise level that she stumbled out of the house and on to the Street where she was joined by other women. There was silence throughout Weatherfield.

For years the workers had met in small groups, grumbling about working conditions and the way they struggled to feed their families while the mill owners grew fat at their expense. Fred Piggott was one of the first trade unionists in Weatherfield. He had been heavily influenced by the soviets and saw no harm in

•No. 13•
CORONATION STREET

• Like father, like sons. Fred Piggott (left) was proud of his two boys (below) when they joined up to fight the Hun. Even after they were killed, he maintained that they had done the right and honourable thing.

• Enid and Lizzie Harrison (above) were killed in a Staffordshire train crash. Emma Piggott (right) nearly died when she fell from the front-bedroom window while attempting to clean it.

demanding a minimum wage of one pound for a fifty-five-hour week. He stirred up his fellow workers and, on that fateful morning, called on them to take action and strike. It was carefully planned and fellow trade unionists brought all the local factories and mills to a grinding halt.

Fred set up strike headquarters in the select bar at the Rovers. Charles Hardcastle warned him that he stood to lose his job and his home, but Fred remained defiant, pointing out that every working man and woman in the north of England demanded better working conditions and pay: they were sick of seeing loved ones have limbs amputated after being caught up in machinery, sick of seeing babies die of starvation because the meagre pay the men brought home was not enough to feed every mouth. A week into the strike the local dock workers joined in, leaving ships floating in the Irwell, full of cargo. The mines closed down and suddenly the only people working in Coronation Street were the Corbishleys at the Rovers and Cedric Thwaite at the Corner Shop. Not that they were happy with the situation: the strike made the locals penniless and the credit given by the kind-hearted publicans and shopkeepers started to strangle them.

Fred led the march on the council offices, waving a placard demanding a fair wage. He was one of the strongest men in the Street but even he couldn't walk far without resting along the road side as his body doubled over with hunger. Along the way the men and women passed the coal mine where children scavenged for pieces of slack with which to make a fire to boil watery broth. Officials stood guard at the pit entrance with sticks to smash at the youngsters' legs if they dared to touch the prime coal. One burly guard lashed out at a young girl, laughing as he ripped her dress, and caught her ankles with his stick. She fell screaming down a slag heap, the coal cutting her legs and arms until she landed on the rocks at the bottom. The sickening sight gave new strength to Fred and the marchers, who let out a roar and crossed the cobbles towards the coal pit. The children stood in silence as men used their placards as weapons and women picked up rocks to throw at the guards. The police arrived, as if from nowhere, many on horseback, forcing the beasts over the top of the slag heaps, sending lumps of coal in all directions.

Chaos ensued. The police lashed out with their truncheons at the men and women, who tried to pull them off their mounts. On the outskirts, butcher Roderick Elliott secured rope around an injured police horse and recruited men to help pull the beast into the alleyway with the promise of horsemeat. Eventually, the police overwhelmed the people with well-fed re-inforcements. The people limped home, defeated.

The next day the mill owners announced that pay would be increased and machinery would be replaced. The victory had been won by the workers, but at what price? The battle had taken the fight out of Fred and he decided to give up the union to a younger man. His last act as shop steward was to lead the workers back to Hardcastle's.

The call to arms in 1914 petrified Emma. Her father Nat Peel had been killed in the Boer War and she dreaded her sons being taken. At first the boys showed no signs of wanting to enlist but changed their minds after the sinking of the *Lusitania* and the rape of Belgium. They joined the Lancashire Fusiliers in 1915 and were persuaded by Fred to spend the night before embarkation in the Rovers. Father and sons drank heavily that night, and Victor made an unexpectedly passionate goodbye to Alice Buck. The next morning the boys bade farewell to their parents and walked away down the Street.

On discovering that she was pregnant Alice went to Emma for help, but Emma refused to believe that Vic was the father and slammed the door in Alice's face. In July 1916 she regretted her actions when, a month after Alice and her son had left the area, a yellow envelope arrived with the news that a stray shell had hit the dugout on the Somme where her boys had been sheltering. They had both been killed instantly.

For three weeks Emma refused to leave the house. At night she dreamt her sons were calling her name and during the day she stared into the factory window where the twins had waved to her from work. In the winter of 1918, she went down with influenza. The virus grabbed hold of her frail body and she became hysterical. She had spent the last two years searching for Alice and her baby but the trail had gone cold until she discovered that the girl had travelled to London but without her little son Ben. No one knew what had happened to him. Fred watched as his wife faded away before his eyes. When the influenza caught her, there was hardly anything left of her but skin and bones and she died on Christmas Eve. In January, Fred packed up the house and moved to Norwich to help his widowed sister run her draper's shop.

In January 1919 a new family moved in. Head of the household was Tom Lingard, a young man employed as gardener in the borough. His wife Nellie had been a shining light at Hardcastle's: under Fred Piggott's watchful eye, she had quickly risen to the post of weaver at the unheard-of age of fourteen. Now, eleven years later, she was married with a daughter, Ada, and

Nellie's fingers were crippled with premature arthritis. She had always remained true to Hardcastle's and had stuck with the firm throughout the war years when many girls had left for better-paid munitions work. The tenancy of No. 13 had been given to her by way of a thank-you.

Throughout the twenties Tom worked on a huge project: as the Town Hall was being built on the site of the old pit face, Tom was employed with other senior gardeners in landscaping the area, creating parks and gardens. While he worked Nellie stayed at home, looking after Ada and baby Mary, who was born in 1921. She found housework hard as her fingers were stiff and she could not pick things up easily. Ada came to act as her hands, working throughout the day under her mother's instructions. Nellie relied on Ada and kept her home from school to look after Mary.

• *During the war, Tom Lingard (below) had worked with the Red Cross. When his body was found under Blackpool's Central Pier in 1929, no one knew how he had got there.*
George Hardman (middle) saw action in the Second World War and escaped without serious injury.
He also saw another sort of action altogether during wartime: alongside his sister-in-law Madge Mason (far right).

The Town Hall was completed in 1928 and Tom was proud of his work. On Christmas Day he took the family for a walk in the new park and they stood listening to the Fusiliers play on the bandstand. Tom took Nellie in his arms and waltzed her through the trees. They laughed a lot, that holiday, and Tom started the new year's work with a spring in his step. But that night he failed to return home.

On 30 January 1929, Tom's body was found floating in the sea under Blackpool's Central Pier. There wasn't a mark on his naked body and the police were baffled as to how he had met his end. Suicide? Murder? Accident? No one would ever know, and Nellie and her daughters were taken into council care, their belongings piled on to a hand cart.

May Hardman took an instant dislike to gloomy No. 13. At the home in Irlam where she had been brought up she had been used to a bay window that overlooked rose bushes. Her father Frank Mason worked as a solicitor's clerk, and May and sister Madge had been expected to make good marriages. May, however, had married for love, falling for George Hardman, a bank teller in his late twenties. George assured her that he had plans to succeed in life and to open a high-class grocery shop, the like of which he had seen while holidaying in far-off Brighton. May had been pampered all her life, was not very bright

● May Hardman (above left) returned to Coronation Street a subdued woman, turning herself into a recluse and dreaming of the affluent lifestyle she had enjoyed in Oakhill. Her daughter Christine (above) didn't mourn the old days. She enjoyed being back in the Street of her youth.

and had had her parents' traditional values drilled into her. She was not an asset to George.

George had rented No. 13, seeing it as the ideal starter home: being small, it would be economical to run and it was only a ten-minute walk from the bank, which would save tram fares. While George went out to work, May sat at her piano or did needlework by the fire. She was not a good cook and did not see the point in cleaning the house every day. As all the neighbours tried to struggle through the Depression, May employed neighbour Mary Hewitt to clean the house and prepare the evening meal. George objected at what he considered a waste of good money but soon gave way as he had no wish to upset delicate May.

May had not made many friends in the Street – the local women thought her a snob and Mary Hewitt had added fuel to their opinion of her with her gossip about May's slovenly ways. The women felt it outrageous that George had to make his own breakfast and take May a cup of tea every morning as she lay in bed until he had left for work. There was also the way in which May blocked all communication. While every front and back door on the Street was left unlocked to encourage neighbouring, May Hardman kept hers firmly bolted. Her only friend was Elsie Foyle from the Corner Shop.

1939 saw the arrival of their daughter, Christine, and May's sister Madge moved in to help care for May and the baby. George's enjoyment of early fatherhood was brief: war erupted and he joined the Navy. May and Madge were left at No. 13 with Christine, who suffered terrible colic for months on end, her screams echoing around the little house night and day. May feared an immediate invasion and gas attacks: she decided to evacuate to the coast with the baby but Madge decided to stay on as she was enjoying her independence away from their domineering father. Madge took a job in munitions. She refused to stay at home as her sister had and instead threw herself into socializing. When George came home for forty-eight hours before being posted abroad he found the house lit up with Madge's jovial spirit. George found himself irresistibly drawn to Madge, and he was thrilled when she made it obvious that the attraction was mutual. They had only a day and a half together but most of that time was spent in bed where George lost himself in Madge's loving embrace.

A few months later, in May 1940, May complained when the butter ration was cut back to four ounces a week, George was shot in the leg as he helped soldiers clamber into a boat at Dunkirk, and Madge, seeking shelter in the back yard coal hole, was killed: glass sliced through her body when No. 10 Mawdsley Street suffered a direct hit from a stray bomb.

The Hardmans were reunited after the war. George returned to work at the bank but his travels had changed him. He now saw no point in saving for a future that could be wiped out by a bomb or a carefully aimed torpedo. His savings added up to nearly £1,000 and he decided that the time had come to spend it. May was thrilled when he bought a car and drove her up to Oakhill and showed her their new semi on Abingdon Road. Just as she was picturing the right curtain material for the morning room he gave her another surprise. Further up the hill, in Oakhill's exclusive parade of shops, stood a grocer's with a neat new sign bearing the word Hardman. George's dreams had come true.

No. 13 stood empty for a long time. The neighbours felt that it was fated to be unlucky and that anyone living in it was doomed. First the Harrisons, then the Piggott boys, followed by their mother, Tom Lingard and Madge Mason. Death, they said, stalked No. 13. This might have been why none of the locals

approached Hardcastle to rent the property, even though after the war there was a housing shortage.

Kezia North wasn't local: she was from Liverpool and was looking for a place to start afresh following the death of her husband, Ralph, in an industrial accident. The neighbours warned her about the house, but she swore she was not superstitious and that the house looked cosy enough. The neighbours waited to see what fate would befall the unbelieving Mrs North and were disappointed not to hear her screams in the night as she was murdered by a madman, or to see her body swaying from a beam after she had hanged herself. Seven months later, Kezia announced her intention to return to Liverpool, saying she couldn't settle and that she found life in Weatherfield too dull.

Again, the house stood empty, but in May 1955 Elsie Lappin announced to the drinkers in the Rovers that she had secured the tenancy of No. 13 for an old friend. Everyone wanted to know who the unfortunate soul was and they turned out in force to welcome the new resident when the removal van – the first ever to trundle over the Street's cobbles – came into view.

It was just the sort of reception committee that May Hardman had been dreading. She sat with the driver while Christine jumped down and unlocked the house. Elsie Lappin opened the van door and told May she had to put on a brave face: these were her neighbours and they had to be faced sooner or later. May climbed down on to the Street and, with as much dignity as she could muster, walked purposefully into her old home.

George had died of a heart attack brought on by anxiety. The business had gone bad and George had fallen into debt, which he had kept hidden from the family. Only after his death had sixteen-year-old Christine discovered the awful truth. The shop and house had been sold to repay the bank and the creditors, and the Hardmans had been forced to seek charity.

Christine wasn't too bothered by the change in her circumstances. She adapted easily to life on the Street, taking a job at Elliston's raincoat factory and falling in love with Kenneth Barlow at No. 3. May, though, returned to No. 13 full of shame. She refused to open the front door and became a recluse, talking to herself and complaining of pains in her head. Ena Sharples said she'd gone pots for rags. On New Year's Eve 1960 May died in the hallway: she had been suffering for a long time from a brain tumour.

Christine did not mourn May's passing: instead, she bottled up her emotions. She embarked on a relationship with plumber Joe Makinson and to the outsider appeared to be coping well. No one saw her tears as she lay alone in bed, and no one saw her the day she spent trembling by the fire as she watched photographs of her past burn, followed by her father's

• • • • • • • • • • • • • • • • • • • •

The neighbours stood about on the cobbles watching her every move. Didn't they understand she couldn't jump while they were there?

• • • • • • • • • • • • • • • • • • • •

letters and her mother's collection of piano music. It was only when she started to let her appearance slide that workmates asked if she was feeling all right. She began to skip meals, and was given a warning by the foreman when he found her at her sewing machine staring into space.

Then, one lunchtime, she climbed out of the factory window and made her way on to the roof of the four-storey building. She looked down on Coronation Street and then across to the cemetery where her parents shared a grave. What was the point of carrying on? Endless hard work for paltry wages, a dismal little house where she was haunted by the cries of the dead. The neighbours stood about on the cobbles watching her every move. Didn't they understand that she couldn't jump while they were there? She did not want to injure someone who might try to break her fall. As she contemplated her end, she was joined by Ken Barlow. He said he understood her feelings: his mother was buried just along from her parents and he, too, found the Street suffocating, but this, he said, wasn't the way to escape it. She asked him if he would marry her and whisk her away from it all. He said that

he couldn't, but that someone would. She allowed him to take her hand and lead her off the roof.

Ken was right. Someone did want to marry her. Colin Appleby, whose parents had lived near Abingdon Road, read of her suicide bid in the local paper. He called and asked her for a date. They went bowling together and, two weeks later, eloped. Christine was no longer tormented by thoughts of her mother: she had finally escaped No. 13 and was starting afresh.

Jerry Booth was a young plumber who worked with Len Fairclough in his Mawdsley Street builder's yard. He was an easy-going lad who had been carried away by his enthusiastic fiancée Myra Dickenson. Myra had pushed him into buying No. 13 with a mortgage, forcing him to go against his own instinct which had been to rent it. Still, he reckoned, Myra was worth the responsibility of house-ownership: she was beautiful, caring and thought the world of him. Jerry told Myra firmly that he wouldn't allow her to seek employment as it was his place to support her. Myra smiled sweetly, then went out and secured a job as assistant to Emily Nugent in her shop Gamma Garments. She affectionately told her 'Pudding' that the extra money would come in handy.

Jerry was keen to improve the house: he converted the third bedroom into a bathroom and removed the old range from the kitchen, replacing it with a tidy fireplace. He had plans to make his own furniture but found that Myra had already bought brand-new cupboards and chairs. Her spending did not stop there: she needed a bedroom suite, a sofa, curtains, carpets, and, of course, they had to have a summer holiday. Their joint wages should have been enough for the hire purchase payments but Myra was extravagant in other areas too, feeding her beloved husband on steak and buying fashionable clothes to look nice for him. Suddenly there was no money left. The electricity was cut off and the next thing was that Myra discovered she was pregnant.

Jerry asked Len Fairclough for a rise but Len had money problems of his own and sacked the lad. There was nothing for it but for Myra to seek her father's help. George Dickenson agreed to sort out the mess

• *Myra Booth was a pampered only child. Her father had always allowed her to have her way, and on marriage her fairytale views were soon shattered.*

on the condition that the Booths gave up the house and moved in with him in his detached home on Bolton Road. Myra readily agreed, and Jerry followed.

Yet again No. 13 stood empty, but this time not for long. Irma Ogden was an assistant working at Florrie Lindley's shop. She had left home, changing her name from Freda and seeking a new life away from her violent father Stan. When Stan tracked her down, she refused to return home to Chapel Street, saying she was sick of the way that Stan was absent most of the time and when he returned was violent towards the family. Stan swore he was mending his ways and said that he had given up being a long-distance lorry driver. Irma challenged him: she would return home if he bought No. 13. She was stunned when he found a £200 deposit and bought the house for £550. It was June 1964 and the Ogdens had arrived.

There were four in the family – Stan, his wife Hilda, Irma and Dudley. Dudley followed Irma's lead and changed his name to Trevor. Two younger children had been taken into care after one of Stan's drunken rages. The Ogdens could easily have been gypsies as they wandered from home to home. Stan had spent most of his time away at work and Hilda had scraped by, feeding the family on her wages as a char. It was hard but she longed to do her best for the children for Stan's sake: she had loved him since the moment she had fallen over him in the blackout – he was her man and no matter how hard-handed he was, she did everything for him.

Hilda wasted no time in gaining employment as cleaner at the Rovers Return, where Irma worked as barmaid. All went well until landlady Annie Walker discovered that Trevor was using her beer cellar to store six sacks of onions he had bought and was hoping to sell at a profit. Annie was all for sacking the Ogdens but her husband Jack saw the funny side and kept them on. It was Stan Hilda blamed when fourteen-year-old Trevor absconded to London after stealing money from the neighbours. He wrote to his parents asking them not to attempt to find him and to forget they had a son. While Hilda wept into her pinny, Stan took Trevor's letter at face value and refused to acknowledge his existence.

Irma also gave her parents cause for concern. In 1965 she was nineteen and announced that she was in love. The object of her desire was David Barlow, who had returned to his roots after his professional football career had slid to an end. Hilda had plans for a beautiful white church wedding. She herself had married in a register office, in a green serge suit, and had harboured plans for Irma's Big Day since she had walked her first Whit Walk. Irma, however, was not prepared to walk down the aisle as Stan's pride and joy: she knew that the cost of a church wedding would cripple the family and, more importantly, she did not want a fuss made. Instead the happy couple planned to elope.

David's brother Ken lived in the Street but he had shown his disapproval at the idea of David marrying an Ogden so they had no qualms at making plans behind his back. But Irma felt guilty at keeping Hilda in the dark. On the morning of 18 December 1965, David and Irma were married at the register office; the witnesses were a couple of footballers up from London. After the ceremony, Mr and Mrs Barlow treated themselves to a reception for two in an exclusive hotel. Behind their table stood an ornate screen which they ignored until suddenly a two-tiered wedding cake was placed before them and all their neighbours, headed by Hilda, burst out from behind the screen. Somehow the secret had got out, and Hilda confessed to Irma that she had been terribly hurt when Irma had gone off 'to work' in the morning without confiding in her. Irma gave her a hug and confessed that it had been the hardest thing she had ever done.

With Irma and Trevor both having left home, No. 13 seemed strangely empty. For a while Stan's drinking partner Jim Mount rented the back room, but Hilda grew fed up with sitting alone sewing while the lads boozed the night away. Jim ran off with the temporary manager of the Rovers, Brenda Riley, and Stan and Hilda were left staring at each other across the newspaper laid out on the kitchen table. Suddenly it dawned on them that this was it, probably for the next thirty years, Darby and Joan, till death do them part. Neither was alarmed by the prospect: they had never set much store by conversation and they had their hobbies. Stan's favourite pastime was drinking and he had never taken to bottled ale: a true pint, he believed, had to be drawn by a buxom barmaid and that meant in a pub. His other interests were darts, following racing form, and eating. These, he decided, could be his indoor pursuits, with a dartboard on the back of the scullery door, his newspaper by his armchair and Hilda cooking. Hilda's hobbies were 'showing an interest in her fellow humans and their activities' and the supernatural. As the best place for following the former was out of the house, Hilda agreed with Stan that instead of spending their spare time staring at the wallpaper at No. 13 they could save on coal and socialize in the Rovers, partaking of their hobbies at the same time.

When she left school Hilda had taken a job in a greengrocer's. It was next to the undertaker's where

her father worked and here Hilda had served time on Saturdays. At the greengrocer's she had been spotted over the sprouts by Amy Longhurst, the owner's mother, who declared that she had 'the gift'. Over the following weeks and months, she encouraged Hilda to put her psychic powers to the test and showed her the art of tea-leaf reading. Hilda had been incredulous when an early prediction came true and from then on, she nurtured her gift, sharing her insight with only a few. Stan never believed in her powers but once, when times were hard and after he had read of the prices charged for sessions by the likes of Madame Pandora on the Golden Mile, he convinced her to turn professional. Using a goldfish bowl as a crystal ball, he charged the neighbours two shillings a sitting with Madame Hilda. Hilda took the sessions seriously and the local women were drawn out of curiosity to No. 13, just in case Hilda could really see into another world. Stan decided to give Fate a helping hand by ensuring all Hilda's predictions came true. When Hilda saw 'a nasty surprise' for Annie Walker, Stan let a white mouse loose in the Rovers, but even he was stumped when Hilda predicted another child for Valerie Barlow. He was forced to confess his hand in the proceedings to horrified Hilda when the local press became interested in her. She hung up her brass earrings and decided to stick at being a professional char.

Depression was no stranger to No. 13, having struck at Emma Piggott, May and Christine Hardman, and, some said, Tom Lingard. In the sixties, it returned to haunt Hilda Ogden. It was 1967 and next door at No. 11 Elsie Tanner had married a handsome American and had flown off to a new life on the other side of the Atlantic. Meanwhile, back in Weatherfield, Hilda saw her future as bleak: her bedroom window looked out on to a factory wall, her back yard was full of rubbish, and the only green she ever saw was of the weeds poking out from between the cobbles. Each day found her scrubbing floors, scrubbing clothes and scrubbing lavatories. The end of each week found her sitting at the table with the tins before her, coal money, gas money, Christmas club, always robbing Peter to pay Paul. One day she had simply had enough. She walked out of the house, down Rosamund Street where she caught a bus to town and then on to the station. At the end of the day Stan worried when he found her missing. He crumbled without her, like a helpless baby, and Irma called in the police. Two days later Hilda was found wandering in Liverpool, her slippers still on her feet. She was brought home in an ambulance, and the doctor, diagnosing paranoid psychosis, ordered Stan to bring some hope into her life. The breakdown was something to which the Ogdens never referred again. Stan tried his best to buck his wife up but they both knew that life held little promise for them.

As part of her therapy Hilda took to walking in the park. She met the keeper, George Greenwood, who made it obvious that he found her attractive and Hilda pondered the possibility of having an affair. Stan, she

● *The Ogdens' forty-year marriage was built on a six-day courtship. Their own children disappointed them, but lodger Eddie Yeats became like a second son.*

knew, had had plenty of mistresses; she had accepted them as part of him, secure in the knowledge that he always returned at night to her bed. However, Hilda had always remained faithful, even during the war. She decided against romance and settled for friendship. George gave her a budgie, Mabel, and entertained her to tea in his shed. However, even those little moments were too much for Hilda: she felt she was cheating Stan merely by being alone with another man. Sadly, she ended the liaison.

While Hilda cleaned at the Rovers, Stan tried a variety of jobs before opting for the life of a window cleaner. Labouring jobs came and went; for a while he worked as a milkman, enjoying his afternoons in the pub, as a coalman, an ice-cream salesman, a chauffeur and a street photographer. Twice he turned to art. The first time, he was talked into putting his weight into performance by becoming a professional wrestler. He appeared in the ring only once, at the Viaduct Sporting Club, where he was counted out after being thrown

from the ring on to Hilda's lap. Years later he channelled his creativity into producing sculptures created from old junk and scrap iron. A gallery boss saw the work and enthused about it, but unfortunately the binmen saw it as junk and took it to the tip.

The Ogdens' children continued to be a source of confusion. Irma and David, for a while, ran the Corner Shop, next door to the Ogdens. Hilda was thrilled with the endless credit, and helped out occasionally behind the counter. When the couple emigrated to Australia in 1968, she planned to go with them but Stan put his foot down and refused to leave England. Irma wasn't gone long: within two years she had returned a widow. David and Darren, the grandson the Ogdens had never seen, had been killed in a car crash. Stan borrowed money to buy Irma a share of the shop but she wasn't grateful and emigrated again to start afresh in Canada.

Then there was Trevor, whom Hilda managed to track down in Chesterfield. She and Stan made a special journey to see him, in his fancy detached house, and walked in on him after a separation of thirteen years. It broke Hilda's heart when his wife Polly confessed that Trevor had always told her that his parents were dead.

During its occupation by the Ogdens, No. 13 underwent some changes in its décor. First, to prove his worth as a handyman, Stan knocked a hole in the wall dividing the kitchen-living-room from the front parlour. He used some old plans to make a serving hatch but did not realize until he was half-way through that the plans had been for a hatch in a works canteen. Hilda was staggered when she saw the huge hole with wooden shutters but fell in love with it when it was finished – even though, as she pointed out, she'd never serve anything through it as they never used the front room. A few years later, Hilda put up a mural of the Swiss Alps in the living room, across a whole wall. She finished off the effect by placing her aunt Edie's plaster ducks high in the sky, flying over the mountains. The mural was ruined when Stan took a rare bath and the water overflowed when he fell asleep. To replace the ruined vista, he bought a new scene, this time of cliffs and rolling waves.

After a run of extreme bad luck – the house being fumigated, Stan being suspected of being a peeping Tom, a downfall of soot from the chimney which ruined the soft furnishings – Hilda decided that No. 13 was unlucky, not the Ogdens. She sent Stan out to buy new numbers from Woolworths and cooked roast lamb to celebrate her brainwave in changing the house number from 13 to 12a. Stan put up the numbers and Hilda admired them on the front door, before realizing that the door was shut, the key was safe inside and the roast was burning. Stan smashed a window to gain entry but he was too late and the meat was inedible. Furthermore, the Ogdens discovered that as they hadn't sought council permission for the number change they had acted illegally and faced a fine. Quickly they fished the old numbers out of the bin and put them back in place. Hilda concluded that it wasn't the house, after all, that was doomed, it was her.

During their marriage the Ogdens had plenty of ups and downs, but always seemed able to bounce back at life. One particularly bad patch, though, found them separated for three long weeks. Hilda was fed up with scraping to make ends meet while idle Stan made excuses for his glass back in an attempt not to work. In the height of anger, she turned on him and ordered him out of the house. To her surprise he went. He didn't return for his tea and when closing time came and went at the Rovers Hilda began to worry for her man. She turned for help to Stan's drinking pal Eddie Yeats.

Eddie was an ex-con from Liverpool who had drifted to Weatherfield in the early seventies. He and Stan were like-minded in their mistrust of the law and their fascination with get-rich-quick schemes. As well as befriending Stan, Eddie grew fond of Hilda, seeing in her a kind heart which, he believed, would one day welcome him into No. 13 as a permanent lodger. Eddie took up the search for Stan and tracked him down to Hilda's brother's chippie, where he saw him making free with the chips and with his brother-in-law's fancy piece Edie Blundell. Alerted to Stan's whereabouts, Hilda fought off Edie and dragged Stan home. Eddie hoped for a reward in the shape of the spare bed but Hilda was quick to point out that the Ogdens' marriage

● *After Stan's death Hilda relied heavily for support on the young people she surrounded herself with. When she left No. 13, she sold the house at a bargain price to two of her lodgers, newly married Kevin and Sally Webster (right).*

had suffered a blow and would need building up again, which would be awkward with a third party in the house.

Eddie did finally become the Ogdens' lodger in 1980 when he took his first full-time job – as a binman – on sixty pounds a week. As Stan became weaker, Eddie helped him on the window round, eventually buying it and employing Stan, whom he grew to see as a father figure. As Stan continued to slow down, Hilda took in more work: as well as the Rovers, she cleaned for factory boss Mike Baldwin and Dr Lowther in Oakhill. When the Graffiti Club opened in 1983 she was given the position of cloakroom attendant. That year saw two landmarks in Hilda's life: first, in October, Eddie married his pregnant girlfriend Marion Willis from No. 11. Hilda and Stan stood in as the groom's parents and were sad to see the couple move away to Bury to live with Marion's mother, but not until after the Ogdens' big party in December. The occasion was

Stan and Hilda's ruby wedding anniversary: Hilda hired the Rovers select bar for the occasion and all the neighbours wished them well. It was while Rita Fairclough from No. 7 was singing 'My Old Dutch' to the happy couple that the police arrived to tell her that her husband Len had been killed in a car crash.

With Eddie gone from No. 13, the house went quiet overnight. Stan took to his bed, forcing Hilda to become the sole breadwinner. She worked hard and at home spent all her time running around after Stan. The strain was too much. She confessed to Dr Lowther that she could no longer cope with Stan. The doctor arranged for him to be admitted to hospital to give Hilda a break but she didn't want Stan to go: she knew that as soon as he entered hospital he would lose what will to live he had left. She was proved right when on 21 November 1984 Stan died peacefully in his sleep.

Hilda buried him with dignity in Weatherfield, in a plot big enough for two. Trevor supported her on the day, and both Irma and Eddie sent flowers. After the funeral Hilda had a quiet weep and tried to adjust to life alone.

Following Emily Bishop's lead at No. 3, Hilda advertised for a lodger. She took in Henry Wakefield, a quiet soul whose mother had recently died. Hilda secured him a job sweeping up at Baldwin's factory but the other workers threatened a strike when he was recognized as a strike blackleg. Henry left the factory and No. 13, and Hilda accused the factory women of robbing her of her fresh start after Stan's death. In 1985, she took another lodger: Kevin Webster was a twenty-year-old mechanic, whose family had moved south leaving him homeless. Hilda found him respectable and kind-hearted; her only complaint was that he left his oily overalls around the place, while his was that she interfered too much in his love life. In Hilda's opinion Kevin deserved the best girlfriend available: she approved of his romance with Michelle Robinson – she was a neighbour of the Lowthers' – but strongly disapproved of his liaison with Sally Seddon, whose rough family came from Arkwright Street. Kevin, however, thought Sally was fantastic and threw himself into a passionate love affair with her. He was annoyed when after he had told her that she was his first lover she confessed she had had four other men.

Sally was fully aware of Hilda's opinion of her but won the older woman round by introducing her to her parents. Eddie Seddon was a long-distance lorry driver, like Stan, and, also like Stan, he was heavy-handed. His timid wife Elsie cleaned for a living, like Hilda and, again like Hilda, flinched whenever her husband raised his hand. Straight away Hilda knew exactly what went on behind the closed doors at No. 15 Arkwright Street and she made up her mind to rescue Sally. Sally moved into No. 13 as a paying guest on the strict understanding that there would be no 'funny business' under Hilda's roof. Kevin was installed on the sofa and Sally in the back room. To keep them free from temptation in the night Hilda placed a man-trap on the stairs, consisting of mops and pails. Sally decided that nothing was going to keep her from her strong-armed Romeo and nimbly jumped over the obstacle to wake

him. Hearing noises downstairs, Hilda followed, forgot about the trap and ended up with a strained ankle.

In October 1986 Hilda was guest of honour when Sally and Kevin married in the same register office at which she had married Stan. The young couple spent their wedding night at No. 13, unable to afford a honeymoon. Soon afterwards they left the house to move into the flat over the Corner Shop. They were grateful to Hilda and, as a thank-you present, they bought her a washing machine.

The winter of 1987 was a harsh one for Hilda Ogden. In Oakhill the Lowthers planned to retire to a peaceful Derbyshire village and sadly Hilda helped them pack. Late at night the couple were disturbed by

• • • • • • • • • • • • • • • • • •

Hilda handed over the keys of No. 13 to the Websters, telling them they could buy the old place at a bargain price

• • • • • • • • • • • • • • • • • •

burglars, who planned to make off with the silver, and in the struggle that followed Joan Lowther suffered a fatal heart attack while Hilda was knocked unconscious. She was rushed to hospital where she came round but not even a visit from Eddie could cheer her up. Suddenly the world wanted to harm her. Hilda was alone and vulnerable.

Back at No. 13, she had bolts fitted on all the doors and spent her days sitting by the fire with her cat, Rommel. The Websters tried to draw her out of her shell but the bruise on her head and the stitches over her eyebrow warned her that the outside world was not to be trusted. She began to despair that her future would be one of self-imposed imprisonment but then Dr Lowther called to say goodbye. Despite his wife's death he was going ahead with his retirement plans, he said, and asked Hilda to come with him as his live-in housekeeper. Hilda did not need asking twice. On Boxing Day 1987, she left the grimy terraces and back streets of Weatherfield for a world of green pastures and rippling streams. Before she went, she handed over the keys of No. 13 to the Websters, telling them they could buy the old place at a bargain price.

Kevin started work on the house straight away: twenty years of neglect needed rectifying. He put in central heating and papered over the mural. The door between the living room and the scullery (now called the kitchen) was removed and replaced with a Mediterranean-style archway, and a telephone was installed. After a couple of hiccups in trying to get a mortgage – Sally had a bad debt against her credit – the couple settled down to married bliss in their new home.

Kevin had always been a mechanic by trade. He was a man who enjoyed working for a wage, with as few responsibilities as possible. Sally was employed as an assistant at Alf's Mini Market, as the Corner Shop had become, next door. Their first daughter was born in December 1990, and named Rosie as Sally gave birth to her in the back of Don Brennan's taxi on Rosamund Street. After the baby's arrival Sally left the shop and set herself up as a child minder, taking in Gail Platt's son David as well. When David fell downstairs she was investigated by the Social Services and reprimanded for working without a licence.

Desperate to keep her job, she registered as a child minder and took on another little boy named Jonathan Broughton. Jonathan's mother had left home and his father, Joe, was unable to cope. Shortly after placing his son with Sally, Joe decided she was the sort of woman he needed to bring up his son permanently. At the time, Kevin was going through a bad patch at work: he was manager of Mike Baldwin's garage on the Street and had been drawn into deceiving the police by his mechanic Steve McDonald. Steve had been involved in a minor accident while driving Mike's car and had needed to present his driving licence at the police station. As he hadn't passed his test he told the police that his name was Kevin Webster. He persuaded Kevin to go along with his story and Kevin took his licence to the police. A few months later the deception was uncovered and both Kevin and Steve were charged with perverting the course of justice. The court took the view that Kevin, who was the older, had corrupted Steve, and imposed an £800 fine against him. Sally broke down in front of Joe and confessed her fear of

Kevin being imprisoned. She was sick of being dragged down by men – first by her father and now by Kevin – and wanted a strong man to treat her well. Joe thought he was that man and declared his love for her, begging her to leave Kevin and marry him. Sally was tempted by sincere, well-off Joe, but she came to her senses and decided her place was with Kevin.

Money struggles were always an issue in the Webster household. The situation improved when Kevin and Sally were given £5,000 by Rita Sullivan, a lonely widow, once again, and living at No. 10. Rita explained that she wanted to help them as she admired them, but Sally secretly worried that Rita was trying to buy herself a ready-made family. And the family was growing: when Sally announced that she was pregnant again, Kevin walked out on her, unable to face having another mouth to feed. Later he apologized and tried to adjust to the situation. Sophie was born in November 1995, safely in hospital.

1996 saw the Websters enter new business worlds. Sally grew tired of looking after the children day in day out, and took a job as machinist at Baldwin's Sportswear. In no time at all she had been promoted to supervisor and had instigated the setting up of a crèche for the workers' children.

Meanwhile, Kevin lost his job when the garage was taken into receivership. He went into partnership with fellow mechanic Tony Horrocks and bought the business for £25,000, much to the disgust of Don Brennan, the vendor, who had paid much more for it. Sally was disappointed that, true to form, Kevin had decided against buying the garage on his own and accused him of needing someone to 'hold his hand' but Kevin maintained that he was merely being true to himself: he was a good mechanic and not a businessman. He swore to work hard and make a go of the business for Sally and the girls.

In 1997, Kevin's plans fell apart when Tony dropped out of the partnership and was replaced by his mother Natalie. She made it clear to Kevin that she wanted to be more than a sleeping partner and when Sally was called away to nurse her sick mother Natalie set about seducing Kevin.

• Nº 15 CORONATION STREET •

1902 – 1915
Cedric and Lottie Thwaite

1915 – 1930
Tommy, Amelia and Lil Foyle

1930 – 1947
Tommy, Elsie, Hilda and Shelagh Foyle

1947 – 1960
Les and Elsie Lappin, with Hilda and Shelagh Foyle

1960 – 1965
Florrie Lindley, with Sheila Birtles and Doreen Lostock

1965 – 1966
Lionel and Sandra Petty

1966 – 1968
David and Irma Barlow, with Emily Nugent

1968 – 1974
Les, Maggie and Gordon Clegg, with Cyril and Betty Turpin,
Irma Barlow, Bet Lynch and Norma Ford

1974 – 1975
Megan, Idris, Vera and Tricia Hopkins

1975 – 1976
Tricia Hopkins and Gail Potter

1976 – 1978
Renee and Terry Bradshaw, with Bet Lynch

1978 – 1985
Alf and Renee Roberts, with Bet Lynch

1985 – 1986
Alf and Audrey Roberts

1987 – 1988
Kevin and Sally Webster

1988 – 1989
Curly Watts and Shirley Armitage

1990 – 1994
Ken Barlow

1994 – 1997
Unoccupied

1997 —
Bill Webster

The brewery bosses at Newton, Ridley and Oakes intended to dominate the newly built Coronation Street as they had many other terraces. As well as their public house on one corner of the Street, they planned to open a beer-house at the other end. In the designs for the street there had always been a corner shop, as there were in most Weatherfield back streets. The brewery had talks with Charles Hardcastle, the mill owner, before the property was built but the Mission Committee heard of the plans and lobbied Hardcastle, concerned with the availability of too much alcohol in such a small street. Hardcastle had no wish to upset the Mission bosses, who had bought a large area of land from him to build a new Mission between Coronation Street and Victoria Street, and turned down the brewery's offer, advertising a shop for sale.

It was quite a catch at thirty-five pounds. It occupied the large downstairs front room, with its door on the corner facing the viaduct. The living quarters were at the back – a thin staircase ran between the shop and the living room, which led to a small scullery and back yard. Upstairs were three large bedrooms and a tiny store room.

Cedric Thwaite had been running a successful pawn business in Salford and, in 1902, felt that the time was right for him to invest his savings in bricks and mortar. For ten years he had operated from his front parlour, never wanting to risk opening larger premises for fear of taking on too much. He was well used to travelling through Weatherfield as he was also a lay preacher, operating on the Mission circuit. It had been the Mission Committee who had told him about the new shop and recommended that he sought the deeds. In fact they had lent him the extra five pounds he needed to secure the building: with the new Mission being built they felt it a good investment to have a volunteer preacher across the street.

However, the residents of Coronation Street viewed him with suspicion. He was definitely not one of them: as a shopkeeper and lay preacher he automatically demanded respect. It was taken for granted that, as a man of God, he was teetotal and the community was

shocked to discover that he was as fond of brewery bitter as the next man. After a couple of nights Cedric spent drinking in the Rovers the landlord, Jim Corbishley, had to ask him to drink in the select bar as he made the working men uncomfortable in the public: they felt they couldn't swear as usual. Cedric had always enjoyed the odd beer but, deprived of his old drinking partners in Salford and pushed into a different room by his new neighbours, he changed. Concluding that he might as well drink at home rather than in private in a public house, Cedric stopped going to the Rovers and helped himself to bottles from his own shelves.

The life of an unmarried shopkeeper was lonely. During the day, customers filled the premises, but no one came to see Cedric: they were there because he was handy and didn't charge over the odds. As the women waited to be served they gossiped and swapped news but as soon as they reached the counter Cedric found himself excluded from the chat and confronted with formal orders for goods. On Sundays after the mission service he would eat lunch with caretaker Gladys Arkwright and it was only with her that he was able to relax. At home in the evenings, if there wasn't a Mission meeting to attend, he would sit by the fire reading and drinking. Soon he drank whether he had a meeting or not.

• • • • • • • • • • • • • • • • • •

During Cedric's sermon, Ivy Makepiece stood up. Everyone knew he'd been stoking Gladys's boiler for months, she said

• • • • • • • • • • • • • • • • • •

Gladys was the first to guess that Cedric had a drink problem and sought to help by spending more time with him. When she knew he was going to spend an evening alone, she would invite him over or call on him. The neighbours started gossiping about the visits and suspected thirty-two-year old Cedric of sharing his bed with Gladys, who was ten years his senior. The rumours reached a head one Sunday morning in April 1904 when Cedric preached a sermon about sexual continence. His neighbour Ivy Makepiece stood up

● *Aliens in a hostile environment: educated lay preacher Cedric Thwaite and his German bride Lotte, or Lottie as she became known.*

and stopped him, branding him a hypocrite: everyone knew he'd been stoking Gladys's boiler for months, she said. As the congregation roared their approval, Gladys rushed from the hall in tears and Cedric tried in vain to deny the charge. The committee heard of the uproar and demanded an explanation, which caused Gladys to blurt out what she knew of Cedric's drinking. Cedric admitted the offence and was removed from the preaching list. When the news of his dismissal reached the Street, Ivy and her cronies felt justified in their suspicions: obviously he had been sacked for his sexual sins.

Cedric viewed all the suspicion, gossip and jokes as punishment for his own folly. He was sorry for Gladys's upset and the shocking events made him stop drinking so much. Gladys's friendly visits ceased and lonely weeks turned into lonely months then years.

The news that Cedric Thwaite had married spread through the Street like wildfire and immediately the residents pitied Gladys, believing she had been cast aside in favour of a younger woman. When the new Mrs Thwaite arrived all were amazed to discover that she was German and spoke no English. Lottie Hofner had been sent to England by her middle-class family to broaden her mind. At twenty-six she had led a sheltered life with elderly parents and it was decided that a six-month stay with a cousin in Fleetwood would

improve her English and help her seek an independent living. Shortly after her arrival she met Cedric in a Blackpool chapel and fell deeply in love with him. They conversed in French, a language they shared, and were married within two months.

Lottie Thwaite was at a terrible disadvantage as the Street's one and only foreigner. She was mistrusted, ignored and belittled by the neighbours. She tried hard to please, taking English lessons, serving in the shop and playing the Mission organ, but she could never break down the barriers. To the residents she was different and it was as simple as that.

Cedric had always wanted children and now with a wife he saw no reason to put off starting a family. Lottie's discomfort in the Street was not made easier by the four miscarriages she suffered between 1912 and 1914. Cedric and Lottie despaired, but worse was to come. It was just after the fourth miscarriage, in October 1914, that the Thwaites' lives were ripped apart.

Germany and Britain were at war and Lottie found herself an undesirable alien. She was torn between loyalty to her home country and her adopted one, and was plagued with the thought that she should return to her parents. For weeks their letters had spoken of food shortages and then had stopped altogether. One dark night a mob descended upon the shop. The window was smashed with bricks and Cedric was thrown into the street where children threw stones at him and his neighbours punched and kicked him. The women hurled themselves on Lottie, smashing her glasses, tearing her hair out by its roots, ripping her clothes and kicking hard clogs into her body. Gladys Arkwright tried to protect her and received a sharp blow to her head in return.

After the sinking of the *Lusitania* in May 1915, German nationals were rounded up. Lottie was interned on the Isle of Man for the duration of the war. Cedric boarded up the shop and, although Gladys urged him to turn the other cheek, he left the Street and Weatherfield to live with his brother in Newcastle.

In December 1915 twenty-six-year-old Tommy Foyle bought the shop. An invalid – his leg was permanently ulcerated since he had been shot accidentally in India where he had served in the Army – he was not needed to fight the Hun and opened the shop with a show of patriotism at the Thwaites' expense. He hung a Union Jack in the window and painted 'British and Proud' on the glass. The neighbours cheered their approval and flocked to spend all they could.

Tommy was a native of Leeds and had joined the Army at seventeen to escape the notoriety of his family name when his father, Fred, was hanged for murdering his wife, Jean. Tommy had been working at the furniture shop where he was serving his carpentry apprenticeship when the police arrived to break the news that his mother had been found strangled and that his father had admitted to killing her in a fit of anger. Tommy tried to comfort his younger sisters, Kitty and Amelia, and to shield them from the publicity that the case attracted. As Fred pleaded guilty there had been no need for Tommy to give evidence against him, and he had been grateful for that. Leaving the girls in the care of an aunt, Tommy joined the Army where he hoped no one would have heard of Fred Foyle.

Amelia Foyle was twenty when she moved to Weatherfield to lodge with her brother at No. 15. Kitty had married and was busy bringing up her own family but Amelia wanted to move out of Yorkshire and crossed the Pennines for adventure. Tommy was happy for his sister to live with him as she helped out behind the counter during the difficult war years. Food shortages hit hard and Tommy made it a rule to offer limited credit only to those living in Coronation Street. With a shortage of men, as well as food, Tommy found himself an object of desire to young women whose husbands and boyfriends were away at the front. Amelia proved a great protection, discouraging advances before naïve Tommy had realized they were being made.

After the war Amelia decided to leave Tommy to the shop. Before she could head south she went down with an attack of flu. She took to her bed and was dead three days later. Tommy was devastated and closed the shop for a week. He planned to sell up, and only with the encouragement and support of his friend Sid Hayes did he stay on in Weatherfield.

At thirty-five Tommy had considered marriage but had never dreamt that someone as beautiful and vivacious as Lillian Makepiece would ever be his bride. Lil was twenty-three in the summer of 1923 and most men agreed she was the catch of the neighbourhood with her pretty eyes, and enticing hips that swayed as she danced away her troubles. She had worked at the Rovers Return as barmaid since the end of the war and was a big draw for the male customers. Her mother Ivy had kept her off school for many years and the girl was empty-headed. She took guidance only from Ivy, who told her to save herself for her wedding night and to ensure that the man she married had enough money to support the rest of the family too. In Ivy's eye that man was Tommy Foyle. She suggested to Lil that Tommy could do with companionship and pushed the two together. Tommy was so flattered by Lil's attention that he ignored the warning signs until it was too late. When Lil announced her pregnancy, Ivy demanded that Tommy accept his responsibility, and the couple were married. Shortly afterwards, Lil announced that she had lost the baby and many doubted that it had ever existed.

Tommy tried to make the best of the arrangement, and set Lil to work behind the shop counter telling himself that as she had been such a big success at the

• *Tommy Foyle was the local catch and Ivy Makepiece did all she could to ensure her Lil (left) caught him. Throughout their four-year marriage Lil took a string of lovers behind Tommy's back.*

the situation and manoeuvre Tommy into bed where he always forgot his complaints in the arms of his 'little angel'.

The strain of supplying the Makepiece clan with goods without payment caused Tommy's health to fail. Whenever he spoke to Ivy about the debt, he was always visited by some of Lil's well-built cousins who made it obvious that Tommy should think it an honour to help out the family in difficult times. While Lil worried about her husband's chest pains, Ivy rubbed her hands with glee as she thought of her little one inheriting the shop.

Tragically for Ivy her visions of herself in mourning came true but it was Lil and not Tommy who was buried. In 1927 bronchitis carried Lil away and after the funeral Tommy put a stop to Ivy's credit-seeking by taking in a mongrel called Growler after he had discovered that Ivy was frightened of dogs. With Growler in the shop, Ivy never again crossed the threshold.

The next Mrs Foyle came without baggage. As Elsie Castleway, she was an unknown twenty-five-year-old with blonde hair and a cheeky grin, but as Melody Mae she was famous throughout Weatherfield as a leg-kicking glamour-puss. A mill girl who had won a talent show and had topped the bill in the last great days of variety, Melody Mae made famous tunes such as 'He'll Break Your Heart If You Let Him' and 'Those Back Street Blues'. Yet she had always remained true to her Weatherfield roots and turned down offers from London agents, though they promised her success in the capital. She was flying high on the northern circuit but tragedy struck when, aged twenty-three, she injured her vocal cords and was told she would never sing again. While others would have seen this as the end of the world, Elsie shrugged her shoulders and said it had been fun while it lasted. She had saved enough money to keep her for a while and contemplated buying a public house. It was then that she met Tommy and found it refreshing that he had never heard of her, and saw her only as an attractive girl. To the amazement of the residents Tommy married her in 1930 and Melody Mae re-created herself once again, this time as Elsie Foyle, the shopkeeper's wife.

Rovers she would boost trade in the shop. However, he had not counted on the fact that most of his customers were female, and the women of the Street didn't take too kindly to Lil short-changing them and making up wrong orders. Tommy was forced to take command and was amazed to discover that Lil had given her large family endless credit. When he tried to stop it, Lil turned on the charm to talk her way out of

● Holidaying in Blackpool, Elsie Foyle and Shelagh enjoy a break from the shop.

● Before she married Tommy, Elsie (left) was a favourite on the music-hall boards. Les (right), her second husband, was embarrassed to admit he'd had no idea about her celebrity when he met her.

The female customers flocked to the shop to be served by her and no one thought she would stick with Tommy, believing in what they had seen on stage in stockings and garters rather than in what they saw dressed in an apron behind a counter. For Elsie's part she was happy to prove the cynics wrong and was not in the least surprised that she found it so easy to settle in the Street. It was what she was used to – serving a close community in a little corner shop and being a faithful wife, like her mother, to a dependable man, like her father. It was safe and, unlike Lil, she wasn't bored by safety. After ten years on the stage she positively hungered for it.

Elsie produced two daughters for Tommy – Hilda in 1933 and Shelagh in 1935. The celebrations for Hilda's birth were marred by the death of Growler, who was knocked down by a delivery van. Tommy had the flagstones lifted in the back yard and buried him with full military honours. Death also marked Shelagh's birth as Elsie's cousin Armistead Caldwell died of pneumonia the day before. Armistead's death didn't stop his wife Minnie from delivering the baby as planned and after-

wards the Foyles took in the Caldwells' whippet, Tim, as he reminded Minnie too much of her husband.

The Depression had a devastating effect on the community, both financially and spiritually. With hardly any money in their pockets, the residents bought only essentials. Tommy and Elsie cut their losses by ordering only selected goods, which they sold to regular customers at low prices while supplementing the difference from Elsie's nest egg. In this way they kept their shop going while helping to keep their neighbours from starvation.

As war was declared on Germany, Elsie worried for the safety of her girls and joined the queues of mothers taking their children to the safety of rural England. Hilda was old enough to be evacuated with the school but as Shelagh was only four Elsie wanted to be with her. They were billeted in Blackpool but Elsie refused to stay in the cramped accommodation offered in what had once been a rat-infested boarding house and was now a rat-infested hovel. Instead she paid for bed and breakfast in a hotel overlooking the sea. When no bombs fell on Weatherfield she took the girls back to the shop. Elsie found she was certainly needed at home when Tommy became bedridden after a stroke. She took on the running of the shop, helped by Hilda, while Shelagh spent her days sitting in bed with Tommy making up stories to entertain him. With food on ration, Elsie decided to dip again into her savings and purchased black-market goods which she kept in her store room for the neighbours to buy off-ration. The gesture backfired when the police caught up with her. She appeared in court and was fined.

When the bombs started to fall Elsie was sick with worry as she couldn't move Tommy from his bed. He joked that he was happy to die there but as she cowered with the girls in the stock room she was only too aware of her unprotected husband above. But the shop was not hit and the nearest bomb fell in Mawdsley Street. The back of the shop was blasted and all the windows blew in, showering the girls' room with glass. Shelagh was badly cut but Tommy, in the front bedroom, slept through the attack.

Tommy hated being an invalid, stuck in bed, whilst Elsie tired herself out nursing him and running the shop. He prayed for death and eventually his prayers were answered. On 8 May 1945, the rest of the Street celebrated the end of the war with a Street party. Tommy heaved himself up to the window to see his daughters dancing around the bonfire and fell back into Elsie's arms to die of a heart attack. In the months leading up to his death Tommy had urged his wife to remarry as he feared she would struggle on single-handedly with the shop. Elsie had promised she would consider it but it was the last thing on her mind when the family were mourning Tommy.

It wasn't until two years had passed that she allowed herself to be flattered by the attention of sales representative Les Lappin. Les had known Tommy for years as he had been a regular visitor at the shop, selling bootlaces and buttons. He had served in the Navy during the war and had been saddened by Tommy's death. His job had been held open for him and he paid great attention to his 'special' customer Elsie Foyle. At first Elsie feared he was only interested in her because of the shop but he showed her that he genuinely cared for her by treating her and the girls to a day out in Blackpool, telling Elsie that all work and no play would make her a dull girl. For the first time in ages Elsie laughed and the girls, thrilled to see the change in their mother, warmed to Uncle Les.

Elsie and Les were married in September 1947 and Les gave up his job to help out at the shop. While Elsie took the name Lappin she was pleased that Les insisted that the girls remained Foyles in honour of their father. Hilda left school at fourteen and took a job at Elliston's factory in the canteen.

Without Hilda around to look after her Shelagh had a bad time at school. She was a delicate child: aged twelve she looked nine and was picked on by the others. Rather than tell anyone of the bullying she suffered she became withdrawn. When Elsie saw bruises on the little girl's arms she thought Les had hit the girl and, in a blazing row, confronted him in the closed shop. Mild-mannered Les was horrified that Elsie could suspect him of such a thing and Shelagh, upset by the shouting, blurted out her tale of playground torment.

When she was fifteen Shelagh announced her intention to follow in her mother's footsteps and become a singer. Elsie wanted to discourage her, and so she arranged a night's engagement in a rough working-men's club. When Shelagh started to sing, the men jeered at her and made obscene remarks – watching in the wings, Elsie realized that twenty-five years had not changed audiences. Shelagh found she couldn't endure such treatment and burst into tears. She allowed Elsie to lead her off the stage and agreed with her on the way home that she should take up Hilda's offer of a job in the canteen.

In January 1952 Les Lappin dropped dead of a heart attack on the shop floor. He had been serving Ida Barlow from No. 3 and Ida's screams brought Elsie rushing from the back room. After burying her second husband, the spirit went out of Elsie and she threw herself into shop work. The girls left home to work in the kitchens at a girls' boarding school in Surrey and Elsie decided the time had arrived to retire. She selected a bungalow in Knott End and left the Street whistling 'Those Back Street Blues'.

Florence Lena Lindley, or Florrie for short, had been a barmaid for ten years, serving at the Farrier's Arms on Collier Street. During that time she had married engineer Norman Lindley but the marriage only lasted three years. He thought her a nag and took a job working in India, telling her that if he ever returned to England it wouldn't be for her. To save face, Florrie let it be known that she was a widow and at the age of thirty-eight had saved enough to buy herself a little business. Florrie had no big plans to change anything at the shop; a native of Weatherfield she knew the customers wanted well-stocked shelves, handy credit and an eager ear for gossip. Florrie prided herself on supplying all three.

Almost immediately she discovered, as had Cedric, Tommy and Elsie before her, that shopkeeping could be lonely. She socialized as best she could in the Rovers but found that friendly customers were less so when she crossed into their territory. Perhaps, she mused, it was because they worried that she would tell others how much money they owed her. She set her cap at the only eligible man in the Street, Harry Hewitt, but was seen off by barmaid Concepta Riley.

Florrie wisely restricted credit to her regular customers but grew uncomfortable when they failed to settle their accounts. She took the unusual step of employing Albert Tatlock from No. 1 as a debt collector, which caused much offence. Business was still hard and it became increasingly difficult to pay her suppliers when some lines didn't sell. In an attempt to boost her income, Florrie converted two of the upstairs bedrooms into bedsits and took in lodgers. The first were two young clerks from the Town Hall, Messrs Dobson and Braithwaite. Their plans for an escape from the world of complaints and officialdom were shattered when Ena Sharples, the mission caretaker, took it upon herself to use them as an avenue for her complaints and suggestions on how the Town Hall should be run. After a month they had had enough and moved out again.

The next lodgers were two local girls, Sheila Birtles and Doreen Lostock. Sheila worked at Elliston's raincoat factory while Doreen helped behind the counter of the chain store Gamma Garments. The girls shared a love of pop music and dancing, and Florrie's shop ceiling vibrated to the sounds of 'In Dreams' and 'She Loves You'. Florrie had strict rules about gentlemen callers and refused to let the girls entertain. However, when Sheila started to court plumber Jerry Booth, whom Florrie thought a nice, quiet, well-spoken lad, she dropped her defences. What Florrie didn't know, though, was that Sheila had two boyfriends – shy Jerry, and worldly Neil Crossley who, as manager of Gamma, was Doreen's boss. Sheila fell for Neil in a big way and lent him money when he said he was short. She took advantage of Florrie's absence from the shop to let him into the flat. For Sheila it was the stuff of which movie magazines were made – big, handsome, sophisticated man sweeping factory girl off her feet. The reality was sordid: Neil was sacked for helping himself to the petty cash and left the area. When Sheila told him she was pregnant, he retorted that it was her own fault and that he wanted nothing more to do with her. Alone at the flat she took an overdose, planning to kill herself, but Dennis Tanner from No. 11 saved her and she left the Street to live with her parents in Rawtenstall. A month later, Doreen left too, joining the Army to drive tanks.

Without the girls, Florrie became lonely and depressed. She had the shop converted, moving the door from the draughty corner to the front, near the party wall with No. 13, and she employed Irma Ogden as an assistant. Irma was needed as Florrie had sectioned the shop into two parts: the grocery and a sub-post office. The GPO fitted out the sub-post office and installed a telephone booth. Florrie took charge of that area, selling stamps and cashing pensions, while Irma served behind the grocery counter, encouraging the pensioners to spend the money that Florrie had just given them. For a while it worked well but then Florrie began to get jealous of Irma's youth and her popularity with the local men. She turned against the girl then suffered a breakdown: she threw a tin of meat through the shop window and was found in a weeping heap on the floor. The doctor ordered rest but Florrie refused, fearing that the business would collapse without her. And then Norman returned.

For nearly five years Florrie had maintained that she was a widow and had a lot of explaining to do when her husband tracked her down. Norman told her that if she wanted him she'd have to live in Canada where he had taken a job. At once Florrie saw her chance to escape the shop and grabbed it. As she locked its door for the last time she told Norman she was glad to see the back of it.

The shop was sold to Lionel Petty, a Welsh Army man who had retired from the ranks and had dreams of running a chain of shops Army style, with managers and assistants jumping to his every command. As this was his first shop he realized he would have to start small with a staff of one, his daughter, Sandra. Lionel's wife, Mary, had died while he was serving abroad and Sandra hardly knew her father. She certainly resented the way in which he ordered her around as if she were

a squaddie but she was happy enough living in the Street as she had a crush on Dennis Tanner at No. 11.

It wasn't long before Lionel realized that he was a fish out of water: he knew nothing of retail life and his domineering tone and manner drove away the customers. The neighbours resented the way in which he tried to interfere in their lives. He was so busy meddling in other people's domestic problems that he was blind to his own and he was shocked when Sandra announced her intention to leave home. She had found work in another shop and rented a flat, wanting her independence. Lionel thought nineteen-year-old Sandra too young to live alone and tried to stop her by using the only method he knew – brute force. After he had slapped her and shoved her around, Lionel was sickened by his actions and made no further attempt to keep her with him.

After Sandra moved out, Lionel took on Irma Ogden as shop assistant but decided, even with her help, that the sub-post office wasn't good business. He closed that section and enlarged the grocery but he knew that his heart was not in the venture. He tried to talk Sandra into returning home but life for her was blossoming and she had an ever-increasing circle of

• *Lonely Florrie Lindley spent many evenings playing bingo. She once won the £100 jackpot only to have her bag snatched as she jubilantly made her way home.*

MEMBER NAT. UNION OF SMALL SHOPKEEPERS

F. LINDLEY
Independent Family Grocer
CORONATION STREET,
Personal Service a Speciality

new friends. When Lionel sold up, in January 1966, the only person sad to see him go was his occasional dancing partner Annie Walker.

The next owners of the shop did not face the problems that had seen off Florrie and Lionel. They were already part of the Street community and, as a married couple, did not suffer the dreaded loneliness. Irma Ogden had married David Barlow in December 1965. Before this she had lived with her parents at No. 13, while David had been born at No. 3 and had lived with Albert Tatlock at No. 1 for a few months. He had originally left Weatherfield to follow a career in football but had returned to the Street and had decided to settle in his home town. He took a job playing for County, the local team. Shortly after marrying Irma, he was fouled during a game and his knee ligament was damaged; he was told he would never again be able to play football. Stuck in the couple's bedsit on Ackroyd Street, David's future looked bleak. He had grown used to being a schoolboy's hero, the sort of chap for whom other men wanted to buy drinks; now he was washed up with £300 compensation. Irma's solution was to buy the shop from Lionel but David's pride would not let him agree. He felt that living in the Street again would be a step backwards for him and Irma walked out. David understood that he had to go along with Irma's dream and the couple were reconciled.

Irma was a popular member of the community: a natural mimic, she was entertaining and fun-loving. She flirted with male customers and gossiped with the women, encouraging them to stay longer in the shop, spend a little extra and therefore boost profit. David was more conservative but had a good head for business and the couple made a more than adequate living. The only thing that threatened the profits was Irma's habit of giving her parents goods without payment or even credit. She solved this problem by taking a well-paid job as a plastic welder at the PVC factory and employing her mother, Hilda Ogden, as David's assistant. He wasn't very happy with that.

Less than a year after taking over the business, the Barlows were faced with closure when it was alleged that potted meat sold by them to the Rovers had caused food poisoning in the community. The health inspector called and took samples of the meat, and the shop was boycotted by the locals. David feared ruin but the inspectors wrote giving the food the all clear. He pasted the letter on to the shop window so that all the residents could read it. Slowly they returned.

In January 1967 spinster Emily Nugent became the Barlows' lodger. She was well known in the Street as she had helped out for years at the Mission of Glad Tidings. She worked as manageress of Rosamund Street's Gamma Garments and had revamped it, selling the latest fashions. Although the bedsit contained a mini-kitchen Emily had most of her meals downstairs with the Barlows and was regarded as a friend of the family. She proved a great support when Irma lost a baby in the fourth month of her pregnancy.

After the miscarriage she decided she would never be able to have children, even though the doctor assured her that this wasn't so. David tried to help by visiting an agency to ask if they would be able to adopt a baby. He was stunned when he was told that, at twenty-five, he was too young to be considered as an adoptive parent. Irma wanted a child, but not one of her own, so the couple applied to be foster-parents and this time were successful. They hoped that their first charge would be a baby or toddler but she turned out to be an eleven-year-old girl called Jill Morris, whose mother was in hospital. Irma was a natural mother and loved having the child around the shop. When Jill was reunited with her mother, Irma knew she had become too attached to her and asked to be taken off the fostering register. Instead, she told David that she was ready to try again for a child of their own.

David put his football skills to use once more when he took the job of coach to an all-women team, the Hotspurs. David swore that the sex of his players made no difference to him but Irma grew jealous of the time he spent with the girls and joined the team to keep an eye on him. Watching his team play stirred old passions in David and he longed to return to the pitch. Behind Irma's back he tested his damaged knee by taking part in his first game for two and a half years. After that he sought medical advice and was told his knee

•*Jill Morris was David and Irma Barlow's guest over Christmas 1967. After they emigrated she returned, and Hilda Ogden hid her from Social Services.*

had healed and that he could start playing football regularly again.

Irma was upset when David announced that he had been approached by an Australian football team and wanted to return to professional playing. She hated the thought of leaving her parents in England but realized that Australia offered more to them as a family, especially as she was now three months pregnant. The Barlows packed up the shop and flew off to a new life in Adelaide.

Emily Nugent was a casualty of the Barlows' emigration. Some months before she had been depressed to be single on her thirty-ninth birthday so had joined a marriage bureau and had been introduced to a series

of men seeking wives. The most hopeful had been a farmer, Frank Starkie, but Emily was forced to drop him after she discovered she was frightened of his dairy herd. In 1968 she fell for demolition expert Miklos Zadic, who had fled to England during the Hungarian revolution as a refugee. He introduced her to Communism and encouraged her to express herself freely. She danced barefoot with him, to recordings of gypsy violins, and spent a passionate holiday with him. On her return she discovered that the Barlows had left and the new owners needed the bedsit for their own use so she moved into the Rovers as a paying guest.

The new shop owners were Les and Maggie Clegg and they needed the bedsit for their seventeen-year-old son, Gordon. The family moved into No. 15 in April 1968, just after Les's fiftieth birthday. When the neighbours asked them where they had come from Maggie seemed vague and changed the subject.

Les was an alcoholic: when under the influence of drink he stopped being a gentle giant and turned into a raging, violent thug, hitting out at his family and anyone else who happened along, swearing and smashing his way through anyone who came between him and his bottle. Buying the shop was a new start: he had promised Maggie that he wanted to give up the drink and said that with her help he could do it. She told him that the shop would have to be their last attempt at salvaging a marriage that had left her black and blue and an emotional wreck.

For two months Les managed to stay sober and the customers found him an affable gent who was good company over the shop counter. He won back Maggie's trust and, when his bowls team won, she felt happy for him to attend the celebrations on his own. He disappeared on a two-day drinking spree and on his return started to wreck the shop. When Maggie attempted to take a bottle from him he punched her in the face. Then Gordon swiped at him, hitting him full in the face. Les fell down and smashed his head on a stack of tins. He was rushed to hospital and Gordon feared he had killed his father. In hospital, Les came round and was full of remorse. He asked to see a psychiatrist about his drinking and was admitted to a psychiatric hospital.

With Les receiving treatment, Maggie was ashamed to find herself enjoying her relief at his absence. Without him to worry about she stopped having sleepless nights and started eating properly. She refused to let Gordon help at the shop as he was studying for accountancy exams and employed Valerie Barlow, Kenneth's wife, as an assistant. However, when Maggie began to enjoy living in the Street, she found something else to worry about: Gordon declared his intention of marrying Lucille Hewitt from the Rovers. Maggie refused to let him become engaged to her as she feared he would throw up his future in accountancy but Gordon refused to listen to his mother and believed his love for Lucille would overcome any obstacle. The couple ran away together, intending to marry at Gretna Green, but the train was delayed at Preston so they returned home.

Maggie herself wasn't short of admirers and surprised Gordon by starting a friendship with Len Fairclough from No. 9. She told Len she was only interested in a platonic relationship as she was still married but she was pleased to have a man to confide in. At Len's advice, Maggie took a step back from Gordon and told him she wasn't going to mother him any more; he was free to follow his heart. No longer having to fight his mother's objections, Gordon began to see his engagement to Lucille more clearly and realized he was too young to settle down. With less than a month to go before the wedding, he told his fiancée that they were making a mistake and that he couldn't go through with it. Maggie's delight in the broken engagement was short-lived as Gordon decided he couldn't stay around the Street and he took a job with an accountancy firm in London.

With Gordon gone, Maggie's dreams of a quiet life ended with the arrival of her elder sister Betty Turpin. Betty descended, with husband Cyril, to console Maggie over Gordon's departure and to help out in the shop. Maggie was horrified by her presence on two counts: first, the domineering Betty had always bossed her about and tried to run her life, and second, she feared that with Betty around there was a strong chance of the residents discovering their secret. After the war, when Maggie had married naval hero Les, she had miscarried and had been told she would not be able to have a child. At the time, Betty had been having an affair with a married man, which had left her pregnant. She moved with the Cleggs to Les's native Birmingham and when her son was born gave him to Maggie to bring up. Gordon had no idea that his auntie Betty was really his mother.

Maggie refused to sack Valerie in favour of Betty so Betty took a job as barmaid at the Rovers. However, Maggie couldn't get rid of her sister altogether: the Turpins moved first into the bedsit, then took over the rest of the shop's living quarters. Cyril was a police sergeant, which discomfited the other Street residents, but Betty soon proved her worth as a champion darts player. The Turpins continued to live at No. 15 until Cyril was forced to retire from the force after he had attacked with an iron bar an ex-con who had been terrorizing Betty as a way of getting back at Cyril for arresting him two years previously. Len Fairclough managed to stop him before he killed the man. The police were sympathetic and hushed up the incident and Cyril took a clerk's job, which came with a house in Hillside Crescent.

After being dry for nearly a year Les left hospital in 1970. Maggie was ashamed to discover that she didn't believe he would remain sober for ever so he returned to Birmingham and they started divorce proceedings. When Gordon was given the chance to buy into a partnership, Maggie sold a share of the business to Stan Ogden for £600. He wanted it as a gift for his daughter Irma who had returned to Weatherfield after

● *Les and Maggie Clegg moved to the Street in an attempt to start afresh. They always tried to keep secret the fact that Les was an alcoholic.*

the death of her husband, David, and their son, Darren, in a car crash.

Irma moved into the shop bedsit with her friend Bet Lynch. The shock of her losses brought on a breakdown and Irma stole a baby from outside a post office, believing him to be Darren. Bet took the child from her and returned him, unharmed, while Maggie attempted to keep Irma's mind occupied by throwing her into shop life. Bet told Irma that she understood her feelings over her son's death and revealed that at sixteen she had had a baby who had been taken from her for adoption. Bet was taken on as barmaid at the Rovers and after a while left Irma alone at the flat while she rented a bedsit in Victoria Street with her young boyfriend, Frank Bradley.

Irma continued to have a bad time at the shop. She fell for American serviceman Joe Donnelli but he became deranged and told her how he had killed his buddy Steve Tanner. Irma wanted to notify the police

but Joe threatened her with a pair of scissors and held her prisoner in the flat where he raped her. Later he shot himself in Minnie Caldwell's house. After this, Irma decided she was never going to be free of her ghosts and left to live in Llandudno.

Faced with having to buy Irma out of the shop, Maggie took on a bank loan rather than let Betty supply the money. She employed Norma Ford as live-in assistant, and when her divorce finally came through she started going out with Councillor Alf Roberts. Norma moved into the bedsit and her father, Jacko, joined her when he was released from Strangeways where he had served a prison sentence for breaking and entering. Maggie felt sorry for Norma, living with her father's past – much as she had with Les – and stood up for Jacko when the neighbours heard of his shady dealings. Jacko took a job as potman at the Rovers and Maggie was angry when Betty refused to work alongside him. She stood by Norma when Jacko was accused of breaking into Benny Lewis's betting shop in Rosamund Street, and in this she wasn't alone: school teacher Ken Barlow from No. 1 took up Jacko's case and proved that he had been framed. Jacko decided to start afresh and moved away but Norma was grateful to Ken and fell for him in a big way. It was left to Maggie to comfort the girl when, after spending the night with her, Ken shrugged off her advances.

Norma felt sorry for Maggie, too, and behind her employer's back advertised in a lonely hearts column through which Maggie met draughtsman Ron Cooke. Their mutual attraction was marred when he admitted to having been an alcoholic. Although he assured Maggie that he was seeking treatment, she felt unable to live with another man with a drink problem and they parted. She also parted from Norma, who was upset when Ken married Janet Reid and, unable to see him with a wife other than herself, left the area.

Alf Roberts made it clear to Maggie that he wanted her as a wife but she felt too comfortable with him: he was solid and reliable, a man who would take care of her but with whom there would be little romance and passion, which Maggie felt she needed in her life. She feared for the future when, following Cyril's death of

a heart attack, vulnerable Betty suggested pooling their resources. With Alf and Betty crowding in on her, Maggie was thrilled when Ron Cooke, having been dry for over a year, re-entered her life. He told her he had been offered a job in Zaïre and suggested that they both needed a fresh start. They married at St Mary's Church, with Gordon giving her away, and flew off to live in Africa.

Gordon took control of the shop and let it to the Hopkins family on the understanding that if they decided to buy it the rent money already paid would be deducted from the price. The Hopkinses were a rough-and-ready bunch from Wales. Megan was a fierce Welsh dragon, who dominated the family and ruled her son Idris. Idris's wife Vera waged a constant battle with her mother-in-law and struggled to keep her teenage daughter Tricia on the straight and narrow. Megan had run a fish-and-chip shop and wanted to move into the grocery business with Vera as her assistant. Idris worked at Foster's foundry on the night shift and spent his days sleeping to get away from his troublesome females. At seventeen Tricia was boy mad and spent her days dreaming of Prince Charles and David Bowie, when she should have been working as Ken Barlow's secretary at the mail-order warehouse across the Street. She fell for local lad Ray Langton and tricked him into kissing her while her friend Gail Potter took a photograph. Megan found the picture and was horrified, locking Tricia in her room. Vera was too preoccupied to worry about what her daughter was getting up to as her own mother fell ill and she left to look after her.

Five months later, Vera returned after her mother's funeral to find Megan a different person: she laughed at Vera's jokes and called her 'dear' in a pathetic attempt to get her to use her inheritance to buy the shop. Vera had her own plans for the shop and announced that she would buy it, but it would be hers and not Megan's. Idris found himself caught in the middle, refusing to take sides, while the women argued. The issue was decided for them when Megan discovered a copy of Gordon's birth certificate stuck behind a drawer in the sideboard. It revealed Betty

Turpin as his mother and his father as unknown. Megan assured Betty that her secret was safe but Betty alerted Maggie, who came home to tell Gordon the truth. Gordon was shattered by the news but at the same time relieved that his real father hadn't been an alcoholic. When Megan attempted to use the birth certificate to blackmail Gordon into dropping the price of the shop she had no idea that he knew the truth. Gordon was furious with the old woman and tore up the tenancy agreement, telling the Hopkinses to clear out. The family left, under the cover of night, in a van borrowed by Idris.

Not all the Hopkinses left, though, as Gordon had agreed to allow Tricia to stay on in the bedsit with her workmate Gail Potter. Instead of letting the shop again, he put it on the market and employed Blanche Hunt to run it until it was sold. Blanche lived in Victoria Street with her daughter, Deirdre, and enjoyed serving in the shop: it took her away from her established corsetry business, which she found tiring. She kept a motherly eye on the girls upstairs and let them help in the shop when they lost their jobs after the warehouse burned down. Tricia nearly died in the fire as she had been in the toilets when it started in the store room next door.

· · · · · · · · · · · · · · · · · ·

Megan discovered Gordon's birth certificate stuck behind a drawer. It revealed Betty Turpin as his mother and his father as unknown

· · · · · · · · · · · · · · · · · ·

Rather than apply for dull secretarial work the girls answered an advertisement placed by a model agency who were seeking talent for their books. The girls paid their entrance fees to embark on a modelling course before they discovered that the agency was fake. They had lost their savings, but became canvassers and had a telephone installed in the flat. Tricia enjoyed ringing people up, trying to get them to buy replacement windows, but Gail grew to hate the phone as she was subjected to anonymous calls during which a man made suggestive remarks to her. Alone in the flat one night, she was trapped by the caller, John Lane, who posed as a telephone engineer to gain entry. Gail thought he was going to attack her but neighbour Emily Bishop realized that something was wrong and called the police.

Blanche Hunt gave up the job at the shop when she left the area to run Dave Smith's hotel in the Midlands. Tricia and Gail took over the day-to-day running of the business but they allowed youths endless credit and ran the business down. In March 1976 the shop was finally sold to supermarket checkout assistant Renee Bradshaw.

Renee had worked in retail all her life. At thirty-three she decided she was skilled enough to run a small outlet of her own and picked No. 15 because her brother Terry already worked in the area – as a labourer for Len Fairclough. The Bradshaws had been born in Gas Street but had moved to Lancaster after their father Harold's death. Mother Daisy had remarried but the children took against their step-father. Terry left to join the Army and Renee flung herself into work. Now that they were both back in Weatherfield, Renee determined to provide Terry with a stable home life.

After she bought the shop, Renee gave Tricia and Gail notice to quit and moved her brother into the bedsit. Gail found work with Elsie Howard at Sylvia Separates, the lingerie shop on Nightingale Street, and lodgings at her house, No. 11, but Tricia made a clean break and left to join the rest of her family.

In 1973, three years before moving into No. 15, Renee had become engaged to Harry McClean, a merchant seaman. He wasn't happy with the news that she had bought a shop as he feared she was trying to force him to settle down and broke the engagement. Renee wasn't particularly upset as she found she had become married to the shop. The customers were astounded when she refused credit and publicly waged war against Rovers landlady Annie Walker when Annie opposed her application for a licence to sell alcohol from the shop. The two women went to court, but in the end Renee was victorious and began to supply a small selection of wines and spirits.

Terry Bradshaw wasn't happy to be living with his big sister as he felt that under her eye he had no freedom. He fell for Gail and hoped she would go out with him but Renee felt that Gail was beneath Terry and warned her off. Fed up with Renee's interference, Terry returned to the Army – at least you knew where you stood with a sergeant major while women were unpredictable.

Renee now let the flat to barmaid Bet Lynch and was pleased to have another woman in the place to have a laugh with, but wasn't amused when, shortly after moving in, Bet turned off the freezer by mistake and ruined a hundred pounds' worth of stock. They fared even worse when Bet arranged a foursome with two men, arranging to meet them in Ashton. When the men failed to turn up, Renee and Bet returned downcast to No. 15 to find that the shop had been ransacked: they lost four hundred pounds' worth of stock and fifteen pounds in cash.

Maggie Clegg's old flame Alf Roberts became friendly with Renee and helped her out with her VAT return. She enjoyed his attention and was thrilled when he proposed to her. She accepted, even though he had been drunk, and in the morning pretended that she knew he had been joking when he explained that he hadn't meant it seriously. Nevertheless Renee refused to give up on her man and worked on him until he proposed again. This time they married and honeymooned in Capri.

As well as being a councillor, and ex-mayor, Alf worked at the GPO, running the sorting office. He sold his house on Omdurman Street for £27,000 and invested the money in his post-office account. The Robertses were financially set up for life and had no worries, apart from the presence of Bet Lynch. When it had been just her and Bet at No. 15, Renee hadn't minded the way in which Bet strolled around the place half naked but now that Renee's husband was living there too she found it too much. She told Bet to find other accommodation but changed her mind when her mother Daisy suggested that if the flat was vacant she could move in. Both Renee and Alf agreed that they would rather have Bet as a lodger than bossy Daisy.

Alf decided to retire from the GPO to work alongside Renee in the shop. When he announced the news, though, expecting her to be thrilled, she was far from happy: she believed they would be at each other's throats in no time. In her anger she accused Alf of marrying her for her shop and they rowed. He walked out, to drink in the Rovers. Just as he had sat down in the window seat with his pint, a lorry overturned and timber shot into the pub, knocking him unconscious. Renee went with him in the ambulance as he was rushed to hospital and sat by his bedside for three days as he lay in a coma. When he recovered the doctors sent him home but, to Renee's horror, he had undergone a personality change and became aggressive at the slightest provocation. Thankfully, sessions with a psychiatrist taught him to curb his anger and he became once again the old Alf whom Renee knew and loved. Following the crash Renee welcomed him behind the bacon slicer and was pleased to spend her days with him.

In 1980 Bet left the shop flat after upsetting Renee by allowing her lorry-driving boyfriend, Dan Johnson, to spend the night with her. She and Dan took a flat together in Victoria Street and the Robertses enjoyed being alone together for the first time. Renee took driving lessons and the couple decided to sell up and move to the country. They found a sub-post office in Grange-over-Sands and celebrated when George and Maureen Bannister agreed to buy No. 15. After a drink in a country pub, Alf allowed Renee to drive the car home as he was over the limit. She stalled the car down a lane and, just as Alf got out to take her place at the wheel, a lorry appeared from nowhere. It smashed into the car and Alf looked on in horror as Renee lurched forward through the windscreen then fell back into her seat, her spleen and liver ruptured by flying glass. She had to be cut free from the car and whisked to hospital where she underwent emergency surgery but died on the operating table.

Alf cancelled the sale of the shop, feeling he needed the support of his friends and customers. He employed Deirdre Langton, now divorced, as his assistant. She moved into the shop flat with her daughter

• *Alf Roberts married into the Corner Shop when he wed Renee Bradshaw in 1978. After her terrible death, he invested in the shop as a distraction. He had the shop enlarged and opened as a mini-market, and refurbished the upstairs into a comfortable flat.*

Tracy, after assuring Alf that no one would gossip about them living under the same roof. Her stay there was short because soon afterwards she married Ken Barlow and moved into No. 1, but she continued to help Alf behind the counter.

Alf kept the shop open for long hours as a way of occupying himself after Renee's death. He developed a reputation for being thrifty, out to make as much money as he could, and attracted women who hoped to cash in on his savings. One was Gail Potter's flighty mother, Audrey, who talked Alf into letting her look after the shop while he took a much-needed holiday. In his absence Audrey set up a hair salon in the living room and took long lunch breaks so that when he

returned he found his profits down. To the amusement of his friends, Alf swore he didn't care and bought an MG sports car, which impressed Audrey, but the growing realization that Alf viewed her as a future wife made her panic and she left the area.

Bet Lynch returned yet again to the flat when her bedsit was demolished. Alf let her stay rent free until the *Gazette* ran an article on Councillor Alf living with busty barmaid Bet. She caused him further anxiety by having an affair with his council pal Des Foster. Alf warned Bet that Des was married but she didn't care; she needed a man, she said, and was too old to wait for an unattached one to appear on the scene. When Bet discovered that Des had another girlfriend as well as a wife she finished with him, her pride hurt, and Alf was left to comfort her. In January 1985, however, Bet moved out for good when she took over the licence of the Rovers Return.

With nothing but the shop on which to spend his money, Alf planned to change the structure of No. 15. He had the shop enlarged into the back room, knocking down the stairwell, and turned the larger premises into a self-service mini-market. Upstairs he made the bedsit into a flat, with a separate kitchen, bathroom and bedroom, which covered the length and width of the whole shop and had a separate entrance at the side on to Viaduct Street. He made the flat his living quarters and celebrated the opening of his new shop by proposing to newsagent Rita Fairclough. She turned him down, and was embarrassed when he told her she would always be the only woman for him.

Maureen's life was thrown into turmoil by Maud's revelation that her late husband, Wilf Grimes, had not been Maureen's father

Just a few months later Rita remembered his words when he married Audrey Potter. Audrey re-entered Alf's life after realizing that as she wasn't getting any younger she might as well snare a rich man while she still had her looks. She wanted to live near her daughter and grandson, and picked Alf as her husband because he was the richest man for miles. Alf was thrilled with his pretty wife; Audrey was thrilled with her full wallet. The only condition Audrey made when she married Alf was that she did not intend to live in a poky flat over a back-street shop. She had her eyes firmly set on a detached house going for £44,000 on Bolton Road. Instead, Alf splashed out £11,000 and bought No. 11 Coronation Street.

For nearly two years no one lived at No. 15 Coronation Street. During the day Alf and Audrey ran the shop, with the help of Deirdre Barlow, but at night the premises lay empty, which bothered Alf as he feared break-ins. In 1987, he lost his council seat to his own shop assistant when Deirdre stood against him in the elections. He put his defeat down to the long hours he worked in the shop and the lack of support Audrey gave him – she hated serving behind the counter. He employed newly-wed Sally Webster as an assistant and allowed her to move into the flat with her husband Kevin. Their stay was short-lived, though, as they bought No. 13 from Hilda Ogden and settled

there, although Sally assured Alf that it was still handy for work.

Shortly after Kevin and Sally left, student Curly Watts moved into the flat with his girlfriend Shirley Armitage. At first Alf had not been keen on this arrangement, which led to neighbours calling him a racist as Shirley was black. He backed down and the young couple set up home together. Neither anticipated the problems they would face because of their different backgrounds. Curly was a grammar-school boy, an only child brought up by elderly parents, encouraged to take an interest in astronomy and stamp collecting. He had been awarded a *Blue Peter* badge for collecting 500 silver milk bottle tops. Shirley's large family lived in an overcrowded terrace in Nelson Street. She had left school with no qualifications and was working in Mike Baldwin's sweat shop on Coronation Street. Curly tried to educate Shirley and encouraged her to read up on his favourite subjects but Shirley wanted to spend her spare time going to clubs and having a wild time. They were poles apart and the crunch came when Shirley threw a party to celebrate their first year together: Curly ordered everyone out of the flat as he had to revise for an exam. Shirley was upset by his attitude and left him to return to her mother's. Alf wasn't happy at having a lovelorn student above the shop, and Curly was taken in by Vera Duckworth at No. 9, who saw that the boy needed some mothering.

When Curly passed his exams he took a job as assistant manager at Bettabuy supermarket, working under Reg Holdsworth. Reg moved into the mini-market flat after his wife Veronica threw him out for having an affair with the Bettabuy store detective. Alf didn't like having a supermarket boss living over his shop because he held supermarkets responsible for his fall in custom. When Reg decided that the bus ferrying customers to the supermarket should stop right outside No. 15, Alf saw red and evicted Reg, throwing his belongings into the Street.

Alf played safe with his next tenant, school teacher Ken Barlow, whom he had known since Ken was a schoolboy. However, they clashed during the 1990 elections when Ken supported his ex-wife Deirdre in the campaign and put a 'Vote Deirdre' poster in his window, directly above the shop. When Alf entered the flat to rip it down, Ken called the police and lodged a complaint against his landlord.

Alf decided to retire from business at the age of sixty-seven and sold the mini-market to Brendan Scott, Bettabuy's area manager. Brendan had ideas to revolutionize the shop, seeing it as the first rung in his 'caring community' chain shops 'Best Buys'. He favoured traditional retailing and employed Emily Bishop in a mob cap and apron behind the counter while he sported a boater and Nicky Platt delivered orders on a rickety old bike. However, the dreams died with Brendan who suffered a fatal heart attack on the

● *Reg and Maureen first met at Llandudno in 1968 but Maureen's mother was firmly against marriage. Twenty-five years later they rekindled their love.*

shop floor. His young widow, Debi (Miss Bettabuy 1977), had no wish to hang on to the shop and put it up for auction. Alf Roberts bought it back and made a profit by selling it for £68,000 to Reg Holdsworth.

Reg took over the business with his second wife, Maureen. They had worked together at Bettabuy and carried away with romance, they thought it would be wonderful to spend every hour of the day together. They even decided to open on Sundays. The reality was harsh, though, and Reg found the small shop stifling after his supermarket arena. Leaving Maureen to run it with her disabled mother, Maud Grimes, Reg took the post of manager at Firman's Freezers supermarket. Maud was confined to a wheelchair and Maureen had a ramp built for her behind the counter so that she could serve while still in her chair.

Stuck with her interfering, critical mother all day, Maureen grew tired of working at the shop. Then she got a shock. Her life was thrown into great turmoil by Maud's revelation that her late husband, Wilf Grimes, had not been Maureen's father, and that she was the result of a wartime fling Maud had had with an American. Maureen suffered an identity crisis and found herself ignored by Reg, who became obsessed with his age and bought a wig for £300 in an attempt to turn back the clock.

The Holdsworth marriage was placed under immense strain when Reg took promotion and moved to Lowestoft. For a while Maureen spent her weekends making the four-hour journey to see him while Maud struggled with the shop. Finally, Maureen discovered that Reg had given up his job and run off with a secretary, Yvonne Bannister, who was expecting his baby. Maureen agreed to divorce Reg on condition she was given the shop as settlement. She changed its name from 'Holdsworth's' to 'Maureen's' and started a relationship with builder Bill Webster. Maud, who had never liked Reg, approved of solid Bill and was thrilled when he moved into the flat over the shop to be nearer to Maureen.

Her delight did not last long. Maureen had a passionate moment with Curly Watts, and afterwards she and Bill split up.

THE OTHER SIDE OF
• THE STREET •

Hardcastle's Mill

The Mission of Glad Tidings

Elliston's Raincoat Factory

Viaduct Sporting Club

PVC Factory

Maisonettes

Community Centre

Mark Britain Mail Order Warehouse

Baldwin's Casuals

No. 2 Coronation Street

No. 4 Coronation Street

No. 6 Coronation Street

No. 8 Coronation Street

No. 10: The Kabin

No. 12 Coronation Street

Unit 14

HARDCASTLE'S MILL

Although in 1902 Sir Humphrey Swinton had been the man behind the building of Coronation Street and Mawdsley Street, Charles Hardcastle was identified as the champion of the people. He owned the four-storey mill, founded in 1882 in Victoria Street on disused mining land, for whose workers the back streets had been built. The mill's imposing back wall and loading area towered over Coronation Street.

Charles Hardcastle was pleased to see his workers housed in the shadow of the mill: they were never late for work and he took a percentage of the rent they paid to Sir Humphrey's estate. Charles was a widower, his wife Elizabeth having died in 1901 leaving him with a son, Matthew. In July 1904 he married landowner Mabel Grimshaw, securing his hold on the community, and built a large house for her on Ashdale Road.

Matthew Hardcastle oversaw the work of the mill, which boasted seven weaving sheds, a dyeworks and a separate four-storey warehouse. At the height of Hardcastle's empire he was responsible for the well-being of over three thousand people, including his workers' children who were educated at the factory school. At the age of eight, the children were moved from school to mill as half-timers, spending mornings in class and afternoons working, running in and out of the looms retrieving broken threads and spare bobbins. Hardcastle had a good reputation for safety, but if a worker or child was killed he always paid for a decent funeral.

The workforce maintained a monotonous routine, working from 6 a.m. to 7 p.m. with an hour's break at lunch. They were deafened by the noise of the looms and learnt to lip-read to communicate. Work conditions were never addressed and slowly unrest spread through the community. Fred Piggott at No. 13 was union representative for the mill workers and, following the coal workers and other mill hands, called a strike in 1911, which shut down production at the mill for the first time since it had opened. The strikers requested better conditions and higher pay, and Charles, worried about meeting orders, was inclined

to agree to their demands, shocked though he was by the behaviour of his employees: he considered himself a kind-hearted employer. However, when the disruption spread across the country the Government became involved and forbade Charles to settle with his workers. The strike lasted throughout the summer and he despaired: he thought he would be out of business by the end of the year. Eventually, the Government backed down, the workers were given a basic wage rise and Fred Piggott led them back to the mill.

When Charles Hardcastle died in 1926, Matthew took over the business. When the Depression gripped the country, businesses folded throughout the north-west. Matthew struggled to keep hold of the mill but no one seemed to want the cotton goods he manufactured, even when he cut prices. It was a sad day in 1931 when he called the workforce together to announce closure. The mill was stripped bare and boarded up. The Hardcastle family were forced to sell the Ashdale Road house and Mabel bought a small house in Oakhill.

THE MISSION OF GLAD TIDINGS

In 1902 Weatherfield had a fast-growing Mission circuit. Many of the inhabitants were Nonconformists and viewed the parish church with suspicion. Of those who were practising Christians, the majority were chapel- or Mission-goers. When Coronation Street was planned, the Mission committee used its funds to buy the land between Hardcastle's mill and the viaduct; building started in 1902 and by the end of November that year the sixth Mission in Weatherfield was completed. The building had its main entrance in Victoria Street, next to Jackson's chip shop. As worshippers entered through the porch they came to a huge hall furnished with wooden pews. The pulpit was built into the wall facing the double front doors and behind it a door led into a one-bedroomed vestry flat. The stained-glass windows looking onto the viaduct had a carefully crafted design of ivy leaves at the bottom representing the souls of the worshippers on earth. Bells were depicted half-way up the windows to

The other side of the Street

● *The wooden interior of the Mission Hall was dark. Brightness could not come in through the huge windows because the close-by viaduct cut the light off. Gladys Arkwright (right) employed two daily ladies to help her scrub the floor each Saturday night. Her nephew Harry (above right) helped by mending broken chairs and lighting the gas mantles for Wednesday-night Bible classes.*

represent sinners turning to God. At the top of the window, the ivy leaves were twisted together, showing the holy community rejoicing in Heaven.

The Mission opened its doors for the first time on Christmas Eve 1902 and the opening sermon 'Love Thy Neighbour' was preached by shopkeeper Cedric Thwaite. Widow Gladys Arkwright was employed as caretaker and moved into the vestry. As her address was 16 Coronation Street, she linked herself more with the Street's residents than those living on Victoria Street. Gladys was forty when she took over the Mission; before that she had attended the Salvation Army chapel on Clarence Street and had lived above the neighbouring tripe shop. Her husband, William, had died of fever after only a year of marriage and

Gladys had no children. She considered herself married to Jesus and set herself the task of evangelizing the residents of Coronation Street.

Gladys's biggest battle was with having a public house so close to the Mission. She was a member of the temperance movement and urged the congregation to sign the pledge to abstain from alcohol, the brew of the Devil. She despaired of her brother, Arthur Moss, who helped her with manual work at the Mission, as he had a drink habit that he refused to shake off. When Arthur died of alcohol poisoning Gladys felt vindicated in her condemnation of him and made a home for his orphaned son Harry.

Gladys took Ena Schofield from Inkerman Street under her wing when she discovered that the girl was a gifted pianist. She allowed her to practise on the Mission's harmonium.

Ena married Alfred Sharples in 1920 and remained a worshipper at the Mission; Gladys became god-mother to her daughters Vera and Madge. Apart from Ena's welcome visits, Gladys lived a lonely existence in her vestry. Those residents who weren't part of the congregation found it hard to pass the time of day with her as they always feared she would condemn their behaviour. After the war the size of the congregation dwindled and sometimes preacher Sid Hayes found that only his own family attended the Sunday service.

In 1937 Gladys gave her last admonishment and died. She had taken to standing outside the Rovers to deliver sermons to those brave enough to ignore her to enter the pub. Although she was now seventy-five she refused to be deterred by the weather and pulled her shawl closer round her when she felt cold. Billy Chad from No. 3 was annoyed when she reprimanded him for never attending the Mission. He shoved her out of the way, which caused her to fall and crack her head on the cobbles. She was killed instantly.

Ena Sharples took over as caretaker on the same day that she buried her husband Alfred, who had died after catching a cold demonstrating over workers' rights outside the Town Hall. Ena was glad to move into the vestry as she found her marital home in Inkerman Street too full of memories. Not all the mem-ories were of Alfred: her only son Ian had died there

● *Ena Sharples's links with the Mission went back to before the First World War, when she spent her Saturdays repairing hymnbooks with Gladys.*

aged just two days and her ungrateful elder daughter Madge had fled the house during the harsh years. All that was left to Ena was her eighteen-year-old Vera, who had been dropped as a baby; ever since then Ena had been convinced that she was backward.

During the Second World War Vera took a job sewing uniforms at Elliston's and shamed Ena by joining the local girls as they travelled to Burtonwood to dance with the GIs. Ena locked her in the vestry on the night the Americans threw a party at the Rovers as she had no intention of seeing Vera disgrace herself in front of folk who knew her. Ena served as an ARP warden as well as spending her days welding breech bolts on to rifles. The Mission basement was allocated as the Street's air raid shelter and it was Ena's job to settle everyone and keep up their spirits with singsongs. When the Street was hit, and people were killed or hurt, Ena comforted the grieving.

With Vera married and living elsewhere, and her contemporaries enjoying retirement, Ena seemed to gain more energy in her sixties. She liked to tease Mission secretary Leonard Swindley over the way the congregation dwindled whenever he preached, and was saddened when the committee ripped out the old pews and replaced them with folding wooden chairs. In 1966 she was humiliated to be caught shoplifting at Summit supermarket. Fined ten shillings by the court she was placed under the care of Social Worker Ruth Winter, who moved into the Mission to oversee its conversion into a community centre. Ena was horrified to learn that the committee had decided to make use of the empty hall during the week to encourage the local people to run a play group, poetry classes, youth dances and whist drives. Ena swore to oppose the changes but found that her opinion was not sought.

In January 1967 Vera stayed with her mother at the vestry complaining of headaches. She died of a brain tumour in Ena's bed, and after that Ena gave up fighting the march of progress. When the committee decided that the Mission should be demolished she moved out to lodge with her friend Minnie Caldwell at No. 5, while the Street's place of worship was ripped down before her eyes.

ELLISTON'S RAINCOAT FACTORY

The summer of 1932 brought the wondrous news that the mill was to reopen. Black Jack Elliston, the ward's councillor for ten years, bought the disused building and opened a factory to make raincoats.

He strongly believed in giving the workers what they wanted and set up a good social club in the factory. He had wireless Tannoys fitted in the workrooms so that machinists could be entertained while they were working and encouraged special days off when the social club organized outings. One outing to Bridlington ended in tragedy, when the coach bringing the workers home crashed into a bridge and twelve machinists were killed. In 1936 he had a huge canteen built inside the factory, which served hot food at cheap prices. During the Second World War, the factory switched to producing service uniforms and the BBC broadcast an edition of *Worker's Playtime* from the canteen.

The only drama that the factory ever saw took place in 1962 when Christine Hardman, from No. 13, climbed on to the roof and threatened to throw herself off. Kenneth Barlow from No. 3 managed to talk her down and Jack Elliston insisted that the foreman shouldn't sack her.

In 1964 Elliston sold off the basement under the factory to theatrical agent Laurie Fraser. Laurie transformed the dusty hole into a casino-cum-sports club, but the venture folded through lack of custom.

PVC FACTORY

In the spring of 1966 Jack Elliston died and his son Jocky took over the factory site. He closed down the sporting club and stopped production of out-of-date raincoats, shifting to manufacturing the more modern PVC coats and hats, replacing the old style sewing machines with welding machines.

John Benjamin from Nelson Street was given the job of running the factory, and Jocky turned a blind eye to his methods. All he asked was that the profits were high and costs low. John employed local girls, including Lucille Hewitt from the Rovers, Sheila Birtles from No. 11, Irma Barlow from the shop and Bet Lynch from

Pear Street. He selected busty Bet as his favourite and made her his sex interest while demanding high output from the girls, who struggled to work the welding machines after little tuition. Lucille Hewitt proved expert on the machine but her speed produced shoddy work. John cut all the wages when she refused to own up to producing the sub-standard goods, which caused Bet to give her a black eye.

When John's practices came to light, Councillor Len Fairclough threatened an investigation by the Town Hall's Works Committee. Jocky decided he couldn't be bothered with the factory and closed it. In January 1968 the demolition men moved in.

MAISONETTES

Seven maisonettes were erected on the site in 1968, the plumbing contract going to Fairclough and Langton. On the ground floor three one-bedroomed

• *Many of the Street's female inhabitants left Bessie Street School to start work at Elliston's Factory.*

'Fabiola' RAINWEAR

Elliston's
(1932·LTD)

Reg'd Office & Works

CORONATION STREET,

Hands Wanted :

BASTERS - - PRESSERS

FINISHERS - BUTTONHOLERS

ALTERATION   HANDS

single-storey OAP flats were built with a walkway through to the shops on Victoria Street. Above these ran a balcony with four two-storey maisonettes. They were council-owned and each new flat consisted of a large living room with small kitchen and bedrooms.

Valerie Barlow was shown the plans and persuaded husband Ken to sell their home at No. 9 so that they could move across the Street to be the first occupants of No. 14, one of the two-storey flats. Directly beneath them, at No. 16, Ena Sharples was allocated one of the OAP flats, opposite the Corner Shop, just where her vestry had been.

There was drama in the Street shortly after the maisonettes were built when an escaped convict, Frank Riley, broke into the Barlows' flat when Ken was out. Riley held Valerie captive while their three-year-old twins slept upstairs. Valerie feared that he planned to rape her and, telling him it was the only way to get the water working, she banged on the water pipes under the kitchen sink. Down below Ena heard the banging and called the police. The flats were surrounded and sealed off before two detectives burst through the kitchen window and arrested Riley. Valerie was shaken after her ordeal but received no comfort from pacifist Ken, who refused to believe that Riley hadn't touched her and struggled to work out how he would have reacted if Riley had killed her or the children.

Sixty-eight-year-old Effie Spicer moved into No. 4. She was the widow of a well-known sports journalist, and for the first time in her life found herself having to cope on a pension when she lost her savings in bad investments. Ena tried to give her advice but Effie was too proud to accept it and gave up the flat to rent No. 1 from Albert Tatlock as it was cheaper.

The maisonettes were a huge structural failure. They had been put up quickly and costs had been kept low: the rooms were damp and those not filled immediately remained empty, attracting only squatters and tramps. Ena moved out to take the post of caretaker at Ernest Bishop's camera shop and the Barlows decided to emigrate to Jamaica, where Ken had been offered a teaching post. On the eve of their departure Annie Walker threw a farewell party for them at the

● *Tea break at Ellistons: Jean Stark, Doreen Lostock, Sheila Birtles and Christine Hardman take a rest.*

Rovers. Struggling to get ready, Valerie used a faulty plug socket and was electrocuted. As she fell she knocked an electric fire into a packing case and the flat was engulfed in flames. The fire brigade pulled her body from the maisonette and the council decided to have the block demolished.

COMMUNITY CENTRE

Councillors Len Fairclough and Alf Roberts led the fight to have the maisonette site put to good use. They bowed to commercial pressure to have a warehouse built at the Rovers end but stuck out for a community centre to be erected on the site of the old Mission. Ena was given the job of caretaker.

As the centre was to serve the needs of people from Coronation Street and Victoria Street residents were invited to stand for election to the committee. Both Ernest Bishop and his girlfriend Emily Nugent stood and were elected. Emily was living at the Rovers and Ernest had a camera shop on Victoria Street. The building was completed in late 1971 and included a one-bedroomed flat at the front of the building, directly opposite the Corner Shop with the address No. 16 Coronation Street. A door from the flat led into the centre, which had three small offices and a huge hall, with a main entrance to the side on Viaduct Street. It was to be used for the recreational pursuits of the community and was opened by the Mayor.

Ena found working at the centre much harder than it had been at the Mission. In the old days everything had been geared towards getting ready for Sunday services but now each day had a different agenda and rota with groups meeting all the time in the hall and small rooms. Seats had to be set out, refreshments laid on and sports equipment locked away. At seventy-two she was too old to run the centre but refused to acknowledge this until the shameful day when the new colour television set was stolen after she had fallen asleep and left the main door unlocked. There were calls for her to be replaced but Emily and Ernest fought to keep her on, and eventually won by dint of making pensioner Albert Tatlock assistant caretaker.

Over the years the hall was used for wedding receptions (including Emily and Ernie's), flower shows, dances, plays, concerts and pantomimes. When Ena suffered a stroke and moved away she was replaced by Gertie Robson, a widow in her fifties more suited to the hard work. However, she left to become housekeeper at the Flying Horse public house and the Bishops insisted that Ena was given the flat while cleaners were employed to look after the centre.

Ken Barlow from No. 11 became community development officer at the centre. He struggled to give everyone what they wanted and was disappointed by parents' attitudes when he employed ex-convict Eddie Yeats as child group leader. Eddie was a natural with the children but parents demanded his removal and Ken was forced to comply with their wishes.

When old age finally forced Ena Sharples to retire she moved to Lytham St Anne's to keep house for an old friend. The caretaker's job was briefly given to Fred and Eunice Gee, newly-weds in their forties who upset centre users by their lazy attitude. Councillor Ben Critchley called to complain and ended up running by off with Eunice.

After this the Council decided that a single man would be best suited to the job and employed retired baker Percy Sugden. Percy was a widower, his wife Mary

● *When Valerie Barlow was once trapped by an escaped convict, her concern had been not to let him know her children lay asleep in the room above.*

having died of cancer in 1978. He was of the old school, believing in a world where youngsters respected their elders, and gentlemen opened doors for ladies. During the war he had served as a sergeant in the Catering Corps; he brought a military bearing to his new job as he worked out rotas and guarded the ping-pong bats until they were issued from his lock-up. Using the centre as his headquarters he ran the local home watch and started a dance formation troupe. All his good work ended, though, when he reached sixty-five and the council told him he had to retire.

In 1989 the council decided to sell the site, feeling that the community it had been created to serve no longer existed. No one wanted to put on plays and concerts for the old folk, no one was interested in dances when they could go to night-clubs, and the sporting activities were too limited to justify the centre staying open. The site was sold to developer Maurice Jones, who moved in the bulldozers.

MARK BRITAIN MAIL ORDER WAREHOUSE

The residents strongly opposed plans to build a warehouse on the site of the maisonettes. Led by militant Emily Nugent, the womenfolk formed a human chain in an attempt to prevent the workmen starting on the site but their efforts were fruitless: the men dumped a load of sand over them and broke through the chain. The PR men at Mark Britain called a public meeting at the Rovers and showed the designs for the warehouse, pointing out that there was no need to fear a huge building like the old factory; the new warehouse would be two storeys high and would have many windows to make it light and airy. The company that explained nothing would be produced on the premises; goods would merely be stored and packed there before distribution via their mail-order catalogues.

The residents had been right to worry about having the warehouse opposite the houses: although the building itself didn't impose, the lorries travelling in and out of the loading bay did. The warehouse was open all night, taking deliveries of goods, and the

● *Cigar-puffing, whisky-drinking Mike Baldwin demanded loyalty from his workers. After all, if he did not employ them, who would?*

noise of the engines echoed around the Street. Ken Barlow from No. 11 complained to the chairman, Sir Julius Berlin, and so impressed him that Sir Julius employed him as north-west executive. Ken's first task was to reorganize the deliveries so that the locals didn't complain.

Sir Julius hated unions and Ken had to squash the workers' attempt to form one, even though he thought they should have one. He was sympathetic towards trade unionist Peggy Barton but made the mistake of having an affair with her. His executive rival, Edward Pollard, found out and reported him to Sir Julius. Rather than give up Peggy or his principles, Ken resigned from his job.

One October night in 1975 three lads broke into the warehouse storeroom. They spent the night sleeping on blankets and in the morning ran off, leaving a cigarette smouldering. A fire started, which quickly took hold in the room, finding plenty to ignite. When Edna Gee opened the door, intending to sneak in for a crafty cigarette, she was engulfed in flames. The fire tore through the building and the Street was evacuated as containers of gas threatened to explode. After seven hours the fire brigade managed to dampen it. It was then that Edna's body was found. The building was gutted and Sir Julius moved operations to his warehouse in Leeds.

BALDWIN'S CASUALS

In November 1976 the old warehouse site roared into action again when Londoner Mike Baldwin had the place renovated and opened his second denim factory. He had moved north because he believed wages for his workforce would be cheaper. Many of the girls who had been employed at the warehouse were still out of work so he employed them as machinists and packers, working on long rows of industrial machines, sewing seams on denim outfits which arrived pre-cut. Ernest Bishop from No. 3 was taken on as wages clerk but was gunned down in an armed wages snatch.

Twenty-year-old Steve Fisher replaced him as Mike's right-hand man. Mike planned to train him up in management so that he could run the factory. As it happened, when Ivy Tilsley called a strike they nearly ended up as the only two on the workforce. Mike had sacked Hilda Ogden, the factory cleaner, when he accused her of wilfully damaging her broom and Hilda was thrilled by her colleagues' show of solidarity but did not want to join the picket outside the factory. To get an important order through Mike brought in non-union workers by the back door but they were spotted and the factory was besieged by Ivy's gang. They smashed windows and threatened the blacklegs with violence until the police arrived to get the workers safely out. Mike backed down and reinstated Hilda.

In 1982 Emily Bishop stepped into her dead husband's shoes to become Mike's wages clerk. At the same time, machinist Vera Duckworth introduced a cat, Cleo, to the factory after finding a mouse in the stock room. When Cleo knocked coffee over his accounts Mike took against her and ordered her destruction. However, the girls made the cat a union member to protect her. Mike had the last laugh, though: he shared out the workers' bonuses to include Cleo, and pocketing the cat's share, he told the girls he was putting it in 'the kitty'.

Mike's love-life had its many ups and downs. In 1986 he fell for Ken's twenty-one-year-old daughter, Susan, and married her, despite her family's opposition.

Susan had been trained in market research and put together a business plan showing Mike the openings in children's wear. He humoured her by setting her up in her own business, Hopscotch, using his workers to run up her designs. Susan threw herself into the venture, which annoyed Mike who wanted her to settle down and have children. When he saw that Hopscotch's profits were low he closed the firm and ordered Susan to work in the new factory shop he had opened in the factory to sell the denim. When Susan told him she never wanted children, he sacked her and the marriage crumbled. She later had a secret abortion.

In 1988, as Mike closed down denim manufacturing and reopened as Baldwin's Curtains, student Curly Watts wrote a thesis on the factory and Mike's business practices. It cast Mike in a bad light, likening him to a Victorian sweat-shop owner and listing the bad conditions in which he forced the women to work on poor wages. Mike ripped up the report up but Vera Duckworth told Ken Barlow about it and Ken wrote a critical article which he published in his newspaper, the *Recorder*, saying that Mike sold as first quality any sub-standard curtains he produced. This led a client to withdraw an order so Mike threatened to sue Ken for libel, pointing out that sub-standard items were sold on as seconds. Ken apologized and Mike enjoyed his humiliation before he agreed not to take legal action.

When property developer Maurice Jones bought the community centre land from the council, Mike was tipped off that he was after the factory land too. When Maurice approached him, Mike raised the asking price to £180,000 before agreeing to sell as a going concern.

He assured the girls that Maurice would find work for them but was amazed by the speed at which Maurice moved in the bulldozers the day after closing the factory down.

NO. 2 CORONATION STREET

Maurice Jones drew up plans to change the face of the Street for ever. As well as homes and a factory unit, he decided to build two new shops in the area. One was erected directly opposite the Rovers, with a back room and two-bedroomed flat above and a separate entrance facing on to the Street. In order to have the shop occupied he gave a cheap six-month lease to the Friends of Weatherfield Hospital, who opened the premises as a charity shop. Friends' committee member Emily Bishop took the role of manageress and rallied her band of volunteers to run the shop. The venture was not a success and closed after a few months, the stock being transferred to the established Rosamund Street branch.

In December 1992 twice-divorced thirty-seven-year-old Denise Osbourne bought the shop lease and opened a hair and beauty salon called simply 'Denise's'. Her second husband Neil Mitchell fitted it out for her, hoping for a reconciliation, but she took up with businessman Hanif Rupparell on a strictly no-strings basis. She kidded herself that she could enjoy a sexual relationship without commitment but soon found herself falling for him. Hanif reminded her that she had only wanted to have fun and made it clear that he was not interested in a long-term liaison. After paying back to Neil the £3,000 he had lent her to start the business Denise ran into financial problems. Hanif refused to lend her money so she finished with him. Taxi driver Don Brennan eventually put up the cash, but Denise's friendship with him came to an abrupt end when she discovered that he was responsible for the frightening telephone calls she was receiving. In the meantime, Neil started a relationship with Angie Freeman from No. 7.

After her divorce came through from Neil, Denise celebrated by embarking on an affair with teacher Ken Barlow. Again she never intended it to become a heavy relationship but then discovered she was pregnant. Immediately she knew that she wanted the baby, seeing it as her last chance to be a mother. However, she didn't want Ken and broke with him, telling him that she had no need of him. That all changed, though, when she went into labour and begged Ken to help her through the pain. In January 1995 Daniel was born and shortly afterwards Denise moved in with Ken at No. 1. She kept the flat on at No. 2 as a secret love nest, where she entertained Brian Dunkley, who happened to be married to her sister Alison. When Ken found out about the affair, he threw Denise out and she and Brian went off together. She rid herself of the salon by selling the lease to her assistant, Fiona Middleton.

Twenty-year-old Fiona moved into the flat from her old place above Jim's Café on Rosamund Street. She renamed the salon 'Hair by Fiona Middleton' and closed down the beauty parlour. Like Denise, she was troubled with rocky relationships and broke with mechanic Tony Horrocks when he discovered she was visiting her old boyfriend Steve McDonald in prison. Tony didn't waste much time pining for her as he bounced back by dating Fiona's assistant, Maxine Heavey.

Alec Gilroy discovered that Fiona had a talent for singing and tried to persuade her to swap crimping hair for stardom but Fiona found showbusiness too demanding and gave it up. During one of her club appearances she caught the eye of Alan McKenna in the audience and he whisked her off her feet. But Alan was elusive and Fiona worried that he might be married. She was relieved to discover he was wed only to his job – in the police force.

Fiona had borrowed £4,500 to buy the salon's lease from her brother Lee, who had given her a year in which to repay him. She was thrilled when he wrote the debt off as a twenty-first birthday present to her.

NO. 4 CORONATION STREET

1990 saw Mavis and Derek Wilton buying their first home together. Although both were in their fifties the couple had only married in 1988, but they had been going out with each other on and off for twelve years. Mavis fell in love with the house as soon as she saw it: it appealed to her artistic nature. The downstairs was open-plan and so benefited from both morning and afternoon light. The garden was just a rough plot, but as soon as she saw it Mavis could picture the ornamental pond, the fruit trees and the swinging hammock where she would escape the madness of the twentieth century.

Shortly after moving in Mavis was delighted to discover an urban fox in the garden. She called him Freddie and fed him dog food but he preferred Jack Duckworth's pigeons. Much to Mavis's horror, Jack organized a fox hunt and Mavis pressed Derek into acting like a fox to put the hunters off the scent. When they tried to enter her garden, having tracked Freddie, Mavis attacked the men with a saucepan to give the fox time to flee.

In an attempt to cheer Mavis up Derek organized an outing to London to take in a show but during a mix-up at a service station he was left stranded on the motorway. He was given a lift home by fellow salesman Norris Cole and put a brave face on the situation, calling himself Dirk and lecturing Norris on how to handle women. A week later Norris turned up on the Wilton's doorstep to say he had taken Derek's advice, had left his wife and had come to stay at No. 4. Mavis took an instant dislike to him and was furious when Derek used his savings to join Norris in a new venture, selling Envirosphere ecological products. Derek was put out to find Norris the better salesman, and while he struggled to sell the products Norris rose quickly

● *It was a proud moment for Fiona Middleton*
when her name replaced Denise's above
the Salon.

● *Derek and Mavis Wilton knew they were the butt of their neighbours' jokes as they attempted to turn their home into an oasis of peace and tranquillity. They suffered most from Des and Steph Barnes (below), who loved to tease and shock them.*

and soon had enough profit to take a dockland flat. Mavis demanded that Derek moved the Envirosphere boxes out of their house so he sold them to his ex-wife Angela Hawthorne, who mischievously employed him at her own firm, upsetting Mavis who viewed her as a sexual rival.

The Wiltons' love of animals encompassed budgerigars as well as Freddie the fox. A few days after moving in, their budgie Harriet died of shock. They replaced her with a new bird called Harry, but he died in 1995 after Derek had walked out on Mavis during a row over Angela. The death brought the couple back together and Derek bought a third bird, Beauty, as a replacement. While Mavis grew passionate about her feathered pets Derek formed a relationship with two garden gnomes he called Arthur and Guinevere. He was annoyed when Arthur disappeared from the garden and started to send postcards from around the world. At one point Derek was sent Arthur's ear, along with a ransom note, and he began to guard Guinevere fearing that she, too, would be taken. The mystery was

solved when drunken Norris confessed to having taken the gnome. In an act of vengeance Derek made Norris late for the wedding when he married Angela in 1995.

The Wiltons took on one of the council allotments and set about producing organic vegetables, then bought the Malletts' unwanted conservatory and had it erected in their back garden. Having turned their home into an oasis all they longed for now was the time to relax and enjoy it together. But Derek suffered a fatal heart attack on Mavis's birthday and she was left alone at No. 4.

NO. 6 CORONATION STREET

When Maurice Jones's daughter Stephanie married Des Barnes in February 1990 he gave the couple No. 6 at cost price. They moved in immediately after the wedding reception, although she locked him out after he banged her head on the door frame while trying to carry her over the threshold. The marriage was stormy – Steph was a spoilt only child with a fiery temper, who demanded her own way in all things, and Des was a joker, who had no idea about commitment. Straight away they upset the neighbours by throwing a rowdy house-warming during which Steph plied Kevin Webster with drink then took him upstairs to shave off his moustache.

After leaving his native Newcastle, Des had worked as a courier in Spain before settling down to the life of a bookie. He was employed by Alex Christie in his Rosamund Street betting shop while Steph worked as a perfume salesgirl at Ashcroft department store.

Des wanted to have children but Steph refused, pointing out that Des was the child of the family. She suggested that instead he took up a hobby so he bought an old boat, which he kept in the back garden while he lovingly restored it. When the engine was delivered, Des couldn't wait to test it and, despite warnings not to touch it, started it up. The boat vibrated with the action and toppled over, crashing into the Wiltons' garden.

The boat was the scene of more drama when it was launched. During a day-trip to christen it, Steph con-

fessed to Des that she had been having an affair and was planning to leave him. The object of her affection was architect Simon Beatty and he had made her realize that she couldn't go on living with a man who enjoyed watching children's TV. Des was devastated and, in an attempt to frighten Steph into staying with him, set fire to the boat. Then he slashed her suitcases but Steph walked out of the marriage.

There wasn't a shortage of women wanting to help Des get over his marriage break-up and barmaid Raquel Wolstenhulme moved in as his lodger. She spent one night in the back bedroom before moving in with Des. Cleaner Phyllis Pearce was pleased to discover that he was fighting back after Steph when she found one of Raquel's earrings in the bed. Des enjoyed having Raquel around but she cared more for him than he did for her. When Steph arrived with a suitcase, Des insisted that she stayed and Raquel walked out. Des hoped that Steph was back to stay but she explained that she was using him only as a half-way house between Simon and her new lover.

Lisa Duckworth used Des's garden for her son Tommy to play in during the Summer of 1992. Her husband Terry was in Strangeways and she lived with his parents at No. 9 but missed the company of young people. Des loved having Tommy around the house and he and Lisa found themselves drawn to each other. Terry's mother Vera worried about the relationship and warned Terry. Lisa was horrified when Des was set upon by thugs, who beat him up and told him to stay away from her. Disgusted with Terry for using such tactics, she told Vera that the marriage was over and returned to her native Blackpool.

With Lisa gone, Des had time to sort out his feelings for her and decided that she was the girl for him. He visited her in Blackpool and brought her back to the Street to live with him at No. 6. They planned a fresh start and looked at houses in Withington but the plans came to nothing. Lisa was knocked down in the street in front of Des. She was rushed to hospital and lay in a coma for two days before she died. Des was devastated by her death and by the way in which Vera took Tommy from him. He was attacked by Terry at

● *Lisa Duckworth did not live at No. 6 for long. She and Des were planning a life together with baby Tommy when she was killed crossing the Street.*

Lisa's funeral and for a time couldn't see any point in carrying on.

In 1994 Raquel moved back in and looked upon No. 6 as the house where she would live as Mrs Barnes. Des tried hard to make a go of this relationship but found himself drawn to Raquel's workmate Tanya Pooley, who teased him and encouraged him to be unfaithful to Raquel. For months he led two lives, being domesticated with Raquel while having passionate episodes with Tanya, which were all the more complicated because she was also his boss Alex Christie's lover. The whole sordid mess came to a head when Des decided he had to have Tanya to himself. He confronted her when she was in bed with Alex and told his boss all about the affair, unaware that Raquel had

followed him and heard every word. She fled back to the Rovers where Bet Gilroy comforted her. Tanya looked on in horror as Des and Alex fought over her. Alex sacked Des and finished with Tanya but she refused to stick with Des, telling him he'd ruined everything as she really loved Alex. One minute Des had two women, the next none.

Steph Barnes re-entered Des's life briefly when he found her working in a burger bar. She had finished another relationship and was heavily pregnant. She was also in dire straits so Des took her under his wing, found her a new flat and paid two months' rent on it. She realized Des had matured and wondered if they could start afresh. He refused, pointing out that her baby needed love and he didn't think he could give it the love it needed. This time when he walked away from Steph he felt a weight lift from him.

Widow Claire Palmer was the next to move her toothbrush into Des's bathroom. They had met at the market where she helped out on her in-laws' crockery stall. Her husband Jeff had been killed when he became trapped in an aircraft hangar which had caught on fire. Des had a hard job matching up to RAF hero Jeff in the eyes of Claire's thirteen-year-old daughter Becky but slowly he broke down her defences and worked hard to win her round when she moved in with her mother. The relationship became strained when Des discovered that Claire stood to lose her £16,000 annual pension from the RAF if they discovered she was cohabiting. He urged her to hang on to the money and arranged for her and Becky to move into the flat over Sean Skinner's betting shop where Des now worked as manager. Claire hated the deceit involved in having the flat as her address and spending her nights at No. 6 and was relieved when her father-in-law Charlie shopped her to the RAF. The pension stopped and she took a job at Maureen Holdsworth's shop, telling Des that she hoped he was worth £16,000 a year.

She didn't have long to wait before discovering he wasn't. Des made a pass at Samantha Failsworth from No. 7 and she had some fun with him – throwing his trousers out of her bedroom window. Claire witnessed the spectacle and packed her bags, leaving with Becky. Des decided to leave and set off for pastures new in his boat. He rented the house to Angie Freeman who took in mechanic Chris Collins as a lodger. A few weeks later they became lovers and he moved into her bedroom.

NO. 8 CORONATION STREET

This three-bedroomed house, with open-plan downstairs, internal garage and large garden, stood empty for two years after Maurice Jones built it. It was bought in Christmas 1991 by Martin and Gail Platt for £38,000, the bulk of the money coming from the £20,000 insurance that came to Gail after her first husband Brian's death. The couple moved in with their three children – eleven-year-old Nicky, Sarah Louise, five, and David, one. Martin and Gail had only been married a year and Martin had adopted Gail's two older children. Brian's mother, Ivy Brennan, who was still living at No. 5, was pleased to have her grandchildren living across the Street but disliked Martin, seeing him as replacing her beloved Brian.

Someone who did like Martin was Carmel Finnan, who was training to be a nurse with him. Carmel fantasized about Martin and convinced herself that he loved her. Representing herself as a willing baby-sitter she talked her way into the Platt home and, after complaining of a prowler in the nurses' home, moved in as their lodger. Gail thought it wonderful to have Carmel around the house because she cleaned, cooked and took care of the children. What she didn't know was that Carmel made the children think that their own mother was too busy to be with them. When Gail was out one night, Carmel lay in bed with Martin, who

● *Gail Tilsley refused for a long time to marry Martin Platt. Eventually he made her realize he'd never leave her, and that she'd never be too old for him.*

● *The Kabin became Rita Fairclough's haven after her ordeal with Alan Bradley. The peace was shattered when she was twice targeted by burglars.*

was drunk after a party and had no idea that he wasn't snuggling up to his wife. In the morning he was horrified to find Carmel beside him and stunned when she declared her love for him. She tried to seduce him into joining her in her bedsit, telling Gail that she was too old for Martin and had to release him so that he could be happy with her. The Platts threw Carmel out but she returned to announce her pregnancy with Martin's child. Martin swore his innocence and Gail did battle with the girl after she tried to abduct David. She pushed Carmel down a flight of stairs and feared she'd lose her baby, only to be told by the doctor that Carmel wasn't pregnant – it had all been in her mind. The Platts breathed a sigh of relief when Carmel's grandfather took her home to Ireland.

When Martin qualified and became a staff nurse at Weatherfield General, he made the mistake of having a brief encounter with a nurse called Cathy Power. Gail found out about the fling and had a breakdown: she had always feared that Martin would stray as he was ten years younger than she was. He swore it had been a one-off and had been nothing but sex but it took months before Gail could begin to trust him again.

Nicky Platt was upset when Granny Ivy died of a stroke but amazed when he discovered she had left him No. 5. The issue threatened to split the family as Ivy's condition of his inheriting the house was that he changed his name back to Tilsley. While Gail supported Nick's claim, Martin sympathized with Ivy's husband Don, who swore to contest the will. Eventually Don bought the house from Nick, for £12,000, half its market value. Martin hoped that the matter had ended then but Nicky remained a troublesome teenager. In 1996 while the rest of the family holidayed in Wales he disappeared on an adventure. Gail was frantic with worry and the police issued missing-person posters while pointing out that, at nearly sixteen, Nick, as he now preferred to be called, was going to be hard to find. Just when Gail had convinced herself that the lad was dead, he casually returned home, explaining that he had spent the summer in Torquay in a bed-and-breakfast. The Platts realized he was dissatisfied with his life and agreed to let him use his inheritance to pay for entrance to a boarding academy in Canada, under the watchful eye of Gail's half brother Stephen Reid.

NO. 10 THE KABIN

Rita Fairclough had run the Kabin newsagent on Rosamund Street for seventeen years. When she saw that Maurice Jones had built a shop unit opposite her house she felt certain that the time was ripe for change. She sold the old shop, let her home, No. 7, to students, and bought the new shop from Jones, moving into the two-bedroomed flat above. It ran along the front and side of the shop, its entrance beside an internal garage facing the forecourt off the Street. When the new Kabin opened its doors in 1990, it was much the same as the old shop in the sense that Rita and her assistant Mavis Wilton were still behind the counter but the shop area was much larger and they were able to stock items such as lunch boxes and party plates for which there had not been room before.

One disadvantage of living above the shop was that Rita felt vulnerable to attack and twice in the early nineties she was woken at night by the sound of the burglar alarm. Even when she had shutters fitted at the windows, thieves still managed to smash through and steal cigarettes. Upstairs she would worry about youths breaking in to get to her and the attacks brought on a nervous collapse.

A solution to her problems arrived in the shape of retired sweet-salesman Ted Sullivan. He swept Rita off her feet and asked her to join him in his retirement plan of living in Florida. She went with him to view the community there and decided to agree but then he broke the news that he had a brain tumour and that he was dying slowly. Rita was heartbroken and told Ted that she still wanted him in her life, even though they wouldn't have long together. She did, however, refuse to leave England and told him that she would need her friends around her for support. After they married Ted moved into Rita's flat and began to deteriorate. In less than six months he was dead and Rita was a widow once again.

Rita still lives alone above the shop. She involves herself with the Websters at No. 13, her surrogate family, since she never had children herself. When she is not working in the Kabin she can generally be found sipping a vodka and tonic in the Rovers.

NO. 12 CORONATION STREET

This one-bedroom flat was built in the same block as the Kabin, its entrance looking out on to the edge of the mini market. The front door leads straight to a flight of stairs and the flat is all on one level to the side and back of the Kabin below. It was first bought by Reg Holdsworth in 1991 after his wife Veronica had thrown him out, accusing him of having an affair. Reg had bought the flat to be close to Rita Fairclough, the Kabin owner, but his hopes of romance were dashed when she made it clear that she wasn't interested.

Reg worked as manager of Bettabuy supermarket on Albert Road, and it was there that he found true love in the shape of divorcée Maureen Naylor. Twenty-five years previously the pair had met while holidaying in Llandudno. They had planned to marry then but Maureen's mother had taken a dislike to Reg and had driven them apart. Reg told Maureen that Fate had brought them back together and the pair became engaged. Maud continued to try to break them apart but Reg did his best to ignore her. Eventually, frustrated that his love for Maureen hadn't been consummated, he whisked her off in the middle of the working day to make love to her on his water bed. Unfortunately Derek Wilton, in the Kabin store room below, drilled a hole in the ceiling and punctured the bed. Reg had to admit defeat as the bed, and Maureen's passion, sank.

After Reg married Maureen in January 1994, he moved into Maud's house in Nightingale Street. He bought the mini market and rehoused sitting tenant Ken Barlow from the bedsit over the shop in No. 12. Ken did not have a happy stay in the flat as first he watched his ex-wife Deirdre marry a younger man and then his daughter Tracy suffered kidney failure after taking Ecstasy. When she came out of hospital, Tracy stayed at No. 12 before leaving for London.

In 1996 Ken bought No. 1, where he had lived years previously with his uncle, Albert Tatlock, and with Deirdre, and moved in with his girlfriend Denise Osbourne and their baby son Daniel. The same year, the Holdsworths separated and Reg sold the flat for £29,500 to Alec Gilroy.

Alec lives alone in the flat, although he employed Joyce Smedley to clean it for him until he discovered she was helping herself to his ready cash. He views the flat as a base rather than as a home, spending his days managing Sunliners Travel Agency. His evenings are devoted to roaming the night-clubs looking for talent to sign up for his theatrical agency.

UNIT 14

When Maurice Jones planned the redevelopment he built a unit which could be used as a small factory. He leased the property to Phil Jennings, who used it as a base for his company PJ Leisure, which ran amusement arcades. He made his girlfriend, then Deirdre Barlow, manager of the site but she grew puzzled as she never had any work to do. When she investigated the company she discovered that the unit was just a front for Phil's dodgy deals, but before she could confront him he had fled the country with his wife Valerie.

Mike Baldwin took over the lease and set up a T-shirt printing company, MVB Print, and employed school-leaver Steve McDonald to run it for him. It didn't take long for Steve to use the operation to undercut Mike and supply T-shirts on the side, pocketing the money. Mike was furious when he found out and sacked him, but Steve bounced back threatening to set up in opposition, pointing out that he had all the contacts now, not Mike. Mike admired his cheek, and decided that the lad reminded him of himself at the same age. He agreed to rent the unit to Steve for £120 a week and made a point of sending him a £1,200 rates bill almost immediately. Steve struggled financially with the business, turned to gambling and had some success on the horses. Then he landed a big order to produce merchandise for a pop group but failed to get a bank loan to raise the £20,000 needed to buy new equipment. Mike stepped in and the pair formed a partnership. However, after using all Steve's contacts, Mike dumped him and did a separate deal with the group, dissolving the partnership.

Steve's next financial backer, eighteen-year-old heiress Vicky Arden, ensured that she was actively involved with the business as she wanted a good return on her investment. She renamed the unit 'Dun 2 A T' and installed computers. She kept putting money into the business: she wanted Steve and the money drove a wedge between him and his girlfriend Fiona Middleton. Even so, she was not prepared to cover Steve's gambling debts until he was beaten up in the unit by a thug with a baseball bat.

Fiona threw Steve out of their flat on the day before his twenty-first birthday and he slept rough at the unit, only to be joined by Vicky. The next day he proposed to her and, despite opposition from her grandfather Alec Gilroy, they married in St Lucia. After their month-long honeymoon, Steve was surprised to discover that Vicky intended to keep the business going – he had thought they would live off her inheritance. He made a pretence of running it but his heart wasn't in it and Vicky was horrified when police searched the unit and found stolen whisky. The marriage collapsed as Steve pushed Vicky into bribing a convict to withdraw evidence against him then expected her to take the blame when the police became involved. Vicky closed down the business, filed for divorce and began a hotel and management course in Switzerland while Steve was sent to prison for two years. 1997 saw the opening of a new factory in the unit, with partners Mike Baldwin and Angie Freeman designing and manufacturing lingerie.

Residents of the Street

APPLEBY Christine,	13: 1939–53, 1955–62
née Hardman	
ARDEN Victoria,	Rovers: 1992–5
m. Steve McDonald	
ARKWRIGHT Gladys	16: 1902–37
ARMITAGE Shirley	15: 1988–9
ARMSTRONG Jamie	1: 1995, Rovers: 1996–7
ARMSTRONG Tricia	1: 1995, Rovers: 1996–7
ATKINSON Janey	Rovers: 1903
BALDWIN Mike	5: 1976–7
BARLOW David	3: 1942–62, 1: 1965,
	15: 1966–8
BARLOW Deirdre	*See* RACHID
BARLOW Frank	3: 1938–64
BARLOW Ida	3: 1938–61
BARLOW Irma	13: 1964–5, 15: 1966–8,
	1970–1
BARLOW Janet	1: 1973, 11: 1973–4
BARLOW Ken	3: 1939–62, 9: 1962–8,
	14: 1968–71, 3: 1971–2,
	1: 1972–3, 11: 1973–6,
	1: 1976–90, 15: 1990–4,
	12: 1994–5, 1: 1995—
BARLOW Marjorie	3: 1939–40
BARLOW Peter	9: 1965–8, 14: 1968–71,
	3: 1971
BARLOW Susan	9: 1965–8, 14: 1968–71,
	3: 1971
BARLOW Tracy,	5: 1977–8, 3: 1979–80,
m. Robert Preston	15: 1980–1, 1: 1981–94
BARLOW Valerie, *née Tatlock*	1: 1961–2, 9: 1962–8,
	14: 1968–71
BARNES Des	6: 1990–7
BARNES Steph	6: 1990–1
BIRCHALL Suzie	11: 1977–9, 1983
BIRTLES Sheila,	15: 1962–63, 11: 1966
m. Neil Crossley	
BISHOP Emily, *née Nugent,*	15: 1967–8, Rovers: 1968–72,
also m. Arnold Swain	3: 1972—
BISHOP Ernest	3: 1972–8
BOOTH Jerry	13: 1963–4, 9: 1971–5
BOOTH Myra,	13: 1963–4
née Dickenson	
BRADLEY Alan	7: 1987–9
BRADLEY Jenny	7: 1986–92
BRADSHAW Renee	*See* ROBERTS
BRADSHAW Terry	15: 1976
BRENNAN Don	5: 1988–97
BRENNAN Ivy, *formerly Tilsley*	5: 1979–95
BRIDGES Sarah	Rovers: 1905–16
BUCK Alice	9: 1910–16
BUCK Avis, *née Grundy*	9: 1920–26
BUCK Ben	9: 1916
BUCK Ian	9: 1923–6
BUCK Jim	9: 1913–15, 1918
BUCK Joe	9: 1910–15
BUCK Kelly	9: 1913–15, 1918

BUCK Larry	9: 1910–26
BUCK Lucy	9: 1923
BUCK Ned	9: 1910–25
BUCK Sarah	9: 1910–19
BURTON Amy	9: 1987–8
BUTLER Bernard	11: 1969–70
BUTLER Sandra	11: 1969–70
CALDWELL Minnie	5: 1962–76
CHAD Billy	3: 1920–24, 1926–38
CHAD Flo, *née Makepiece*	3: 1902–38
CHAD Iris (*Granny*)	3: 1933–6
CHEVESKI Ivan	9: 1961
CHEVESKI Linda, *née Tanner*	11: 1940–58, 9: 1961,
	11: 1966, 1984
CHEVESKI Martin	11: 1980
CHEVESKI Paul	9: 1961, 11: 1966
CLAYTON Andrea	11: 1985
CLAYTON Connie	11: 1985
CLAYTON Harry	11: 1985
CLAYTON Sue	11: 1985
CLEGG Gordon	15: 1968–9
CLEGG Les	15: 1968
CLEGG Maggie, *m. Ron Cooke*	15: 1968–74
CORBISHLEY Charlie	Rovers: 1902–16
CORBISHLEY Jim	Rovers: 1902–18
CORBISHLEY Nellie	Rovers: 1902–18
CRAPPER Albert	9: 1902–6
CRAPPER Bertie	9: 1907–10
CRAPPER Jack	9: 1902–6
CRAPPER Pearl	9: 1902–10, Rovers: 1910–18
CRAPPER Ronnie	9: 1902–10
CRAPPER Rose, *née Weaver*	9: 1909–10
DIGGINS George	Rovers: 1918–38
DIGGINS Mary	Rovers: 1918–38
DONNELLI Joe	5: 1970
DUCKWORTH Cliff	9: 1994–5
DUCKWORTH Jack	9: 1983–95, Rovers: 1995—
DUCKWORTH Lisa, *née Horten*	9: 1992, 6: 1993
DUCKWORTH Terry	9: 1983–8
DUCKWORTH Tommy	9: 1992–3
DUCKWORTH Vera	9: 1983–95, Rovers: 1995—
ELLIS Edna	*See* TATLOCK
FAILSWORTH Samantha	7: 1996—
FAIRCLOUGH Len	9: 1968–82, 7: 1982–3
FAIRCLOUGH Rita	*See* SULLIVAN
FLEMING Audrey	3: 1968–70
FLEMING Dickie	3: 1968–70
FORD Norma	15: 1972–3
FOYLE Amelia	15: 1916–19
FOYLE Elsie	*See* LAPPIN
FOYLE Hilda	15: 1933–57
FOYLE Lil, *née Makepiece*	11: 1902–23, 15: 1923–7
FOYLE Shelagh	15: 1935–57
FOYLE Tommy	15: 1915–45

FREEMAN Angie	7: 1990–3, 6: 1997
GASKELL Sharon	9: 1982, 7: 1982–3
GEE Eunice	Rovers: 1981, 16: 1981
GEE Fred	Rovers: 1976–84, 16: 1981
GIBSON Amy	9: 1950–60
GIBSON Ted	9: 1950–60
GILROY Alec	Rovers: 1987–92, 12: 1996—
GILROY Bet, *née Lynch*	15: 1970, 5: 1976–7,
	15: 1977–80, 1982–5,
	Rovers: 1985–95
GRIMSHAW Aggie	1: 1902–07
GRIMSHAW Daniel	1: 1902–06
GRIMSHAW Percy	1: 1902–06
HARDMAN Christine	*See APPLEBY*
HARDMAN George	13: 1930–53
HARDMAN May	13: 1930–53, 1955–60
HARRIS Hetty	11: 1910–11
HARRISON Enid	13: 1902
HARRISON Lizzie	13: 1902
HAYES Ada, *m. Matt Harvey*	5: 1910–49
HAYES Alice	5: 1908–52
HAYES Esther	5: 1924–62
HAYES Fred	5: 1915–16
HAYES Sidney	5: 1908–40
HAYES Tom	5: 1926–47
HEWITT Alice, *m. Sam Burgess*	7: 1920–39,1961
HEWITT Betsy	3: 1902–05
HEWITT Christopher	7: 1962–4
HEWITT Concepta, *née Riley*	Rovers: 1960–1, 7: 1961–4
HEWITT Dolly	3: 1902–05
HEWITT Flo	*See CHAD*
HEWITT Frances	7: 1922–3
HEWITT George	3: 1902–06
HEWITT Gertie	3: 1906–26
HEWITT Harry	7: 1921–64
HEWITT Lizzie, *née Harding*	7: 1948–59
HEWITT Lucille	7: 1949–64, Rovers: 1964–74
HEWITT Mary	11: 1902–19, 7: 1919–36
HEWITT Molly,	3: 1909–30
m. Artie Lonswaite	
HEWITT Samuel	3: 1902–09
HEWITT Thomas	3: 1902–19, 7: 1919–47
HOLDSWORTH Reg	15: 1990, 12: 1991–4
HOPKINS Idris	15: 1974–5
HOPKINS Megan (*Granny*)	15: 1974–5
HOPKINS Tricia	15: 1974–6
HOPKINS Vera	15: 1974–5
HOWARD Alan	11: 1970–3
HOWARD Elsie	*See TANNER*
JINKS Jack	11: 1930
KHAN Flick	7: 1990
LANGTON Deirdre	*See RACHID*
LANGTON Ray	3: 1969–70, 9: 1970–5, 5: 1977–8
LANGTON Tracy	*See BARLOW*
LAPPIN Elsie,	15: 1930–60
formally Foyle	
LAPPIN Les	15: 1947–52
LATIMER Ian	5: 1986
LEATHERS Nancy	3: 1961
LEEMING Jack	5: 1902–04
LEEMING Maggie	5: 1902–04
LINDLEY Florrie	15: 1960–5
LINGARD Ada	13: 1919–29
LINGARD Mary	13: 1921–9
LINGARD Nellie	13: 1919–29
LINGARD Tom	13: 1919–29
LOSTOCK Doreen	15: 1962–3
LOW Dinky	1: 1917–18
LOW Madge	1: 1917–18
LYNCH Bet	*See GILROY*
MAKEPIECE Alfred	11: 1902–08
MAKEPIECE Frank	11: 1902–16
MAKEPIECE Iris, *née Morgan*	11: 1926
MAKEPIECE Ivy	11: 1902–38
MAKEPIECE Lil	*See FOYLE*
MAKEPIECE Mary	*See HEWITT*
MAKEPIECE Ralph	11: 1902–16
MAKEPIECE Susie	11: 1906–24
MAKEPIECE Vi	*See TODD*
MAKEPIECE Will	11: 1904–26
MALLETT Gary	9: 1995—
MALLETT Judy	9: 1995—
MARSH Alfie	1: 1915–16
MARSH Mo	1: 1915–16
MASON Madge	13: 1939–40
MATTHEWS Cissy	*See O'CONNOR*
MATTHEWS Jake	5: 1904
MATTHEWS Millie	*See O'CONNOR*
McDONALD Andy	11: 1989—
McDONALD Jim	11: 1989—
McDONALD Liz	11: 1989–96
McDONALD Steve	11: 1989–94
MIDDLETON Fiona	2: 1996—
MOFFITT Charlie	5: 1964–5
MOUNT Jim	13: 1966
MYERS Ethel	11: 1958
NARKIN Ned	Rovers: 1943–4
NIGHTINGALE Wendy	11: 1976
NORTH Kezia	13: 1954
NUGENT Emily	*See BISHOP*
NUTTALL Alf	9: 1946–50
O'CONNOR Cissy,	5: 1904–08
formerly Matthews	
O'CONNOR Mollie,	5: 1904–07
formerly Matthews	
O'CONNOR Reg	5: 1908
O'CONNOR Tom	5: 1904–08
OGDEN Hilda	13: 1964–87

OGDEN Irma | See BARLOW
OGDEN Stan | 13: 1964–84
OGDEN Trevor | 13: 1964
OSBOURNE Daniel | 1: 1995–6
OSBOURNE Denise | 2: 1992–5, 1: 1995–6
OSBOURNE Mary | 1: 1907–15
OSBOURNE Thomas | 1: 1907–15

PALMER Becky | 6: 1996–7
PALMER Claire | 6: 1996–7
PEACOCK Ashley | 5: 1996—
PETTY Lionel | 15: 1965–6
PETTY Sandra | 15: 1965
PIGGOTT Emma | 13: 1902–18
PIGGOTT Fred | 13: 1902–19
PIGGOTT Robert | 13: 1902–16
PIGGOTT Victor | 13: 1902–16
PLATT David | 8: 1991—
PLATT Gail, *née Potter, formerly Tilsley* | 15: 1975–6, 11: 1976–9, 5: 1979–80, 1983–5, 8: 1991—
PLATT Martin | 8: 1991—
PLATT Nicky | 5: 1983–5, 8: 1991–6
PLATT Sarah Louise | 8: 1991—
POPPLEWELL Clara | 7: 1902–18
POPPLEWELL Emily | 7: 1902–15
POPPLEWELL Ernest | 7: 1902–04
POPPLEWELL Harry | 7: 1902–18
POPPLEWELL Herbert | 7: 1902–18
POTTER Audrey | See ROBERTS
POTTER Gail | See PLATT
POTTS Walter | 11: 1963–4

RACHID Deirdre, *née Hunt, formerly Langton and Barlow* | 5: 1977–9, 3: 1979–80, 15: 1980–1, 1: 1981–94
RACHID Samir | 1: 1994
RIGBY Jackie | 9: 1946–50
RILEY Concepta | See HEWITT
ROBBINS Dave | 9: 1963
ROBERTS Alf | 15: 1978–86, 11: 1986–9
ROBERTS Audrey, *née Potter* | 11: 1981, 15: 1985–6, 11: 1986–9
ROBERTS Renee, *née Bradshaw* | 15: 1976–80
ROBOTTOM Henry | 11: 1931–2
ROBSON Gertie | 16: 1974

SEDDON Sally | See WEBSTER
SHACKLETON Joss | 9: 1990
SHARPLES Ena | 16: 1937–68, 6: 1968–9, 16: 1971–80
SHARPLES Vera, *m. Bob Lomax* | 16: 1937–46
SPENCER John | 9: 1981
SPICER Effie | 8: 1968–9, 1: 1969
STONE Jed | 5: 1962–3, 1966
SUGDEN Percy | 16: 1983–8, 3: 1988—
SULLIVAN Rita, *née Littlewood, formerly Fairclough* | 9: 1977–82, 7: 1982–90, 10: 1990—
SULLIVAN Ted | 10: 1992
SUTTON Jenny | See TANNER
SWAIN Arnold | 3: 1980
SWAIN Emily | See BISHOP

TANNER Arnold | 11: 1939–45
TANNER Dennis | 11: 1942–68
TANNER Elsie, *also m. Alan Howard* | 11: 1939–73, 1976–84
TANNER Jenny | 11: 1968
TANNER Linda | See CHEVESKI
TATLOCK Albert | 1: 1919–84
TATLOCK Alfred | 1: 1914–15, 1921–4
TATLOCK Beattie, *m. Norman Pearson* | 1: 1933–53
TATLOCK Bessie | 1: 1919–59
TATLOCK Edith | 3: 1971
TATLOCK Edna, *née Ellis* | Rovers: 1920–1, 1: 1921–3
TATLOCK Joyce | 1: 1923
TATLOCK Valerie | See BARLOW
THOMSON Kelly | 1: 1996
THWAITE Cedric | 15: 1902–15
THWAITE Lottie | 15: 1910–15
TILSLEY Bert | 5: 1979–84
TILSLEY Brian | 5: 1979–80, 1983–5
TILSLEY Gail | See PLATT
TILSLEY Ivy | See BRENNAN
TILSLEY Nicky | See PLATT
TODD Clark | 9: 1943–5
TODD Daisy | 9: 1940–3
TODD Dot, *m. Walt Greenhalgh* | 9: 1926–45
TODD Jack | 9: 1926–46
TODD Jim | 9: 1926–39
TODD Sally | 9: 1926–45
TODD Vi | 11: 1902–14, 9: 1926–44
TURPIN Betty, *m. Billy Williams* | 15: 1969–70
TURPIN Cyril | 15: 1969–70

WAKEFIELD Henry | 13: 1985
WALKER Annie | Rovers: 1938–83
WALKER Billy | Rovers: 1938–62, 1970–4, 1984
WALKER Jack | Rovers: 1938–70
WALKER Joan, *m. Gordon Davies* | Rovers: 1940–60
WATTS Curly | 3: 1983–8, 15: 1988–9, 9: 1989–91, 7: 1991—
WATTS Raquel, *née Wolstenhulme* | 6: 1992, Rovers: 1992–4, 6: 1994, Rovers 1994–5, 7:1995–6
WEBSTER Bill | 11: 1984–5, Rovers: 1995, 15: 1997–
WEBSTER Debbie | 11: 1984–5
WEBSTER Kevin | 11: 1984–5, 3: 1985, 13: 1985–7, 15: 1987–8, 13: 1988—
WEBSTER Rosie | 13: 1990—
WEBSTER Sally, *née Seddon* | 13: 1986–7, 15: 1987–8, 13: 1988—
WEBSTER Sophie | 13: 1995—
WHITELY Bob | 9: 1982
WHITELY Chalkie | 9: 1982–3
WHITELY Craig | 9: 1982
WILLIS Marion | See YEATS
WILTON Derek | 4: 1990–97
WILTON Mavis | 4: 1990—
WOLSTENHULME Raquel | See WATTS

YEATS Eddie | 13: 1980–3, 11: 1983
YEATS Marion, *née Willis* | 11: 1982–3